FAITH

AND

CULTURE

Bernard Eugene Meland

SOUTHERN ILLINOIS UNIVERSITY PRESS

Carbondale and Edwardsville

FEFFER & SIMONS, INC.

London and Amsterdam

Preface

THE PROBLEM OF THIS BOOK is the problem of every contemporary person who has remained restive and unreconciled under the
barrage of reaction in recent years; but who, nevertheless, has felt
the emptiness of the liberal's defense. It has been argued that the
liberal era has ended, and that, except for the ashen words that fall
from surviving liberal pulpits, its declarations of moral faith are
but echoes of another age. I am not willing simply to contest that
argument; for I am convinced that the apologetic for liberalism
cannot be a defense of what has been historically established as
liberal. The Liberalism of our time is a new emergent. It is the
spirit of faith and of free inquiry which has come through the
chastening fires of war, disillusionment, despair, and tragedy; and
which has confronted evidence of evil in man's world, evil that is
shocking beyond the power of any reasonable mind to grasp. Out
of these same harrowing circumstances there has emerged also a
decisive theology of reaction which contests every premise of historic liberalism and declares itself irrevocably at odds with what
it calls a sanguine and superficial gospel. The liberal spirit reborn [1]

[1] The literature expressing this renascent liberal spirit in a chastened
and realistic mood is not vast; yet it is important because it operates at
present as the seed bed for a significant theological thrust beyond both
the sterile liberalism of the 'twenties and the literal forms of reaction
which have been content simply with reversing the liberal premises. The
most articulate voices in behalf of a reconstructed liberalism are to be
found among members of the Federated Theological Faculty at the University of Chicago. Cf. Bernard M. Loomer's essays, Christian Faith
and Process Philosophy, *The Journal of Religion,* vol. XXIX, July 1949,
181–203; Daniel Day Williams, *God's Grace and Man's Hope,* Harper,
1950; and my own writings since 1945, particularly *Seeds of Redemption,* Macmillan, 1947; and *The Reawakening of Christian Faith,* Macmillan, 1949. See also Wilhelm Pauck, *The Heritage of the Reformation,* Beacon and Free Press, 1950; H. N. Wieman, *The Source of Human Good,* University of Chicago Press, 1946; Charles Hartshorne,

is a contemporary of this theological reaction. It is at home
in the situation of crisis. It partakes of the impatience with premises that ignore the irrationalities of existence and that fail to
take serious account of the creatural limitations of man in the use
of reason and in the appeal to human experience for guiding
truths. It partakes also the recovery of Christian faith as a
mediation of God's grace and forgiving love for repentant man. In
the restoration of this resource for modern man it finds the chief
incentive for its labors.

Yet the Christian realism that rises out of the ashes of moral
disillusionment and defeat takes a guarded view of the leap beyond liberalism, convinced that reaction can issue in sheer negation when the flame of its prophetic fire subsides and the air clears
for constructive effort. The road to realism in witnessing to the
Christian faith, it contends, is not a reckless reversal of every
idealistic premise, but a sober probing of the depths of experience
which the more surface-like rational dialectics and pragmatic
empiricisms of the liberal era failed to discern. Faith, it argues, is
not to rout reason, but to counter its claims on the appropriate
occasion when the overreaching intellect needs to be restrained.
Faith is an initial situation of depth which precedes and underlies
the reasoning mind. It is therefore a primal resource which both
nurtures and re-creates the mind. In so far as the modern, autonomous intellect of man has lost a sense for this deeper dimension
of thought, the renascent liberalism of our day cries out against its
arrogance and its willful folly. This critical liberalism, in so far as
it has been reborn of a penitent mood, speaks out with prophetic
judgment upon the lethargy of intellect that permitted practical
considerations and preferences to obscure, even to displace,
fundamental issues of theory pertaining to ultimate problems. In
this respect the re-creation of liberalism implies a reorientation of
mind which refuses to shunt off any basic inquiry that pertains to
the life of faith. This concern with theory and basic issues is no

---

Man's Vision of God, Harper, 1941 and *The Divine Relativity,* Yale
University Press, 1949. Other works speaking in a similar vein and drawing upon some of the same resources include: Charles Clayton Morrison,
What is Christianity, Harper, 1940; John Bennett, *Christian Realism*
and Roger Hazelton, *Renewing the Mind,* Macmillan, 1950.

new scholasticism. It is a recovery of proportion in relating concrete and abstract values, insisting that these may not be torn apart or be truncated to suit the occasion or the individual temperament.

The critical liberalism of this post-crisis mood insists that clarity of meaning and a consequent intellectual respectability in religion are not enough in themselves. Complexity in existence is of the essence. We see in part and we know in part; but the vision of attention shades off into obscuring horizons where the way may not be readily charted. Depths and discontinuities harass the inquiring mind as it moves through the sequences of even common events. These may not be glossed over or subsumed under a generalized notion of continuity or immanence for purposes of clarity or intellectual convenience. What is given in experience as an actuality is to be reckoned with. And in these stark terms of being what it is, it is to be taken into account. If the complexity of existence leaves us in part baffled, then the bafflement of man's intellect is a fact of our existence; and the adjustment of our mental sights must follow accordingly. Mystery need be no source of embarrassment to the enlightened mind, nor a stumbling block, if the chastening of mind and spirit, which the modern liberal has encountered, is accepted. Nor is the pursuit of clarification, within bounds appropriate to the mind's capacity, an idle effort. In the renascent, liberal mood of our time, faith and inquiry become two inseparable rhythms which continually alternate in the course of human experience.

In so far as my effort succeeds in this volume, I shall point a way to consolidating some of the advances which penitent and critical thinking has made in recent years to reconstruct the liberal position in Christian theology. The reconstruction, I feel, must be radical and pervasive, reaching to fundamental notions which underlie basic premises. I am confident that the resources for such a reconstructive effort are available to us; and that the time is ripe for such a renewal.

B. E. M.

University of Chicago
July 1953

Table of Contents

PREFACE   v

PART I
THE RECONCEPTION OF FAITH

CHAPTER I   New Sources of Insight   3
       II   The Dissipation of Faith   14
       III Clues to Reconstruction   32

PART II
FAITH, THE DYNAMIC OF CULTURE

       IV   The Energy of Faith   63
        V   Faith, Myth, and Culture   80
       VI   Structure of Experience   98
       VII The Discernment of Faith   117

PART III
FAITH AND ITS ULTIMATE ISSUES

       VIII The Depth of Man's Nature   131
       IX   The Source of Human Evil   147
        X   The Problem of Human Goodness   169
       XI   The Redemptive Good   190
       XII God as Hidden and God Discerned   209
            Index   225

PART I

THE RECONCEPTION OF FAITH

I

New Sources of Insight

THE RECONSTRUCTIVE MOOD in liberal Protestantism is prompted not simply by an impulse toward reaction but by a recognition of new resources of insight into the meaning of faith and its role in the life of the individual person and in culture. It becomes increasingly clear to the person who ponders this problem that the divergence between those who simply cling to liberalism in its historic form and those who press for its reconstruction is to be explained in large part by the differences in the resources with which they interpret the liberal's faith. The earlier, historic liberalism was basically neo-Kantian in its philosophical method and perspective, Darwinian or Spencerian in its view of evolution, and Newtonian in its understanding of the fundamental notions relating to the physical universe. This applies to American liberals who followed in the pragmatic tradition as well as to the Ritschlians, Hegelians, Personalists, and Positivists who stem from European sources. Kant's dissociation of the subjective ego from the context of objective relations persisted with remarkable tenacity, causing the human dimension of consciousness to be regarded as the source and center of spiritual meaning and value. Darwinian, and later Spencerian, conceptions of evolution reinforced this humanistic bias because in these interpretations the human species stood at the peak of the process in a rather stark and ultimate way. What has developed with striking results in recent critical scholarship has been the placing of man in a context of concrete relations where the fuller datum of nature, including man, has been more completely envisaged. Idealistic perspectives, elaborated out of the dissociation of the human ego, have given way to a realism of structured life and events in which the full passage of events as a spiritual process comes into view. Because this fact of relationship, lifting up patterns or configurations of meaning, has become so formative in our thinking, it would be difficult today to be humanistic or individualistic or atomistic in the sense that earlier liberals tended to be.

The reconstructive mood of our time, which is responsive to these turns of thought, goes beyond historic liberalism in the sense that James, in his radical empiricism, and Bergson advanced beyond Kant and Hegel; and in the sense that emergent evolutionists like Lloyd Morgan and Jan Smuts went beyond the biological conceptions of Darwin and Spencer; and in the way that the new physics, following late nineteenth-century research, displaced Newtonian mechanism. Many liberal Protestants seem to assume that criticism of their premises constitutes a reaction against the liberal spirit and a recession of critical thinking in religion. This ignores completely the revolution in the fundamental notions of liberalism itself. Instead of advancing the liberal outlook, these apologists for liberalism arrest it at a point that places liberal Protestantism outside of these critical turns of thought in all of the major spheres of research. A brief look at some technical sources of insight which are yet to be assimilated by liberal theology will give some indication of the possibilities of a reconstructed liberalism.

I

The most singular source of new appreciation of the import of faith for culture has come from the recent literature which has been informed by cultural anthropology. Patiently, scholars in this field have worked through the rather disillusioning data which had accumulated during the positivist era, and with an uncanny sense of proportion have detected its limitations. Fresher minds, more concretely informed and with their imaginations quickened, have addressed themselves anew to problems of religion and culture which the older literature assumed had been fairly well settled. The outcome has been a rewriting of the story of man's climb to faith, revealing not only a more sensitive and discriminating handling of data that exemplified the life of faith in the community, but a far richer and, we might say, more clarified intellect in the elaboration of its meaning. The biases against religion that motivated much of the technical inquiry into problems of religion and society a generation or more ago have subsided markedly. We can detect in many of the current writers in this field an impressive degree of wholeness of personality which enables them to deal more forthrightly and fairly with facts and relationships than was possible among research minds that had suppressed an unclarified hostility to religion in whatever guise.[1]

The resources that are in process of forming as a result of this more sympathetic study of man in his sensitive outreaches provide a wholly new approach to understanding the subtleties of faith as they are woven into a cultural fabric. No longer is Christian faith, for example, to be interpreted and justified simply as a set of intellectual beliefs. Apologetics need not deteriorate into the tactics of argument; for faith can be seen to be of deeper import, both to the individual and to culture. It is the formative ground

[1] Works that may be said to exemplify such a chastened and clarified view of the cultural role of religion would include: Ruth Benedict, *Patterns of Culture*, Houghton, Mifflin, 1934; Peter H. Buck, *Anthropology and Religion*, Yale University Press, 1939; Ralph Linton, *The Study of Man*, Appleton-Century, 1936; Robert Lowie, *Primitive Religion*, Boni and Liveright, 1924; R. R. Marett, *Faith, Hope and Charity in Primitive Religion*, Macmillan, 1932; *Sacraments of Simple Folk*, 1933; *Head, Heart, and Hands in Human Evolution*, 1935; Margaret Mead, *Coming of Age in Samoa*, 1930; *Growing Up in New Guinea*, 1933. Robert Redfield, *The Folk Culture of Yucatan*, University of Chicago Press, 1941, and *Levels of Integration in Biological and Social Systems*, Cattell Press, Lancaster, Pa., 1942. The works of Malinowski could also be mentioned here, particularly *Myth in Primitive Psychology*, Norton, 1926; and *A Scientific Theory of Culture*, University of North Carolina Press, 1944. His functional view of culture and his tendency to conceive of religion solely in terms of ritual or ceremonial greatly restrict his interpretation of the role of religion in culture. Certain philosophical works dealing with the nature of man deserve to be included here because of the use they make of anthropological materials in this newer vein: Ernst Cassirer, *An Essay on Man*, Yale University Press, 1944; and Susanne K. Langer, *Philosophy in a New Key*, Harvard University Press, 1941.

of man's valuations, reaching the inmost parts of the human psyche, where the meaning of the person or of personality and the sense of meaning relating the person to the wider life about him is subtly fashioned. Faith emerges before articulate speech formulates its communicable symbols, thus giving rise to intellectualized belief. This is as true of the growing child as it is of the emerging culture. The elemental forms of sensibilities and the imaginative poesy which rises into songs and chants of praise, or sober inquiry, becoming formalized into ritual, prayer, and celebration, voice a discerning consciousness of profound proportion, however simple or lacking in sophisticated expression.

The anthropologist peering into the culture-forming observances and practices has come to recognize the different dimensions of the human response, distinguishing between acts and modes of behavior that simply emulate pre-human forms of life, and the kind of human activity that exemplifies the distinctly human structure of consciousness. In this area of human response, where symbol and gesture assumed a higher order of physical sensitivity and meaning, the cultural anthropologist has been able to delineate the myth-making consciousness out of which the early structures of religious experience have emerged.

For the modern anthropologist, myth-making and the myth-consciousness are not to be dismissed as fashions of phantasy. These hold the key, not only to the beginnings of man's psychical activity reaching toward a religious depth; but also to insight into the nature of the feeling context of the race in which sensibilities have emerged and in which the controlling valuations of the culture have taken form. A more discerning grasp of the meaning of faith as a cultural resource and as a social energy is possible as a result of their findings.

II

Working somewhat independently, yet with a measure of rapport with the anthropologist, modern psychologists, who have outgrown the earlier, restrictive brand of behaviorism, have become impressed, possibly for the first time, with the whole complex of feeling responses in which motives, incentives, and aspirations are generated; or in which blockages, resentments, and psychical defeat occur. This is no simple return to the subjectivist point of view of earlier years, but an extension to the data of psychology of the very resources that have deepened the methodological procedures of cultural anthropology. Man is being dealt with as man: a psycho-physical organism with tendencies toward qualities of spirit, not simply as mechanism. In this approach to the meaning of man and to human responses, the deeper emotions that relate man more profoundly to other men and to the events of his world, come in for more careful consideration. One result of this more sensitive inquiry in psychology has been the discovery of love as a powerful social energy and of its importance in the formation of personality as well as of communal relations. In becoming aware of the creative force of love in human relations, the psychologist has come to discern also the diabolic force of hate and of indifference. While at the moment inquiry remains at a fairly elemental level in dealing with these feeling responses, the indications are that psychology is moving into a more profound orientation of its subject matter than it has attained since its emergence as a science.

What is emphasized in this maturing of psychological inquiry is, again, the force and relevance of the religious relationship and the importance of those resources within the culture which nurture the human spirit at these deeper, emotional levels. Psychology, in deepening its course, has come upon the very vein of human nature with which the Christian faith has been chiefly concerned all these years: namely, the human hunger for love and the human proneness to dam up this psychical resource through indifference; or to dissipate its reserves in acts of violence and hate. In this convergence of insight, traditional theological analyses of man are not necessarily confirmed or justified; but the resources of the Christian faith to which theologians have sought to give interpretation are certainly declared to be indispensable to the modern man, even to secure his sanity in living.

III

Underlying both the work in cultural anthropology and in modern psychology is a third area of research bearing upon the nature and destiny of man which has materially transformed procedures and the course of scholarly inquiry into the meaning of the higher dimensions of man. For lack of a more definitive caption, this area might be spoken of as the wide-ranging field of inquiry into emergent evolution. The literature in this field, dating back to the early stimulus of Bergson and James, had its most extensive elaboration in the 'twenties when the British school of philosopher-biologists, C. Lloyd Morgan, S. Alexander, Jan Smuts, and others, were making their distinctive contributions.[2] It cannot be said that any one exponent of this impressive movement of thought, sometimes referred to in technical circles as *organicism,* ever made a completely convincing case in his argument for emergence. Each of them, in his enthusiasm for the insight that had become controlling, seemed to claim too much in his speculative venture. Yet the fact of emergence and the differentiation of structures making for levels within the evolutionary process have been decisively established as essential features of the natural perspective in which competent discussion of man's nature is to proceed. Scientists as well as modern metaphysicians and theologians have accepted its premises and have appropriated its imagery.

This more recent understanding of the evolutionary process, vastly more mature and realistic in its conception of man's emergence than earlier theories, creates a framework of thinking in which the insights of the Christian faith become at once more pertinent and more illuminating. As I shall try to make clear in later chapters, the whole rationale of the Christian witness, attesting to the sovereign rule of love as a controlling principle of consciousness, and to the consciousness of Christ as exemplifying this higher good as a revelation within history, is made in-

---

[2] S. Alexander, *Space, Time, and Deity,* Macmillan, 1920; C. Lloyd Morgan, *Emergent Evolution,* Macmillan, 1923; *Life, Mind, and Spirit,* Holt, 1926; Jan Smuts, *Holism and Evolution,* Macmillan, 1926.

estimably more persuasive and revealing within this perspective. Man as distinctly man appears vividly. The distinguishing features of the human creation stand out in their own right. Likewise, the limiting factors of the human consciousness, which sets man clearly apart from what is more than man, and which impels man not to think more highly of himself than he ought to think, are made vivid by this understanding of human emergence. Thus the exaggerated strokes of the liberal estimate, bequeathed to it by a romanticist view of man, and the deceptions concerning human fulfillment that followed therefrom can be corrected by this saner realism. Not only does the meaning of man as spirit — and the good discerned in Christ — become intelligible within its perspective, but the formative power of faith, operating within the structure of experience which is continually forming and being transformed, assumes a greater clarity.

IV

Finally, we may take notice of the impressive efforts of recent years to formulate a metaphysics which faithfully seeks to generalize the categories that have become persuasive to the point of achieving a consensus among competent, scientific minds. This new metaphysics, which is simply the new vision of science imaginatively informed and elaborated, promises to restore a sense of actuality to the meanings of the Christian faith. It may not be denied, for example, that our thinking upon God since the time of Descartes has been suspended in mid-air, as it were. God as actual power, making for righteousness in history, as the Biblical writers were wont to conceive Him, was remote and unreal once Descartes' skepticism had imposed the precedent for conceiving of God simply as Idea. Kant's postulates, Hegel's concept of the Absolute Ego, even liberal theology's Christocentric principle, venturing belief in a God as good as Jesus, left us with a sense of God's unreality; or at best, as being a derivative from what was more logically assured.

The modern metaphysician has come down from this pragmatic scaffolding which had been erected as an act of tentative faith. Again the concrete events of history — of communities and of individual human lives — speak of the work of wonder in the creative God. Creativeness is no abstraction. It is the continual happening appearing in every moment of time. It is the most immediate and persistent occurrence, giving both actuality and character to events as they emerge. However impersonally he may speak of this happening in the technical discourse of his field, the metaphysician knows he is conveying through his abstract symbols, truth about the creative moment which is charged with intimate and personal consequences. Man is not fashioned in a mechanism, a world-machine; he is cradled and nurtured in a creative community of love which extends beyond the visible bonds of human relations; though, in these human relations, there is real God, real good not our own, at work, issuing in grace and judgment.

Because the new metaphysics, giving to scientific categories their full and imaginative meaning, rises out of the living experiences of men in which decisions are made, and where events of tragedy and triumph are forged, it finds an immediate rapport with the imagery and poetic symbolism of the Biblical writers. What this ancient lore set forth through parable and poetry, the metaphysician — attuned to the qualitative meaning of every concrete event — finds himself expounding in what he understands to be more definitive terms. The interrelating of these ancient and modern sources has not gone far as yet; but the possibilities of their interpenetration give promise of a vigorous structure of faith which will at once have cognitive force and poetic appeal.

One who works upon the theological scene with these resources at hand is impelled to feel that, from within this perspective, the Christian faith is more firmly grounded today as an indispensable and persistent force within Western culture than at any time since the opening years of the Enlightenment. In the face of tragic evidence to the contrary, such an assertion must appear hollow and unrealistic; for it has become clear that over vast stretches of Europe, where hunger and death have haunted the minds of men and women for a generation, civilization itself has subsided. Vigorous movements of thought countering the Christian estimate of man and pointing him toward a destiny clearly contrary to the expectations envisioned by the Christian hope are steadily gaining ascendancy. The sensibilities observed by our Christian forebears, which provided a certain pattern for living based upon discipline and restraint and gave direction to existence even when intellectual issues were not wholly clarified, have seemingly lost their hold upon individuals and groups alike. The churches along with schools and other social institutions flounder in their attempts to achieve a sense of function in a society that has become ridden with theories of self-autonomy. Clearly they do not draw upon the unifying resources of a steadying faith.

We can multiply observations which go directly counter to any assertion of confidence in the hold of the Christian faith upon our current culture. The most telling evidence of the current collapse of faith as a cultural energy is provided by many theologians and churchmen themselves, in so far as they openly confess a withdrawal of Christian forces from the scenes of action, insisting that the time is again at hand when the church must disavow its connections with culture and declare itself a cult apart from culture. Others, speaking in a similar vein but with a different intent, say quite bluntly that Christians conceivably may have to enter the catacombs once again to wait out this time of crisis. The hope of our Christian faith surviving the holocaust, they argue, depends upon the readiness to retrench and to consolidate its forces in an effective remnant that will purify and preserve the faith.

Nevertheless, against this current counsel of despair urging Christian faith to secure its hold through acts of retrenchment or to confess its irrelevance to an age grown acrid with unbelief, these resources of fresh insight into faith and culture bear their stubborn witness. As one who has become persuaded by their persistent witness, I venture to set forth this new apologetics for the Christian faith and, in part, to exemplify its meaning through an analysis of certain of its facets within the perspective these resources provide.

The thesis that I mean to establish in this volume is that faith, the indispensable ingredient of the human psyche, persists in a culture irrespective of the ebb and flow of human moods, giving it character, direction, and possibilities of resource in the form of a structure of experience. No one generation characterizes the nature of the faith; nor does it exemplify it in full dimension. Yet each generation stands in relation to its resource as heir and recipient, either to benefit by its beneficence and wisdom or to be judged by the sensibilities that inhere in the structure of experience that must be a 'cradle and a tomb' to every human psyche within its natural orbit.

This would mean that the living faith of the culture is always reflected in the mentality of any period, but never wholly contained in it or circumscribed by its passing moods. It operates, as does character itself, either as an active, assertive force under pressure of stimulus; or as a reserve of possible resource — dormant, but of potential, qualitative import.

The faith, understood as an accumulative consensus of sensibility and valuation, giving quality and range to the psychical thrust of the culture, determines the dimension of depth in feeling and conception within the culture. Thus the range and depth of perception and of imaginative power in any given period is proportionate to this persisting, elemental source of qualitative meaning. To live *in character* in this sense of being responsive to the faith is to live with integrity in the culture. To have character in this sense may or may not connote qualitative differentiation in human personality. It is possible to be in character at a low level of conformity. It is also possible to be in character with a high degree of discrimination and perceptiveness. But to be lacking in character, to be in total rebellion against the qualitative depths of the culture or utterly indifferent to its demands, is to suffer psychical frustration to some degree; possibly to the degree of psychical impairment or even of utter, psychical defeat. A man might thus become irresponsible or insensible to qualitative disciplines or restraints. He will, in any case, be shorn of aspirational outreach, and thus lose his capacity for joy and wonder.

The loss of faith is thus a serious, psychical matter. It most certainly must mean the dissolution of structures through which the grace of God is mediated and made redemptive in personality and in human communities. It may mean the crumbling of culture and the atrophy of its creative sense. In time, once the will to live significantly has subsided, it may rout the will to live. Meaninglessness in a society or in any individual life implies the collapse of those subtle connections that enable the person or the community to avail itself of the resources of spirit that inhere in the structure of experience as a persisting faith.

II

The Dissipation of Faith

FAITH, wherever and however expressed, exemplifies a dimension of thought and feeling which serves simultaneously to restrain, or humble, rational effort and to heighten sensitivity to the complexity of man's existence. Being allied with the mythical consciousness, and being a form of psychical energy arising from the depth of orientation implied in the mythical response, faith evinces the elemental outreach of the distinctly human dimension of consciousness. Wonder and expectancy are its barest psychical manifestations. Trust, connoting a psychical resolution of issues raised by wonder and expectancy, or by their negation through apprehension or despair, can be regarded as a more settled form of faith. I would not call it a more mature or sophisticated form of faith because maturity is not always manifest in this resolution; nor is it always its pre-condition. Acquiescence to authority, issuing in credulity, can be an expression of trust. On the other hand, the resolution of tensions and of critical issues, raised and resolved by the restive mind, as implied by Whitehead when he defines religion as 'the transition from God, the void to God the enemy, and from God the enemy, to God the companion,'[1] may exemplify the mood of trust in its mature and sophisticated form.

Wonder, expectancy, and trust, as exemplified in faith, convey implicitly a sense of the human limitation of being which, when expressed constructively, becomes a more-than-human dimension of experience. In minimum form this condition of faith may

[1] *Religion in the Making,* Macmillan, 1926.

be a persistent tinge of nature mysticism, restraining the human mind from laying violent hands upon the works of nature. In its maximum state, it is a bold assertion of theism in some form, confidently distinguishing between what is of man and that which points beyond man's thinking and doing.

The dimension of faith, as conveying an overtone of meaning beyond or deeper than our definitive discourse, is either an ambiguous extension of experience or a penetration of experience which is more subtle and perceptive than the measure of our common sense would imply. Faith deals in overtones and nuances — not that it is simply concerned with the adumbrations of events, but in giving greater dimension to practical vision, faith impels one in any particular grasp of meaning to attend to the fullness of an event. In such an encounter, what is envisaged may not be so readily seized with clarity or precision.

Faith is thus always corrective of the precise measure; although it need not nullify its sharpened focus. If the conclusion dictated by fact yields despair, faith urges a fresh burst of optimism, however tentative, with which to transcend the defeating fact. If the mind, bent on precision, moves toward clarity and toward an economy of terms, faith urges greater perceptiveness and a concern for the complexity of meaning. If decision, in the interest of efficiency and a functional view, cancels out the appeal to tradition, faith awakens a concern for the persistence of value and its claims upon creative experience; but when life loses its creative urge and settles into a visionless routine, faith beckons the eye toward new frontiers. Thus, in addition to exemplifying a dimension exceeding every measured view, faith has a vital character. It resists defeat and dissolution or death because, in its initial and elemental essence, it is an impulse toward life. And this quality of renewal is never lost to it however sophisticated or transmuted faith may become.

Depth and a dynamic power of renewal, then, are the two dimensions that faith imparts to culture and to the individual life. These qualities of faith, however, do not insure it against the indiscriminate or excessive display of sentiment or of power. Because it roots in vitality, faith is given to the exercise of bounty rather than of measured expression. For this reason it is difficult to discipline faith; just as it is difficult to discipline love. Both faith and love are movements within the human psyche which resist all measure; even as their normal inclination is to exceed all measure within space and time.

Faith, which moves mountains, which turns water into wine, which commands the lame to walk and the dead to rise, is a thrust of the human psyche which recognizes no conceptual bounds. In this respect, it honors miracle more than law. But when it pursues miracle with a disregard for law, it assumes an irresponsible character that denies to it structure, discipline, and cultural force. This is the irony of its social situation. It cannot capitulate to form and measure without losing force as an elemental vitality; yet, when it is indifferent to discipline and structure, it dissipates its vital force in sheer sentiment, divorced from the processes of culture. In becoming formless sentiment or aimless wonder, it collapses as a directive of culture.

In this respect, faith is no different from any form of creative art. Art retains character and creative power only as it resists the temptation to become designing in meeting the demands of the critic; yet its force as a work of art, affecting its role in culture, depends upon its acquiring discipline in shaping and executing its imaginative thrust.

Faith, then, as an act of decision, impelling the human psyche toward a transmuted will to live in response to the redemptive grace which brings assurance of a benevolent, infinite will or as a corporate affirmation of the religious community, operates against great odds as a cultural force. It is impelled to transcend the conceptual bounds of the culture as defined by law and logic, or by science; yet its very impulse to exceed these bounds imperils its creative structure. The inclination to define the disciplines of religious thought and practice in isolation from the cultural arts and sciences should be understood as an attempt within the faith to achieve discipline without relinquishing this transcendent thrust. In pursuing this kind of discipline, religion formalizes its acts and symbols, and formulates its dogmas. Ecclesiasticism in rigid form is faith simulating a disciplined structure without recourse to the disciplines of culture. Formalism fixes the faith in durable forms; but in so doing, it tends to arrest its vitality, denying it a creative role in the culture. The inclination, on the other hand, to defy discipline, in whatever form, and to resist all form of thought or structure, even the disciplines and structures of an insulated cultus, leaves faith responsive only to the elemental impulses; or at the mercy of a restricted mode of coercion imposed by fanatic zeal.

Faith thus tends to thrive either as a corporate energy insulated within its own self-imposed bounds or as an individual passion. Once it is cast in either form, the effort to impart its vision or its zeal to the culture itself meets with hostility or frustration. The effort to counter such hostility or frustration, and to relate religious faith to the responsible ends of the culture, tends to take the course of salvaging the intelligible increment of faith, permitting all else to be canceled out or ignored. Historic efforts since the period of the religious wars in Europe, including the most recent pragmatic movements in liberalism, can be characterized as repeated attempts to salvage the functional energy of faith for culture by applying restrictive, conceptual measures to it which might assure it an intelligible course. That the men of these recent years were dedicated to the life of faith cannot be denied. That their faith was of a meager measure, must, however, be acknowledged. By their measures, the problem of faith and culture was, to some extent, met; but only at a level that assured a moral incentive. The deeper range of faith as a perceptive resource of the human psyche, which derived from sensibilities more subtle than ethical discriminations and demands, was made unavailable to the age that followed in their course. This dimension of the Christian faith, pointing to creative and redemptive energies, preceding and transcending the ethical life, was, in effect, lost to the moral appeal to faith, as defined by Kant, Ritschl, and subsequent liberal theologians. And this meant the relinquishment of depth in deference to clarity, and to a practical sense. The present condition in liberal Protestantism which imperils its survival as an effective witness to the Christian faith; and, for that matter, which deprives it of power as a social institution within modern culture, arises from a loss of depth in its envisagement of both man and God, and in its loss of focus. Both the loss of depth and the loss of focus within liberalism can be attributed historically to restrictive tendencies following from the Enlightenment in general, and from Kantian influence in particular, which narrowed the bounds of faith to a rational and moral measure. To an analysis of these restrictive tendencies, which dissipated the dimension of faith, we must now turn.

I

A sampling of representative works from Francis Bacon and Descartes through Kant and Schleiermacher will confirm the common impression that during the years represented by these writers, roughly between the opening years of the seventeenth century and the early decades of the nineteenth century, a radical reorientation of men's minds toward the Christian faith occurred, lessening the hold of faith and dissipating the social force of the Christian mythos within Western culture. This was a time when enterprises of thought and of creative art, including philosophy, literature, painting, drama, music, as well as the professional learning of the schools, broke free from the mores and controlling ideas of a church-controlled culture, and began, each within its own field, to pioneer in the shaping of an independent medium. Art for its own sake, pure science, pure philosophical inquiry, and the independent, critical mind, were to be the normal accompaniments and consequences of this liberated consciousness.

The full account of this changing mentality of the West, of the changing status of the church, and of the relevance of Christianity to culture, all of which are in some degree implied in the emergence of modern culture, has been told and interpreted with varying motives: sometimes from within a perspective that deplores the loss of the church's hold upon culture and its resulting autonomous spirit; [2] sometimes within a very different perspective that glories in the emergence of the free and untrammeled spirit of modern science, art, and culture along with free enter-

[2] Cf. Christopher Dawson, *Religion and Culture*.

prise.[3] Our concern here must be a restricted inquiry, not unrelated to this wider cultural problem but focused upon a specific tendency within this cultural reorientation. The assessment of this cultural reorientation bears directly upon our understanding and judgment of theological liberalism and of the life of the liberal Protestant church which has come to exemplify this liberated consciousness.

That tendency of which we speak may be described as the progressive relinquishment of the Christian myth as a motivating center of sensibilities and of the spiritual outreach within Western culture as it has passed through successive stages of liberation in thought and in institutional development. The problems implied in this tendency have been explored many times, sometimes as an issue over secularism; at other times as a question of the autonomy of scholarship and of free inquiry, implying the separation of religion and the schools; or again, as an inquiry into the relation and differences between Christian faith and democratic faith, implying the separation of church and state. Our problem, though more restricted, is deeper than any of these since we mean to bore into this question: Can any culture be free from the sensibilities of its myth without experiencing a loss of depth in perceptive awareness by which the stature of human existence is envisaged; thus losing, in the last analysis, the sense of meaning in the culture at large, and a sense of direction within its respective institutions?

The premise from which such an inquiry proceeds is that myth reaches a depth of valuation which reasoned thought and the various devices for clarification and communication of meaning cannot emulate or sustain. Or, to put it differently, in any situation, particularly in any relationship, be it the relationship of two people in love, a family circle, or a community gathering under various auspices, silence can be more profound than the uttered speech. I shall not argue the point that this can lead to sheer nonsense or to an unmanageable mysticism. I am only

[3] Cf. G. B. Smith, *Social Idealism and the Changing Theology,* and John Dewey, *Reconstruction in Philosophy.*

concerned here to say that any attempt at utterance gives but a partial and inadequate articulation of the event or situation pressing for interpretation, whether this be the halting attempt of a boy telling a girl of his love or the most eloquent spokesman of the family or community voicing deeply felt sentiments in a public ceremonial. Indirection in speech, as in communication through art and symbol, have been more or less desperate attempts to convey, without loss of perceptive awareness, the fuller meaning of an event under consideration.

A culture in which directness and clarity, above all else, is sought, must of necessity forego some concern with depth and complexity. I should hesitate to make such an observation too categorically lest sheer vagary and credulity be set up as unambiguous goods; while precision and the art of disciplined thought be dismissed as being impoverishing to men's lives. The absurdity and folly of such a position is obvious. Nevertheless, I would hold that the insistent drive toward minimum meanings in the interest of communication, be it the concern with basic English, basic education, or basic Christianity, consciously acknowledges a practical or functional end which either denies the complexity of events, or disavows any concern with the depth of meaning, preferring the process of communication, however meager, to the quality and stature of meanings which are communicated.

The question that confronts us here, however directly or indirectly we may pursue it, is: Can we throw any light upon the predicament of modern Protestantism, not to say the whole of our modern crisis, by assessing the trends in thought and mores which reshaped the Christian conscience and consciousness within the liberal era that followed the age of the Enlightenment? I must confess that I undertook this inquiry with a partial prejudice, having come to the rather vague judgment that liberation from the Christian mythos has meant progressive liberation from the Christian ethos. By ethos I mean here what Webster explicitly states, namely, 'the character, sentiment, or disposition of a community or people; the spirit which actuates manners and customs . . .' And by mythos I mean the pattern of meaning and valuations which has been imaginatively projected through drama or metaphor, expressing the perceptive truths of the historic experience of a people, bearing upon man's nature and destiny. A thorough effort at documenting this judgment will eventually require fuller absorption in the literature of this liberating period; but our modest effort at sampling certain representative documents yields some contribution to a judgment. I shall try to summarize some impressions which seem to me to have become clear from a re-reading of Francis Bacon's *Advancement of Learning,* Descartes' *Discourse on Method,* Locke's *The Reasonableness of Christianity,* Tillotson's sermons, Tindal's *Christianity as Old as Creation,* Hume's *Essay on Miracles,* Kant's *Critique of Pure Reason, Critique of Practical Reason, Critique of Judgment, Religion Within the Bounds of Reason Alone,* and Schleiermacher's *Speeches to the Cultured Despisers of Religion* as well as his *Christian Faith.*

Of the men we have noted above, it cannot be said that they consciously dissociated themselves from the Christian mythos. Each in his own way retained, along with whatever he advocated, some awareness of Christian doctrine, or of Christian revelation, as having some relation and bearing for every man's life. Thus Descartes, who undermined every substance with his skeptical inquiry except the substance of thought, thus retaining the thinking self as the only assured existence on a primary basis, was able nevertheless to derive from this premise that God also exists. And, whether for lack of a heroic spirit or a leaning toward genuine piety, he resisted any implication of impiety in his skepticism, insisting that both science and religion were necessary, though in his own thought no real reconciliation between them was achieved. In his *Principles of Philosophy,* Descartes concludes with the words,

Nevertheless, lest I should presume too far, I affirm nothing, but submit all these my opinions to the authority of the Church and the judgment of the more sage; and I desire no one to believe anything I may have said, unless he is constrained to admit it by the force and evidence of reason.[4]

[4] *Principles of Philosophy,* p. 228.

Bacon, although arguing zealously to separate theology and philosophy and to set up a course of higher learning in the universities which should pursue disciplined inquiry *independently* of ecclesiastical or traditional restraints, acknowledged at the same time the claims of revealed theology.[5] In subsequent instances, say of Locke, Tillotson, Tindal, and certainly of Kant and Schleiermacher, identification with the Christian myth in some respects is forthrightly acknowledged. Hume would probably be the exception; unless it can be said that despite his radical skepticism, dissolving every basis for either rational or empirical knowledge, he reopened the way for a more radical dependence upon faith.

Whether or not this acknowledgment of the Christian myth given in revelation is deemed incidental in the positive convictions which motivated their work, I think that the acknowledgment itself is of some importance for our inquiry.

We may say in addition that, in no instance, was there any conscious effort to weaken or to nullify the constructive force of the Christian faith. The motivation of the men whom we have cited was in no sense iconoclastic. (Were we to explore more extensively the deistic writings and later positivistic studies such as Feuerbach's *What Is Christianity?*, we should have to qualify this observation.) On the contrary, the evidence is clear that in certain instances the concern was to rid Christianity of its debilitating accretions and to streamline its gospel for more effective application in the current cultural scene. This applies particularly to men such as Locke and Tillotson as well as to Kant and Schleiermacher. In the one case, ridding Christianity of its attending tone of mystery was to free it from controversy and divisive tendencies. And simplifying its gospel, thus clarifying its meaning and its demands, was to increase the possibility of its acceptance and of exemplification among reasonable men. Here the readiness to cancel out depth of meaning was obviously stimulated by the immediate experiences of horror and suffering resulting from the religious wars; but it would be a mistake to make this the sole explanation of their appeal to reasonableness. Clearly reasonable-

[5] Cf. *Advancement of Learning.*

ness was, in itself, considered a virtue which applied to Christianity as well as to civic and political affairs. It is here that a deistic strain is detected in Locke and his contemporaries despite all their acknowledgments of revelation. Nothing, in their judgment, which is given by revelation or which remains hidden, unrevealed, or beyond disclosure, is of more significance than that which can be clearly grasped by reasonable minds. This is an understandable lay reaction to specialized expositions of divinity; but it is not simply reaction. It proceeds from a sure sense of an explicit exemplification of God's meaning and intention in natural structures which can be reasonably divined. The whole of this era is obsessed with a conviction of the reasonableness of God and nature which, in turn, associates any notion of depth beyond the reach of the reasoning mind with obscurantism, as in radical deism; or simply sets it apart from rational discourse on the assumption that it is consonant with reason even though it may not lend itself at once to clear, rational exposition.

In Kant and Schleiermacher, to be sure, we meet with a different formulation of this Enlightenment motif; but in the last analysis, their presentations of Christianity draw upon the same basic appeal to the reasonable nature of existence and to the naturalization of existence which brings all meanings, both human and divine, within the range of human experience or human apprehension.

Kant's concept of the thing-in-itself and the dualism which resulted cannot be viewed as a return to supernaturalism. It was simply a way of acknowledging the limitations of thought and of defining the conditions under which the human mind might surmount these limitations in seeking a reasonable ground for faith. If we say that Kant reformulated the appeal to faith, we must recognize the reasonable basis upon which this appeal rested. Kant, in this respect, was as clearly a mind of the Enlightenment as were Locke and Hume.

Kant's motive in seeking a reasonable basis for Christian faith was, of course, prompted in no small degree by the work of Hume, who had dispelled confidence, not only in the reasonable appropriation of religious truth but in a reasonable appropriation of experience itself; but his effort may be viewed in the larger context of the Enlightenment era as well, in which the formulation of truth and of goodness was dictated by a concern for the economy of expression in the interest of a clarified, and thus a reasonable, exposition.

The norm of life, as well as of thought, was the reasonable, moral consciousness. This was not the same as the rational consciousness either of the Aristotelian form or in the Cartesian sense. The latter provided for the extended use of reason in creating an architecture of thought. The motivation here could almost be described as aesthetic in the sense that mathematical construction is aesthetic. The motivation of the thought of the Enlightenment, which appears in Locke and later in Kant, was moral enterprise among reasonable men. This called for economy of thought as well as of action, which created a mind-set against delving into mysteries beyond one's depth or of bending the mind toward effort which lay outside of its capacity or function.

Kant's concern with Christianity was a moral concern as Locke's concern with it was civic and practical. In each case the concern was genuine and wholehearted, bent on a reconstruction of Christian thought in the interest of increasing its motive power and cultural effectiveness.

In Schleiermacher we see the same Enlightenment mentality at work, but with a greater range and diversity of sentiments to enrich both consciousness and experience. Schleiermacher, too, sought to rid Christianity of its irrelevant accretions and to focus it for effectively disciplining culture. In this effort he was not impassive to the appeal for reasonableness, despite his sharp strictures upon rationality and the effort to reduce religion to the bounds of reason; nor was he indifferent to the claims of the moral consciousness despite his impatience with what he regarded as a confusion of religion and ethics. Both of these elements enter into his formulation of the Christian faith as accommodating perspectives, setting his conception of religion as feeling in a context which, to the mind of the age, seemed both responsible and relevant. Schleiermacher, in other words, did not abandon the Enlightenment consciousness; he deepened its range of sensibility by informing moral faith and rationality with the elemental claims of feeling as a prior source and ground of man's religious orientation. But in the last analysis, Schleiermacher, too, worked toward the economy of Christian doctrine in the interest of a reasonable orientation of Christian faith. By specifying the religious consciousness as the normative source of doctrine he excluded a whole range of theological inquiries which might press the mind into speculative ventures. By designating the God-consciousness of the historic Jesus as the religious norm and redemptive center of the Christian community, he purposely canceled out all speculative ideas concerning the Christian life and the atonement. However much we may acknowledge the range and sweep of Schleiermacher's thought, we cannot set aside this defining element in his theology, narrowing the bounds of Christian experience and of theological inquiry. Relating his thought to the Romanticist movement, as did Rudolf Otto in observing that Schleiermacher discovered the sense of the numinous,[6] does not alter matters on this point.

The intention, then, of the men we have considered was constructive with regard to Christianity if their intention is viewed within the perspective of the Enlightenment. Here liberation of the Christian mind from doctrinal complexities and from the sense of emotional depth was clearly related to a regard for religious sanity arising (a) on its negative side from aversion to religious disputes and dissension; and (b) on its positive side from an all-controlling conviction of the reasonableness of God and nature in their relations to the world of men.

II

The consequences of their labors, however, may be judged quite otherwise. The zeal for liberation and for clarification of the Christian gospel meant, in each instance, a shrinkage, not only in the range of theological topics but in the scope of the Christian conception of man and of the meaning of existence.

Bacon's reconception of the content and method of learning, for example, must be judged, not solely by his readiness to retain

[6] *The Idea of the Holy,* Oxford, 1923.

revelation and the imaginative arts as an open horizon extending the learning of the schools; but by the readiness of subsequent educators, scientists, technicians, philosophers, as well as liberal clergymen, to relinquish this horizon in deference to a concerted pursuit of *knowledge as power*. The drift into scientism, which, step by step, transformed the methodology of higher education throughout the entire range of inquiry into one of descriptive analysis, must be considered as one major fulfillment of Bacon's *Advancement of Learning*. To it must be attributed also, motivation for the rise of the so-called scientific outlook with its stress on philosophy and culture in one key, which retired the contemplative arts and other concerns with the nurture of sensibilities to the periphery of the common life, and left purposeful action which arises from knowledge that is power the only serious business at hand.

One can argue that Bacon did not envisage such a single-minded and impoverished human economy; and he certainly did not embrace it himself. Yet the fact remains that his spirited reforms in thought and learning, however guarded, released the vision that gave impetus to what John Dewey has called the radical reconstruction in philosophy and culture.[7] In this new world view, the appeal to the Christian mythos has been wholly lost from view. In its stead, the Leviathan of science and industry looms as the compelling object of men's dreams and the shaper of their institutions.

Again, Locke's simplification of the Christian gospel in *The Reasonableness of Christianity* is to be judged, not solely on the grounds of his own conscientious, civic intent; but as well by the consequences among men of common sense in subsequent periods who continually appeal to this work as a classic model in the interest of reducing Christianity to the proportions of an ethical culture society.

And further, the concern to reduce Christian meanings more radically by way of bringing them within the bounds of reason is to be judged both by the iconoclasm of the early, more impassioned deists, who sought to rid Christianity of its mystery, and

[7] John Dewey, *Reconstruction in Philosophy*, Holt, 1920, cf. Chap. II.

by the almost devout moral earnestness of Immanuel Kant; but not only by the fruits of their labors. It is to be assessed also in the light of Positivism, late mid-nineteenth-century materialism, and religious humanism where, again, the sensibilities and the imagery of the Christian mind are canceled out as confidence in the reasoning mind becomes increasingly assertive.

Again, the reformulation of faith within the range of moral idealism, centering in the worth of the person, as in Kant's *Critique of Practical Reason,* is to be judged not solely on the basis of its accomplishment in overcoming the skepticism of his age; but in the light of the insulating moralism of subsequent periods as well. The consequence of this development for spiritual perceptiveness is difficult to state and more difficult to assess. The difficulty arises from the fact that moral idealism is so obviously a good that we are immediately handicapped in trying to point out its impoverishing or evil effects. There are moments when I feel the impoverishment of this moral consciousness so keenly that I am tempted to cry out against it as a withering blight upon the spiritual sensitivity of modern man; but the irresponsibility of such a remark in the face of our obvious moral crisis quickly impels one to temper his words and to utter them only among friends. It is pertinent to say here, however, that the tendency to enclose the concerns of Christian faith within moral passion, on the one hand, and moral idealism, on the other, had the effect of restricting the range of what might be called the Christian criticism of man as well as of the Christian appreciation of man.

It restricted the range of the Christian criticism of man in that it became a social gospel, bent upon making society and social institutions safe for persons and for personality on the unexamined assumption that the person constituted an assured and unambiguous good. This assumption, to be sure, followed from the prevailing and controlling idea of the period upon which the appeal to moral faith rested: namely, that man as person was the highest exemplification of spiritual good. This idea, formulated by the Renaissance in the dictum that man is the measure of all things, was reinforced both by the Enlightenment and by Romanticist thought. In the one case, the reasoning substance of the self became the criterion of existence and value, and, in the other instance, the individuality of the person became the unique and precious disclosure of the world's deepest interior meaning. Kant lifted these notions to a metaphysical level which he turned to religious ends in fixing upon the moral worth of the person as a controlling and organizing principle, both in ethics and in religion.

To be sure, Kant was aware of what he called a *radical evil* in man. I am in agreement with Emil Brunner when he observes that the liberal's estimate of man would have been basically altered had this notion of radical evil been fully appropriated by subsequent theologies. Actually, it was obscured and ultimately lost sight of altogether when the theory of evolution appeared, providing the scientific ground for saying that sin is the bestiality in man, a vestigial remainder that can eventually be educated out of him as he pursues a more human and personal route.

Personality and spirituality were thus made coterminous. Christianity was interpreted as a guide to confident living as a person. The teachings of Jesus were understood to be explicit delineations of character traits to be emulated by the Christian personality. They who hungered after righteousness could thus be fed; for the conditions of righteousness were clearly envisaged and were within reach of any normal or reasonable person.

By turning the Christian criticism of man into a social gospel for the preservation of persons, and then into a study of character traits for the full-formed personality, the liberal Christian tended to become insensitive to the darker mystery of man's nature. In being indifferent to this aspect, he ignored the vein of human nature to which the Christian faith had pointed its doctrine of sin, particularly in the more radical sense of viewing the person as an ambiguous good. With the obscuring of this deeply perplexing and tragic phase of man's story in theological discussion, there followed a progressive relinquishment of concern with the drama of redemption and with problems of grace and judgment, all of which relate to the vital energies of existence arising from a deeper orientation in faith, giving stature and ultimate meaning to man.

It took alien ideologies (namely, Marxism and depth psychology) and the tragic tyranny of twisted personalities within recent years to reawaken the modern mind to this depth of evil working in human nature.

In saying that liberal theologies, drawing upon the resources of moral idealism, restricted the range of the Christian appreciation of man, I have in mind the oversimplified, moral version of spiritual man. In this portrayal, the complexity of man's nature as a creature and as a child of God was first obscured, then lost from view. For example, the subtleties of the life of the spirit implicit in any contrast between saint and sinner were absent. The overtones of the life of the spirit, the whole dimension of aspiration and of dedicated living which is sacramentally felt or experienced in the act of worship, in contemplation, in great music and poetry, in every form of serious activity in which imagination is quickened, had little meaning for a person committed to the moral measure of man. It is significant that wherever Christian faith was channeled exclusively into a path of ethical action, concern with these overtones vanished. Kant made no place for it. The Ritschlians had no significant place for worship. Liberal Christians with a social passion, like Walter Rauschenbusch, could combine ethical propheticism and a discerning sense for the re-creative values of worship; but for many modernists ritual was to be dismissed as 'the trappings of religion' and the meditative mood as a sentimental dissipation of the ethical nerve in religion.

But this only partly assesses the matter. Ultimately this conception of Christianity as moral idealism amounted to an arrested view of man which made of the moral consciousness the *summum bonum* of spiritual ascent. This, in the last analysis, is a veiled form of humanism. It is to make of the human structure of consciousness the pinnacle of creation and, in turn, the criterion of value for all creation. Even God is then fashioned in its image. Now I submit that this removes the depth of being not only from man but from God as well. The mystery of God's being vanishes, or is made unimportant. God is known either as the moral being discerned in Jesus or the Infinite, Benevolent Will implied in the moral will of man. The holy, the dimension beyond man, beyond the human structure, the not-yet, or the yet-unrealized intimation of God's creative working: all that might properly be termed spirit in contrast to the fully formed structure of human personality — this good not our own which is evident among us, yet not of our making; which interpenetrates our experience with beneficence and judgment — is a dimension that was shorn from the moralistic view of man and God.

Now the problem that presses upon us as we become aware of this impoverishment of mood and of content in the liberal Protestant's conception of faith is: How does a culture, how does a church community, how do theologians recover the sense of depth which can restore this dimension of the holy? Various ways suggest themselves, some of which are in operation in current thought and action. (1) We can return to the thought of some previous period before the dissipation of faith ensued in the hope of reappropriating this larger, Christian vision. (2) We can surround ourselves with an aesthetic stimulus that steadily deepens appreciation of this past heritage in which holiness was a dominant motif. (3) We can set to work at the constructive task within the liberal Protestant tradition in the effort to correct or overcome the turn of thought or state of mind which led to the present impoverishment. I am suggesting that we find a clue to such a reconstruction in the over-readiness of these very men we have consulted to simplify the Christian faith. Simplification of the meaning of faith and existence led to an exaggerated confidence in reason and in the capacity of man to cope with the human problem. Conversely, it obscured the deeper issues involved in the very element of mystery which was cast out — issues that press to the fore in any serious encounter with tragedy, death, or frustration.

The task of our time is to reorient Christian thought in a sounder, more realistic context in which clarity and mystery may be held in tension. The tension must be real such that the capacities of reason and the limits of reason may be clearly envisaged

against the horizon of mystery, both within experience and beyond man's experience. Where the Christian mind is so oriented,
faith as a deeper rapport with the life process and with the living
God, who is creatively at work within its events, can both shape
our course and re-create our minds in the face of these limiting
conditions of creaturehood.

III

Clues to Reconstruction

THE LIBERAL CHURCH has a theological task on its hands which amounts to a major reconstructive effort. It has delayed this task too long. By persisting in the same course it has become the foil of reactionary thought and, within its own ranks, has steadily lost prophetic power. The reconstruction must go deeper than a reappraisal of premises. Its feeling orientation must change radically to accord with the feeling context of all vital existence today and of creative meaning in our time.

In pursuing a constructive solution to the liberal's problem, I shall point up certain clues that seem to me to give promise of a reconstructed liberalism. My procedure here will be to show that within the basic premise of immanence a reconstruction of the theological orientation of liberalism can be effected so as to enable it to avail itself of the dynamic of the Christian faith as an organizing principle.

I regard the doctrine of immanence as a crucial premise to be retained because upon its retention, to whatever degree, however altered or reconstructed, rests what I would call the sanity of the theological enterprise. Notice I do not say *reasonableness* of the enterprise. I am parting company with rationality as an arbitrary norm or generalized feature of existence in the sense in which idealism insisted upon it. Sanity does not presuppose a completely rational order of existence. It simply implies a margin of rationality in the midst of irrational and unpredictable factors which, nevertheless, assures sufficient order and meaningfulness to enable us to function intelligibly in a context of related disciplines.

Now immanence simply presupposes that there are structures within the reach and recognition of man which disclose God's working in some form and to some degree. This does not deny the hiddenness of God. In fact, in reconstructed form it heartily affirms it as a corollary of God's recognizable aspect. This principle of correlating the clearly given and the obscure occurrent will be seen to be indispensable to a reconstructed liberalism.

The first clue, then, to a solution of the liberal's problem is to be found in an appraisal of the doctrine of immanence itself. Here it is discovered how completely liberalism has been dominated by the ideology of idealism and of pragmatic empiricism, wherein the formative meanings have been taken to be mental events. In its present formulation, therefore, the doctrine of immanence is a dated doctrine. Having arisen in the modern period from a deistic conception of mind and natural law, this doctrine became elaborated into a world-view in Romanticist thought and in Absolute Idealism. Nineteenth-century science, once it had been won to the side of idealism, served to reinforce the prestige of this doctrine as the philosophical equivalent of its own scientific empiricism. This was made even more tenable in the philosophy of pragmatism. While the idealistic insistence upon mind as a sovereign category is not expressed in pragmatism, the persistence of this idealistic notion in its empiricism may be clearly recognized.

Now the clue I am pointing up here is that liberalism, through its doctrine of immanence, continues the feeling orientation of idealism and pragmatic empiricism which places it radically out of accord with the feeling context of all vital existence today and of creative meaning in our time. One way of stating it is to say that Liberalism rides upon the surfaces of thought currents that were occasioned by Idealism and by the pragmatic era. In this perspective, reality, man's reality, God's meaning, existence as event, are conceived wholly within the category of conscious experience. The whole of its discourse is occasioned by and retained within the language of conscious experience.

What separates this world of discourse from the contemporary context of thought and feeling is the dimension of depth — the sense of meaning and power that derives from happenings and configurations of events that are deeper than consciousness.

We need not try to delineate the developments in recent years which have brought about this new climate of meaning. It is clear that depth psychology was a precursor of this view of existence, and despite its periodic discrediting, remains a formidable discourse with which liberal Protestantism will have to come to terms. The tortured thinking of D. H. Lawrence was a British counterpart of Freudian thinking, especially such works of his as *The Fantasia of the Unconscious*. The sickness of his mind should not obscure the perceptive quality of his grasp of meaning. Emergent philosophies, dating from Bergson, are of this newer feeling context. And when Whitehead said *we feel with our bodies,* he was articulating a depth of thought that partakes of this context. His philosophy, for all its trafficking with Platonism, is to be understood as contributing to an understanding of this sense of depth. Existentialism, having from the time of Kierkegaard, resisted Hegelian idealism, has persistently sought what it has called the total meaning of the subject — the I — in all human discourse as well as in the divine-human encounter. And in this effort, Existentialistic thinkers insisted upon knowing man in a deeper sense than conscious experience has afforded.

In various ways and to varying degrees these restive forces in modern thought have been breaking free of the restrictive frame of thought and experience in which theological liberalism has remained encased. Liberalism, remaining within the ideology of idealism and of pragmatic empiricism, thus survives as an orthodoxy that cannot speak realistically or significantly to the modern man who has been awakened to tragedy and to irrational forces that plague his world.

The hope of liberalism would seem to lie in the direction of allying itself with a deeper empiricism that will enable it to participate in this dimension of depth without losing character.

A word should be said parenthetically about this phrase *sense of depth*. It should not be dismissed as a mystical shibboleth. In some instances it seems to imply little else. But in the main, it points to a genuine dimension of existence beyond conscious experience which, when related to the conscious life, illumines and enhances it in qualitative ways. I hope to make this clear as I proceed. Whether we are speaking in the context of psychoanalysis or gestalt psychology or modern metaphysics, depth implies relationship and a complexity of meaning defying ready observation or analysis. In modern forms of existentialism, depth has more the implication of irrational qualities, possibly in a demonic sense. In all instances, it restricts the relevance of rationality; or, shall we say, is so sensible to the complexity of events because of their dynamic relations and the unpredictable factors that these entail, that it insists upon reviewing rationality as one among other features of experience, rather than as a controlling concept.

Thus the dimension of depth confronts the liberal doctrine of immanence and its corresponding assumption of rationality, somewhat in the guise of a menacing intruder. In some formulations, to be sure, it implies a canceling out of both immanence and rationality. In these forms, irrationality, transcendence and the dimension of depth appear as inseparable companions. The hope of liberalism, I am trying to say, lies in the possibility of correlating depth and immanence; which in effect, means correlating depth and rationality.

It is the contention of the new metaphysics, as I understand it, that this correlation not only can be made but is made in any adequate description of events. Rationality is assured because events have a structure. But events are known to have adumbrations as well, which fact tempers the import of rationality as a clue to the world's meaning. If idealism was ready to universalize reason as a category and pragmatism could assume rationality or the appeal to reasonableness to be a normative factor, the new metaphysical context in which we believe liberalism has promise accepts both rationality and what is non-rational as twin facets of all events in existence. This means that the 'clearly given' event comes into conscious awareness with a surplusage that points beyond itself to relations that define its meaning with a relevance fully as significant as the descriptive structure that appears.

An illustration is any object taken in its context. A chair that I happen to be looking at, while brooding over this paper, will serve as an example. It is Victorian in style, newly upholstered in brown tones. An interior decorator would estimate it to be a hundred years old. You can take it descriptively as a chair fitting into these general characteristics, of which there are undoubtedly many similar models. But the meaning of this chair is not grasped by such description; for, apart from the fact that it forms part of a setting which creates a certain aesthetic value in a household, it happens to be an heirloom that relates this household to two preceding generations. It is a symbol that recalls to various members of the household former years of family life under various circumstances. The surplusage of meaning involves these connections of sentiment, and much that could be delineated.

The meaning of a person is similarly vast in its multiple and intricate connections which radiate from this visible body that bears a name. But what applies to chairs and persons applies to all events of whatever character — to the life of a family, a community, or a total culture within any given period of time. Context gives to every object, every person, every group, every culture within a given period of time, a surplusage of meaning which accompanies and qualitatively informs whatever may be observed as fact. The clearly given can be described and otherwise rationally noted; the obscure occurrent must be taken as a depth or range of related meaning that must be more subtly envisaged, if it is to be taken into account at all.

Abstractly speaking, this observation merely means, as Whitehead has stated it, that events are inexhaustible. Any object, any person, can become a point in existence from which the whole of the actual world can be deduced. Concretely, however, it points to a sequence of valuations that have an empirical history. It is the feeling-response formed into structural depths which give character to the conscious level of personality and culture. It is this feeling context that I would call the structure of experience.

Conscious experience at any given moment focuses a narrow range of the felt meanings that make up each person. Memory is a thread of recallable meanings that can somehow bring to conscious experience the events of past history which work on hiddenly in our depths until called to mind. But in our bodies, as evidenced by the turn of the head, the look, the stance, the way we receive other people, and more hiddenly still, the probabilities of response, the apprehensions, the concerns, yea the sensibilities — in all that gives character to the person — we carry the fund of valuations that give the total, existential meaning of ourselves as persons.

This fullness of meaning we do not readily apprehend, either in ourselves or in others. Communication and social intercourse demand some simplification of ourselves and of the order of existence that contains us, so we deal with it and with ourselves as conscious events. This practical assumption that we are merely and simply conscious events conceals our deeper meaning and tends to cancel out the dimension of depth which is in the structure of experience of the living culture in which our lives have meaning. For social communication this is no serious loss; and the convenience of this simplified encounter ordinarily justifies this superficial representation of ourselves. But since the meaning of ourselves and the meaning of the present culture in its total range is given in this deeper context, wherein the structure of experience is apprehended, the canceling out of these depths causes one to lose sight of the connections whereby the past of persisting valuations have come into their present emergence as character, collectively made visible in bodies and embodied in the present culture.

The folly of the liberal era, an era of simplification, as we have called it, lay in its readiness to lose this dimension, and thus to lose sight of that continuity of structure in experience by which the past valuations are formed into emerging events. This leads me to a second clue which may aid the reconstruction of liberal theology and thus provide the liberal church access to a sounder orientation in the Christian faith. This clue is given to some extent by cultural anthropology in its understanding of the formative factors in the emergence of the cultural character of a people. It is also given in Whitehead's notion of *causal efficacy,* wherein the past is seen to persist as a formative influence in the present. It is given with even clearer implication in the notion of valuation in dynamic psychology, as it applies to the formation of persons and to the formation of cultures.

The culture, like the person, emerges as a context of interrelated meanings with a given character and also a distinctive psychical pattern of responses as a result of the moment-by-moment valuation or assignment of meaning given to incidents or situations demanding decision. Decision-making, understood as a conscious act of attributing meaning to anything, is a persistent process at work within individual lives and within a definable community life which gradually encloses existence within a frame or within a horizon of understanding. Decisions are more than mental acts. They are psychical events as well, reaching to the interior of the affective processes. Thus the valuations formed in the person or in the culture are more than configurations of meanings; they entail attachments, fixations, interests, aspirations, longings, and hopes which give to the understanding its intensities in the form of tensions, frustrations, expectations, disappointments, satisfactions, and resistances.

This undertow of drives and obstructive processes, though subconscious in character, is nevertheless to be regarded as being of a piece with the conscious experience, and is derived from valuations that follow upon decisions. They cannot be treated as the same thing, for in actual fact, as the psychiatric sciences have made clear, the drives and obstructions may be involved in an independent drama of their own, steadily gathering into a pressure-head that may overwhelm the strategy of the conscious mind and rout its rationality. Nevertheless, the conscious and subconscious levels of experience are two dimensions of the same organic structure of meaning that arises from the accumulative effect of valuations.

What is at work in individual experiences has its counterpart in the culture at large, embracing the individual events of joy and tragedy and fashioning a communal structure of experience. Although this larger structure is continuous with the individual structures of personality, it gathers into itself the persisting, proto-plasmic character of institutional and other corporate processes. Thus a culture at any given period of time presents a public per-sonality, as it were, which tends to be portrayed in the overt transactions that make up its day-to-day life. But it is as surely possessed of imperceptible processes that work on hiddenly as is the individual personality. All that has entered into the public and private decisions of a people through the accumulative effect of valuations resides as a persistent datum in what I would call the structure of experience. In this concept, the structure of experience, I have brought together the sense of depth and the notion of valuation in order to advance it as a reconstructed doctrine of immanence. In this view, the contemporary moment is always a pregnant time span, bearing the accumulative char-acter of past events in a creative passage which compels it to deliver new instances of qualitative meaning through continuous acts of decision and whatever else defines the concrete life of man.

Now the structure of experience is more than the accumulative and transformative complex of men's valuations. It is this together with the creative passage; or, to put it less abstractly, it is the interrelated working of men and God. To separate men's valua-tions and the creative passage too radically, or to speak of them as two different levels that can be only tangential in their relation-ship is highly arbitrary and falsifies the imagery of what actually occurs. This is what is done when we speak of subjective experi-ence and the objective reality as two polar extremes. The occur-rence is one event of actuality. Its meaning is one, and although the grasp of understanding within any single aperture of con-scious experience may be meager and necessarily distorted, it partakes of real events and is to that extent a part of the datum.

Concomitant with the sense of depth in the structure of experi-ence, derived from the complex of relations, is the notion of emergence. Emergence implies a reconception of all evolutionary thinking. Though it holds to the theory of more complex struc-tures arising from simpler ones, it by no means concurs with the notion that therefore these complex structures are reducible to the simple, material levels. There is continuity of a sort between the various levels of structures; but there is also discontinuity of a significant sort. The difference between psychical activity, once it has attained the level of an operational structure, and sheer physical process is so decisive that there is no simple transition between them. Discontinuity here does not suggest dissociation: The psychical structure subsumes the physical structure. That is, in many ways it depends upon it and in some sense is informed by it; but it may never be defined or explained wholly in terms of it.

This situation of continuity and discontinuity occurring simultaneously and inseparably at every level presents the notion of immanence in quite a different light. To speak rapidly and briefly of the implication, it means that the structure of human personality and spirit are to be conceived both as being interrelated and as being distinct.

The third clue pointing to a possible reconstruction of liberalism is the cultural significance of myth. Considerable more work remains to be done on this problem, but I shall indicate at least a direction of thought which follows from this clue.

Myth, as I am using the word, is a term derived from the literature of cultural anthropology to get at the human response to actuality in its ultimate dimension. It is a corollary of the metaphysical term intuition which, as Bergson used it, seizes the meaning of existence in an act of inward appropriation in contrast to the descriptive or observational act of the intellect. It implies discernment which arises from involvement. We can speak of it as being undifferentiated awareness; but the trouble with this way of expressing it is that we may then assume that, by proceeding to a differentiation of explicit meaning which will lend itself to observation and thus reasoning, what is discerned may be literally and descriptively clarified. Actually, only a margin of clarity can be hoped for since the very import of myth is that we stand at a line of vision where mystery abounds. I am not speaking now of something esoteric. I am speaking of a range of vision which can be only partially appropriated by reason of our limited human structure as well as the fullness of data to be envisaged. It is as if we were to assume a perspective that enabled us to get outside of our human limitations and to see this actuality that involves us with the eyes of divinity. This is precisely the imaginative turn that is executed when the theologian or philosopher uses the word *transcendent* or the phrase *beyond history, beyond time and place.* The argument against leaning heavily upon such a word as transcendent is that it becomes self-defeating in so far as the human situation is concerned. It magnifies the limitation of the human perspective in so far as we are able to enter imaginatively into the transcendent perspective. But, on the other hand, in simulating such transcendence, we actually ignore the limitation of the human structure in dealing with the mystery. In one respect, therefore, it tends to negate human understanding. In another respect, it attributes more to human understanding in this transcendent reach than its limited structure actually affords.

If it were possible to formulate this insight concerning the limitation of our human perspective in confronting mystery in a constructive way, we could avoid both of these distortions. Such a formulation would deepen the feeling orientation of mind in the very act of restraining and tempering the work of the intellect. The theological appropriation of the concept of myth is directed toward such an effort. It might be said to be the immanent route to taking account of these limitations of the human consciousness, thus recognizing discontinuities within the stream of experience which constitutes each event of human existence.

This sensitivity to what lies beyond our comprehension, but which nevertheless enters intimately into our every moment of living, is a mode of religious discernment that adjusts the mind to the contradictions of existence. It takes account, on the one hand, of the instrumental function of human thought in clarifying our human situation, yet recognizes the import of the transcendent dimension suggested by the words, 'My thoughts are not your thoughts.' This kind of adaptability of mind is indispensable to the search for actuality if the truth in the notion of emergence is to be taken seriously. For clearly this notion gives us no ground for projecting the apprehensions of the human consciousness into final generalizations. On the contrary, it argues for recognizing that 'we know in part' and that 'we prophesy in part'; but that the horizon of mystery which confronts every human consciousness impels the reasoning mind to move toward wonder and to sustain this tension in thought as a proper act of reverence on cognitive grounds. So much, for the present, concerning the nature of the myth-consciousness and its relation to thought.

We need now to apply what we have been saying to the dimension of meaning implied in the Christian myth which, I am insisting, is important for the liberal churches to retain. I have given the content of the Christian myth in minimum form in a former book, *The Reawakening of Christian Faith*.[1] I shall not repeat that analysis here. It is enough to say that the Christian myth is a pattern of poetic meaning conveying the drama of redemption as an act of God in history. The Biblical narratives have related this drama in elemental language, beginning with the events of the Exodus in the Old Testament and culminating in the death and resurrection of Jesus Christ. What this drama conveys of a transformative working in human nature and in human events, rising above the automatic mechanisms of evil as well as the rigidities of law and of cause and effect is of immense importance to the human situation, not to speak of actualities that extend beyond our vision. The Biblical histories published during the liberal era sought to interpret these narratives in a way that related prophetic history to the ethical passages of the New Testament. This, I think, misses the dimension of meaning that is available in these Biblical accounts. It bends the indirect reference to the level of human comprehension when, in fact, what is important here is to bend human comprehension to the level of witness which seems to suggest a 'transcendent' meaning; to associate man's thoughts with intimations of meaning which are 'higher than man's thoughts.'

The content of the Christian myth is a narrative of grace and judgment, of sin, repentance, forgiveness, and redemption. These words will bear sober re-evaluation by the liberal within the perspective of emergence. They are not ethical terms. They transcend the moral consciousness. They point to operations of

[1] Macmillan, 1947, Chap. ii.

meaning and energy within a medium that moves at a level that just exceeds the reach of the normal personality structure of the human being. By this I mean that what occurs in acts of repentance and forgiveness and what issues in a redemptive situation are not occurrences that can be calculated or even provided for. We should have to speak of them as instances of spontaneity in which a new level of negotiation emerges, rendering the old level of cause and effect, of rights and duties obsolete in this situation. Anyone who has experienced the act of repentance or forgiveness in the human situation will recognize the transmutation of mood to which I am pointing. In these occurrences it is as if a completely new perspective had broken in upon the situation that had reached an impasse. Moral and legal demands are transcended; not in a way that negates their claims but in a way that subsumes them under a higher order of meaningful relationships.

Just as the range and intensity of goodness are heightened under these categories of grace and forgiveness, so the import of evil takes on greater dimension and depth under the concepts of sin and judgment. Without these notions, in fact, it might be said that the religious dimension is not apprehended. The historic way of explaining this fact is to say that it is through these notions that the category of the holy, with its attending emotions of taboo, awe, and reverence, is introduced. This explanation is informing, though perhaps not particularly suitable in the empirical context since the concepts, sin and judgment, when associated with the category of the holy often tend to cast all meaning relevant to this dimension outside of the frame of reference. While it is true that we are dealing here with a datum that extends beyond the range of our comprehension, we are, nevertheless, conversant with it to some degree at the empirical level in terms of emotions, apprehensions, and insights appropriate to the human capacity. The explanation needs, therefore, to be consonant with this empirical reference; not reducible to it, however.

I would suggest that the mythical response can be assimilated into our human frame of meaning by recognizing it as a behavior of man appropriate to emergent moments in his experience when he is confronted with a spontaneous occurrence that transcends the stable relations of ordinary structures at the human level such as men experience in moods of repentance or in acts of forgiveness. These are not ordinary experiences. They do not stand in a one-to-one relation with the representative behavior of the human personality. In such acts we participate in a movement of life that anticipates, if it does not actually reach toward, a structure of meaning to which our structure of consciousness is related, in the same way that all psychic life is related to personality, and to that degree attuned. The only way in which we can speak of these intermittent and spontaneous occurrences, reordering our moods and enabling us to transcend otherwise impenetrable barriers in human relations, is to say that a good not our own interpenetrates experience, releasing the organism from its fixed path of motivation and redirecting it toward a more sensitive order of relations. How much we ourselves contribute to this reordering would be difficult to determine; though I am inclined to think that we have as little to do with it as we have to do with the process of growth or with the emergence of skills. And we may, of course, have even less. This is no easy matter to determine; and there is a serious question whether we should be wise or justified in attempting to determine it. This would argue for a responsiveness as the counterpart of the scientific attitude: namely, an appreciative or receptive mood toward a working of grace and judgment in our midst which may reach and reorder the relations that constitute our organic life as personalities. The import of this attitude of receptiveness toward possible events of new meaning or new relations could, of course, be transforming in itself in that it would shift our course from one of manipulation and calculated effort to one marked by greater sensitivity and wonder, inclusive of horizons beyond our attentive vision. Consequences of a psychological order would certainly follow from such a shift in perspective; but I am suggesting that operations of even greater import than these organic changes would ensue as well.

In speaking this way, I realize I am approaching the position of William James when he wrote in *A Pluralistic Universe:*

The believer finds that the tenderer parts of his personal life are continuous with a more of the same quality which is operative in the universe outside of him and which he can keep in working touch with, and in a fashion get on board of and save himself, when all his lower being has gone to pieces in the wreck. In a word, the believer is continuous, to his own consciousness, at any rate, with a wider self from which saving experiences flow in . . .

There is one side of life which would be easily explicable if (such) were true, but of which there appears no clear explanation so long as we assume either with naturalism that human consciousness is the highest consciousness there is, or with dualistic theism that there is a higher mind in the cosmos, but that it is discontinuous with our own . . .

In spite of rationalism's disdain for the particular, the personal, and the unwholesome, the drift of all the evidence we have seems to me to sweep us very strongly towards the belief in some form of superhuman life with which we may, unknown to ourselves, be co-conscious. We may be in the universe as dogs and cats are in our libraries, seeing the books and hearing the conversation, but having no inkling of the meaning of it all.[2]

This is a sensitive phase of James's metaphysics which was purposely by-passed by his pragmatic colleagues, and which was as readily dismissed by men such as Wieman, who felt that James, in stating the matter thusly, was steering an ambiguous course which could only return him to an uncritical supernaturalism.[3] The literature of emergence since James's time, however, and the growing conviction concerning the social nature of reality because of these experienceable relations, as expressed in the new metaphysics,[4] impels us to take such hints more seriously.

It is possible that James was too much of the scientist to deal sensitively with the insight that he had come upon; though we need to be careful in stating this criticism, for few people have been as sensitive as James in dealing with any problem. Yet the shadow of positivism was upon his inquiring mind, and thus made

[2] William James, *A Pluralistic Universe,* Longmans, 1911, pp. 307–8.
[3] Cf. *Religious Experience and Scientific Method,* Macmillan, 1926.
[4] Cf. Whitehead, *Process and Reality,* Macmillan, 1929; and Charles Hartshorne, *Man's Vision of God,* Harper, 1941.

him prone to press every such intimation to the limit on the grounds that if the human mind were to understand it, science would show the way. The neglect on the part of disciplined minds to pursue James's hunch left the field open for less disciplined ones to exploit it. And in their hands, what could have been an opening of the human spirit into the depths of experience with appropriate religious sensibilities, developed into a variety of manipulative efforts to wrest from these 'untapped resources' spiritual energies to empower man in much the same way that enterprising men since Bacon's time had bent nature to human ends. There is lacking in this orientation the distance of the religious mind which can take a proper measure of the human consciousness and of data beyond its comprehension to which it must attend.

If the appreciative response and an openness to the range of data beyond human comprehension is the best we can do, we do well to take this initial step. Within liberal theology, however, I believe we can go further by availing ourselves of the inherited pattern of mythical meanings centering about the Christian drama of redemption, assimilating them into a discourse of meaning which has become native to us. The interchange would not be one-sided; for once the dimension of man's meaning, implicit in this elemental narrative of human destiny, were assimilated it would re-create both the imagery and the conceptions that make up the language of liberalism. This, in itself, would serve to reorient our thinking toward a more imaginative and perceptive level. Precisely the reverse of what has occurred through acquiescence to psychological and sociological methods would ensue. The earlier liberal effort to appropriate scientific procedures for pursuing religious understanding increased its tendency toward literalizing religious meaning. What it gained in clarity through these procedures it lost through the depletion of meaning which followed.

Language and meaning are subtle creations. They emerge out of an association of symbols and the stimulus of experience, the one playing upon the other in a way that compels reciprocal growth and interrelationship. A theology which is persistently aware of the Biblical events and of the sensitive symbols which were employed to explain their meaning is impelled to retain their poetic reach and probing spirit. One that abandons this resource and immerses itself wholly in the discourse of the sciences or of some philosophy of its choosing will increasingly partake of the restricted range of meaning to which this kind of discourse attends, and thus lose the sensitive outreach appropriate to religious inquiry. Since perceptiveness and precision are both important to theology, its language of analysis and interpretation cannot be indifferent either to imaginative or to analytic and interpretative disciplines; but it must learn to relate these divergent modes of reflection and to assimilate the stimulus of each.

Now we may speak briefly of the meaning of Christian faith as it is conveyed through the mythos of our culture. The motif of our Western culture, which has set the pattern of faith within our structure of experience, can be said to be *the covenant relationship*.[5] It is in this sense that it is said that the root metaphor of the culture is Hebraic, and that the Old Testament, which relates the dramatic unfolding of this relationship in history, is a primal document of the culture. In the teaching of Judaism this covenant relationship is lifted up into a formula which reads, 'Love God with all thy heart, soul, and mind; and thy neighbor as thyself.' This is the pinnacle of the Law cited in the New Testament. Actually many variations on this theme appear within the cultural experience of the West. Legally it forms the basis of justice, though this notion has undergone modification through Greek and, more particularly, Roman mores to the degree that the relationship between man and man is given emphasis. The ultimate reference, however, is not wholly lost. In fact, it becomes a kind of presupposition of the ethics of justice.

Metaphysically, this motif is translated into the problem of the One and the Many. Here, too, under the influence of later perspectives, such as the Newtonian world-view, this motif is modified to accord with a prevailing imagery which the scientific conception of nature provided. Thus mechanism tended to replace

[5] H. Wheeler Robinson, *The Christian Doctrine of Man,* Edinburgh, T. and T. Clark, 1911.

the personal pattern. The imagery of mechanism persisted within intellectual circles until the Newtonian world-machine motif was challenged by the new physics in the nineteenth century, and by the organismic conception of nature following from the work of James and Bergson.[6] Under recent metaphysical stimulus, and developments within the sciences themselves, mechanism has given way to organicism; and more recently to a reconception of the personal pattern of relations.

From the standpoint of the problem of faith it is important to see that around this primary motif, arising from the covenant relationship, the deepest sensibilities of the culture have developed. The strongest sentiment from the point of view of general acceptance is that of justice: giving to each his due. The highest sentiment, that which rises above law and transmutes it, and, in fact, becomes a transvaluation of law, is love. The mystery of relationship centering in this higher order of goodness is, I should say, the chief topic of the New Testament, and can be considered the core of the Christian gospel: the rule of love. To my mind, this is an emergent notion which appears to set aside the structure of law and justice; but actually it does no such thing. The mystery of transcendence here is that of re-creation, given certain conditions. The juxtaposition of sin and recompense yields the judgment of justice. The juxtaposition of sin and forgiveness yields a new relationship in which grace abounds, offering new resources of spirit and a new level of freedom. Yet the freedom that is born of this emergent situation is one that binds people together through the bonds of love.

Out of this gospel of love comes a new reading of events and of the meaning of existence. Love, or this level of meaning in which love, rather than inexorable causation is operative, becomes the key. The new freedom, with its hope and spontaneity, its transcending of limitations, replaces the rigid imagery of cause and consequences. Yet it is always an association of freedom and responsibility.

The familiar formula by which commitment to this new order of meaning and faith has been affirmed within the Christian com-

[6] Cf. Whitehead, *Science and the Modern World,* Macmillan, 1925.

munity is, *Jesus Christ is Lord*. For the Christian, the life, death, and resurrection of the Christ are taken to be both the symbol and the revelatory event in history, exemplifying the concrete actuality as well as the authority of this new order of meaning.

We can say that the new perspective in which love is regulative broke upon the world of Western culture as a result of these elemental Christian happenings in which the primitive Christian community experienced the impact of these events centering in the Christ. Not only did a new dynamic appear within the structure of experience; but a new incentive and new hope. The full import of this hope could never be made explicit, though speculative and imaginary minds did their best to anticipate its meaning. Yet the mature Christian position has always been that of implicit trust in 'the Lord of Life,' and a consequent yielding to the claims of the Gospel of Love with its stark portrayal of man as sinner, of judgment and the cross; as well as its promise of the working of grace in the forgiven man, in the healing of broken relations, and in the resurrected life.

Now whether we speak of this higher order of goodness as *eternity breaking into time,* or as a spirit emerging in the midst of time within the creative passage, we are pointing to a dimension of existence which brings mystery and order into juxtaposition. Living the Christian faith, then, in full dimension implies living with full awareness of mystery and clarity of meaning interpenetrating every moment of existence. Our reconstructed liberal faith must underline the importance of retaining this full dimension of mystery along with the concern to achieve clear and distinct ideas within manageable limits.

We shall see, then, that myth focuses the sensitive values of a culture in the way in which a parable functions; and insinuates their imperative claim upon a people: i.e. impresses it with the gentle force of art. The culture tends to be shaped by the interplay of impulse and sensibility. Impulse is the direct response of the individual organism to any situation without benefit of social sensibilities. Sensibilities arise out of a more delicate feeling into a situation when the individual has had regard for the meanings involved that go beyond his egoistic demands. Every individual may be regarded as embracing a tension between demands of his subjective life and the mutuality of existence which possesses him as a higher demand of his being. The creation of any individual event, as Whitehead has said, launches simultaneously a new center of subjectivity and a new instance of the mutual order of events. Neither is to be denied in the fulfillment of this created event; yet to relate them implies some denial of each. The existence of empathy in the human being, a capacity to feel into another event, precludes isolation in a person's subjective existence and provides the capacity of responding to the demands of this mutual order of events. Without empathy, the psychiatrist would say, the personality cannot escape its own demands or meliorate them in response to the demands of others. Eventually, such a person must reach a dead end in the permanent isolation of his subjective life from all other personal existences.

Now the presence of empathy in human beings opens the way for the individual to reach not only other individuals but the valuations and the expectations of the culture in a way that qualifies his every response, even to the extent of re-creating him. He becomes sensible to the meanings that are cherished, and he is made responsive to their appeal. The sensibilities held up by the myth as a redeeming good in the culture always represent the maximum of valuations attainable or envisioned within the culture. Law is the minimum level of this valuation. Laws impose a minimum good upon the community, rarely, if ever, reaching beyond the condition of order and peaceable communication. The myth transcends the law, in the sense that it holds before the culture the total range of higher sensibilities, while law means to keep it committed to an essential minimum of sensibility. Generally this contrast is described as the contrast between the law of God and the law of man. If they are not conceived as being wholly antithetical, this characterization is not misleading; man's law is a working, minimum version of the larger order of sensibilities, from which in the last analysis it has been derived. For the legal structure, defining the prohibitions and observances essential to an orderly society must, in some sense, remain within the bounds of acknowledged good, though they in no sense may be expected to exhaust that good.

The basic valuations which provide for man's psychical adjustment in its ultimate sense within our culture have been given in the Christian myth. The Christian myth is the elemental ground of all religious structures that have arisen within the culture as the active agents of the good, however discerned. In no instance can the formal religious order or its theology be identified with the myth, for every order has particularized the myth in some way to accord with a theme of its preference. I have mentioned this in discussing the meaning of the Christian faith in an earlier publication [7] but a brief resume of the point may be made here.

Each of the classical forms of Christianity, in its worship, in its theology, has centered upon an aspect of the myth as a focal point which, in turn, has become the organizing center. Roman Catholicism has singled out the *pieta,* the suffering and dying Christ, as the epitome of its faith. The sacrifice of Christ on the Cross sets the theme and mood for the whole of the Roman Catholic faith. The Greek Orthodox Church, building upon the same myth, has found the focal point of its faith in the resurrection of the Christ. 'He is risen!' is the stirring theme that is the epitome of the Orthodox faith. The Lutheran Church has seized upon the act of revelation in the proclamation of the Word, assuring grace and forgiveness and fullness of salvation, as the focal point. Calvinism has made the sovereignty of God the organizing center both of its theology and its worship. In Protestant groups born of the evangelical awakening, the working of the Holy Spirit in the individual heart has been the one feature of the myth that has been given priority. It was made more dramatic by graphic portrayals of an aggressive Satan.

Theological liberalism and modernism seemingly abandoned the myth in the interest of a scientific interpretation of Christianity. Actually, however, the myth persisted in its minimum form, both in Schleiermacher's theology and in the Christocentric the-

[7] *The Reawakening of Christian Faith,* Macmillan, 1949, Chap. II.

ology of Ritschl and Wilhelm Herrmann. In Schleiermacher, the God-consciousness in Christ provided the organizing center. In Ritschl and Herrmann, the person of the historic Jesus, bearing in itself a value-judgment upon the meaning of existence and carrying implications of the Christian God, provided the core of theological reflection. In focusing upon the historical Jesus, however, theological liberalism was on the way to relinquishing the Christian myth. In the Chicago School, both in the theology of Shailer Mathews and in the philosophy of religion of E. S. Ames, the relinquishment was well-nigh complete. In Mathews, the principle implicit in Ritschlian thought, which was to translate religion into ethics, was brought to a clearer formulation. Mathews' *Social Teaching of Jesus* was the pioneer work in substituting for the dogma of revelation, a specific delineation of Jesus' teachings for the modern age. In squaring the modern social mind with this Christian norm, Mathews held, society would be attaining its intended goal. Later Mathews was to take a less Christocentric view of the matter and to center upon the conception of God as the personality producing forces in the universe as the controlling concept; nevertheless, the attitude of Jesus in confronting God as a Father, Mathews thought, remained the pattern by which even the modern man might come into personal relations with these forces.

Mathews argued for the necessity of employing analogical thinking in the historical interpretation of theological doctrines; and in his constructive view he held that the analogy of person was indispensable. Yet, for the most part, he abandoned this procedure in his constructive method, pursuing instead the more definitive course of elaborating the implications of the demands of the personal life along ethical lines. In this the appeal to the Christian myth had no place.

Although the imagery of the Christian drama of redemption retained some appeal as an imaginative construct for Edward Scribner Ames, any attempt to read theological meaning into it appeared offensive to him — he called it a vestige of an astrological age. Ames's thought constitutes a transition between that stage of theological liberalism in which some formulation of the myth persisted, and religious humanism, in which even reference to its imagery is omitted.

These variations in theological construction need in no way obscure or discount the import of the myth as a cultural force. For the Christian myth as a unitary organization of seminal ideas, the origin of which we are in no position to clarify, remains the source of the formative insights of our Western culture in ways that compare with the impress of family traits upon the protoplasm. This figure is misleading, since this transmission of valuations is a social, not a physical process; and the social culture may not be equated with the physical organism. Nevertheless, the impress of the seminal valuations implicit in the Christian myth upon succeeding generations of Western people is of such an intimate and subtle character that no one within that stream of history can be fully aware of the degree to which he has been shaped by it. Other people, removed from its nurturing matrix, can look upon people of our culture and recognize the persistent character, the inherent tendencies toward certain inhibitions, sensibilities, and overt actions. Without affirming the faith that rises as a positive valuation upon existence itself out of this nurturing matrix, all who partake of its psychical and social intercourse, share to some degree in its basic outlook and in its elemental orientation of feeling. In this sense, then, to be Western is to be Hebraic-Christian. It is to be cradled in the accumulative valuations of successive generations which have 'stretched the mind toward large ideas' by having recourse in some sense to the seminal meanings of the Christian myth; and which have felt the brooding restraint and beckoning of the sensibilities rising from its peculiar perception of what is good.

The valuations given in the Christian myth inhere in the structure of experience which defines our living. They persist, in part, as a slumbering wisdom, awaiting articulation. In part they *are* articulated, though more often in formalized ways which restrict their meaning and relevance to the culture; or, as in other instances, in sentimental ways which tend to dissipate their power as a cultural force. When they are permitted to remain encased in symbol or to stand bare in sheer sentiment, their cultural impact, while not wholly negligible, is meager. It is the function of theology, periodically, to rescue these seminal meanings from a growing irrelevance by setting them in a context of relevant discourse which will render them intelligible both as cognitive meanings and as moral directives.

The meaning of the Christian faith in this context, then, is the present affirmation of living Christians, attesting to the formative myth which bears witness to the creative good of existence exemplified in the events pertaining to the Christ. It is, to be sure, inclusive of all groups who, in any way, lift up this cultural myth. But it will readily be seen that there are all grades of articulation, ranging from the most literalistic caricature to the most discerning and sensitive exposition, relating these valuations in ethical and aesthetic ways to the ongoing life of the culture. Bearing witness to the formative myth in the liberal churches should mean compelling the society, 'superficially founded upon the clashing of senseless compulsions,' to come to terms with the qualitative concerns of God's creative love as given in the valuations of the myth. The liberal is charged with rescuing the myth from sheer mythology, not by literalizing it, as his enlightened forebears sought to do, but by giving it a context consonant with the informative discourse of our day that will enable it to become formative both at the level of imagination and of action. Rather than abandoning the myth to orthodox hands, which may only formalize or sentimentalize its meanings, the liberal is called upon to bring the art and literature of an informed imagination, the philosophic acumen of the liberated mind, and the ethically awakened conscience into the service of extending this Christian criticism of man's life into the whole of culture.

A brief explanation about how the liberal witness to the formative myth becomes implemented beyond sheer proclamation and the aesthetic rendering of art may be indicated. This possibly points to its application to religious education.

The structure of experience in any culture is the nurturing context of meanings, feelings, and valuations through which the past is transmitted and emerging events are qualitatively formed. It is, in a general sense, the source of all actualized meaning and value in so far as these are internalized by persons; and it is the carrier of much more that persists as in a social protoplasm — potential, but never actualized in personalized existence. A strict theological interpretation of this point would designate the work of God within the structure of experience as the source of such qualitative emergence; but my concern here is to convey the richness of meaning that is implied by this concept.

Now the personality of the individual, existing in this structure of experience, is formed by a subtle and almost imperceptible process of taking into its consciousness and feelings, the cultural meanings and values thus transmitted. The process is called symbolization. It is difficult not to make of this a passive occurrence, as if the cultural meanings simply flowed into the individual as the water of the sea rises into waves. Obviously this is false. The person, by the very facilities of his organism, their limitations and peculiar propensities, sets a restriction upon this process. And the subjective organization of the person, which is the total, integrated working of these facilities, actually sets up increasing resistance to this process as the internalization matures into critical thought and judgment. The range, depth, and degree of cultural meaning that is internalized through such symbolization varies with the individual; but in a very real sense the content of each person is given by the valuations contained in the structure of experience, through which the formative depth of God's working shapes each destiny. And the level of meaning and of valuation which reaches the emerging person is determined by the opportunities that articulate these resident valuations into formative forces. The structure of experience may bear latent seminal meanings of great force in any given community; but the agencies of articulation may be deficient in sensibility or preoccupied with lesser concerns. In that case the opportunity of emergence passes. The depths of man's nature remain unarticulated.

The relevance of the valuations implicit in the Christian myth to religious education, then, is a qualitative one. The person cannot emerge as a full articulation of the structure of experience except as these valuations become internalized in the process of symbolization that forms him.

The source of the liberal church's predicament may now begin to be apparent. Its concern to become liberated from the restrictive, doctrinal version of orthodox Christianity led it to dissociate itself also from the Christian myth, and thus from concern with the elemental valuations that relate to the deepest appraisal of man and his destiny our culture affords.

Two influences, in particular, contributed to this dissociation. One was the literalizing force of Biblical and historical criticism, which deprived liberalism of an imaginative grasp and a poetic wisdom. The other was the positivistic view which arose from the scientific outlook dating, say, from the time of Francis Bacon, when intellectual slates were wiped clean of the Christian imagery.

The fact that even Immanuel Kant addressed himself to this problem of faith in an age of science attests to the critical state of this issue in his time. His solution in the appeal to moral faith became, as it were, a bridge over which many liberals were able to circumvent the crisis which the scientific outlook imposed.

But the Kantian appeal to moral faith could hardly be regarded as more than a frigid version of the Christian myth, reduced to the abstractions of theses and categories. Through Wilhelm Herrmann and Adolf von Harnack, blood transfusions were successfully administered to the Kantian gospel, so that for the duration of the Christocentric theology, it can be said that liberalism simulated an effective ethical equivalent to the Christian faith.

In like manner, Absolute Idealism, Personalism, and Pragmatism successively furnished rational motivation to a religious faith in lieu of the valuations of the Christian myth. The motivations of contemporary liberal Protestantism may be said to derive from the momentum of these three philosophical sources. The waning of their influence as a constructive cultural force is one of the explanations of the decline in the prophetic power of liberalism.

It has appeared to some of our contemporaries that the solution of modern liberalism lies in its alliance with a new and vigorous philosophy and one that is intellectually alive to the issues of our time. These religious humanists persist in seeking a more adequate scientific formulation of religious faith. Others of us have seen Alfred North Whitehead as our philosophical mentor.

I am convinced that preoccupation simply with the philosophical reconstruction of religious faith only perpetuates the predicament of the liberal Protestant church. Even the efforts of neo-naturalism to provide an alternative to neo-orthodoxy seem to me destined to fail as a theological reconstruction of liberalism unless dissociation from the Christian myth is seen to be a fatal mistake of liberalism, and there then follows an appropriate concern with this problem.

The task then is two-fold: it is a problem of faith, and a problem of truth. It is a problem first of restoring the meaning of the Christian myth in the context of liberal Protestantism, and thereupon, developing an appropriate witness to that faith through liberal churches; it is, second, a matter of attending to the intellectual problem of setting these valuations of faith in a cognitive context which will give them intelligible and communicable power as meanings.

As a constructive solution to the predicament of the liberal Protestant church, this analysis, in its present form, may seem overly ponderous. But it has practical implications that can be stated quite simply. And these statements I would set down as tentative formulations of a reconstructed liberalism:

(1) That the doctrine of immanence, which has given metaphysical orientation to the liberal position, can be substantially retained, though radically revised along lines indicated by the concept of 'structure of experience.'

(2) That revision of this assumption that God works through the concrete structures of history must come at the point (a) where liberalism has followed an idealistic practice of identifying these concrete structures with conscious events; and (b) where liberalism has tended to equate the human structure, either as mind or experience, with the creative working of God.

(3) That these corrections will be somewhat facilitated by a deeper conception of empiricism than historic liberalism has embraced. Instead of continuing within the ideological frame of modern idealism, or of its pragmatic distillation, liberalism must

find an orientation within a context that takes account of the dimension of depth. The alternatives here narrow down to two, only one of which really enables liberalism to remain in character. I have purposely refrained from giving this orientation a name, because no single name suggested thus far adequately characterizes this context. I will say that it is a context in which the features of rationality and irrationality are frankly confronted, and one in which the clearly designated features of God's working and its adumbrative character are forthrightly affirmed.

(4) Immanence in this context presupposes transcendence as a category of differentiation in the sense that individuality and mutuality are simultaneously embraced, and God and man represent distinct though related categories.

(5) In this revised doctrine of immanence, structure of experience becomes a basic concept. The structure of experience, as the immediate context of feeling, embracing the whole datum of cultural history including its persistent valuations, is in this revised doctrine of immanence, the bearer of all relevant meanings, including the seminal insights of the Christian myth informing our Christian faith.

(6) Access to the Christian faith is thus not a problem of relating the contemporary culture to a remote, historic event, as in the modernists' dilemma, but of attending to the depth of the immediate moment of the cultural structure of experience which bears, in its valuations, the witness to God's working in history and in the living moment — even Jesus Christ, conveyed through the persisting drama of the myth.

(7) The meaning of the myth that God works on in history to redeem man through Christ is given in fragmentary form, wherever encountered. The epic poetry of various periods, interpolating the drama of redemption — Milton's *Paradise Lost,* for example — vivifies its meaning. The great musical utterances, the Bach B-Minor Mass, or Mozart's *Requiem,* Brahms's *Requiem,* Handel's *Messiah,* Franck's *Redemption* — all are special forms of witness to the meaning of this redemptive myth. The liturgies of the churches serve in a highly disciplined way within special communions, to communicate the meaning of the myth

and to bear witness to the sovereign good of Christ. Numerous ways beyond these formal expressions could be found by which the Christian myth is made articulate to the culture. We might say that in these formal expressions, the myth is rendered, is symbolically related, and is vivified through pageantry, poetry, or song.

(8) The myth that resides in the depth of the culture as valuation and motivation, and which is celebrated, attested to in the drama of ritual and song, is presented, clarified, and elaborated within a given historical context in the Biblical writings. The Bible is the primal source of the cultural motif that has been shaped into myth and, as such, is the primary document of our culture. Its study is more than a pious act; it is an act of orientation in the feeling context which pervades the whole Western experience, and in particular, the structure of experience that possesses us. The liberal will recover this document, not simply as a source of ethical teaching or of didactic discourse, but as a source of perennial renewal in sensibility to the deeply laid valuations of the culture wherein the sensitive nature of the living God is disclosed to our deepest sight.

(9) The valuations conveying the sensitive working of God are the historic responses to the good discerned in Christ as an event of sacrificial love, persuading men to receive the work of God's grace; yet witnessing to the 'costingness' of this life of love, and to the judgment upon those who deny it.

(10) The church, understood as a community of men and women who have been awakened to the sovereign force of the Christian myth in culture, is the living witness to the revelation of God in Christ.

The clues to reconstruction which have been set forth in minimum form and in a somewhat impressionistic manner in this section may now be explored in greater detail. What follows in this volume is an analysis of the nature and role of faith as a context of feeling and expression, both as it becomes articulated as a motif of culture and as a resource of psychic energy within the human spirit. A fuller understanding of this remarkable creative and redemptive occurrence in its social and solitary aspects will go far toward providing the deepening of orientation in the liberal faith, which it so sorely needs to enable it to bring the resources of Christian faith to the pressing problems of modern culture; and, beyond this urgent task, to enable the liberal mind to speak incisively to the issues of faith and culture.

PART II

FAITH, THE DYNAMIC OF CULTURE

IV

The Energy of Faith

LOOKED AT from within the cultural complex of any society, faith is the thrust of the human psyche which forms the emotional pattern of a people. It becomes manifest, not only in the religious aspirations and valuations of a people; but in their creative labors as well, appearing as a motif in their architecture, art, music, and literature. In the periods of a certain culture when people have lived largely by faith it has determined and defined the pattern of living, providing both the directives and the restraints of conduct and of corporate practice.

Faith roots in the will to live; thus, in its elemental form, it is hardly distinguishable from a biological attachment to life. In the early stages of human living, before the human psyche had assumed corporate expression or had achieved a consensus of sentiments, hopes, and aspirations, this elemental forerunner of faith might have been indistinguishable from the will to live. It had no content, save an inchoate conglomerate of immediate impulses arising from individuals who were propelled by circumstances and an inner urge to pursue various ends. The emergence of faith as a pervasive cultural force, impelling the human psyche in one way or another, and giving direction to purposes and actions, waited upon the coalescence of individuals or small groups into organized units wherein some conscious communication and interchange of felt purposes was attempted. If it is true that crises in the form of a foreign attack or threat of natural disaster stimulated the formation of groups for mutual defense and strategic planning, then we must say that faith as a corporate attitude arose out of the convergence of these felt resources which hitherto had been retained only as individual feelings. The story of any people rising to a self-conscious expression of faith is always an account of articulating sentiments deeply held as a common heritage which hitherto had been only vaguely discerned. The corporate affirmation of these sentiments amounts to a pooling of privately held persuasions which, when publicly affirmed, become a cohesive influence as well as an impelling social force.

Once faith had risen from a state of inarticulate sentiment and persuasion, privately held, to a consensus of affirmation and aspiration, it passed from the individual stage of being merely psychical energy to the level of communicable meanings. The transition here is very subtle, for it is difficult in any culture to determine just when faith assumed a definitive content. The declaration of the content as a public act was always preceded by a prolonged period of private assimilation of meanings such that the act of declaring the faith in bold, public terms was simply felt to be a speaking out of a common experience — the voicing of a common mind. Poets, bards, prophets have been the agents of such expression. Their significance has been measured by their capacity to lift these felt sentiments, hopes, and aspirations which have secretly motivated individuals to the level of a common possession.

Faith as psychical energy, once it became released into the communal stream of meaning, pyramided in power and influence. It persisted as a private motivation below the level of articulate speech or even thought, shaping the structure of individual experience in habitual ways; but it also assumed a self-conscious, articulate character, capable of being institutionalized, dramatized, and nurtured. These private and public dimensions of faith tended to coalesce to such a degree that the one reinforced the other. They were, as it were, the inner and the outer aspects of the same phenomenon. In subtle ways, however, the public expression of faith assumed an ascendancy; for its very articulate and assertive nature, as contrasted with the more inward psychical energy, gave it a recognizable character which could be reiterated, repeatedly affirmed, and thus made durable and continuous. Public ceremonies and practices with their drama and literature developed around these instances of publicly declaring the faith; and these became the carriers of its articulated content.

The agencies for expressing and nurturing the faith often became so assertive and binding that they tended to operate mechanically as an objective medium upon which individuals depended for their aspirational life. Faith in its public character then tended to tyrannize over the subjective life of individuals, even suppressing private manifestations of psychical energy which appeared to be sustaining or, in any sense, directive. Once the dichotomy between the outer and the inner life of faith had occurred, their correlation was well-nigh impossible. It was as if a breach had occurred, driving the one into hostility and rebellion against the other.

Once the process of tyrannization over the subjective life of individuals began in the public institution of faith, the tension between persons in whom individuation had progressed far and the religious institution which presumed to be the bearer of faith was made acute. The rise of individuals, generally associated with the rise of city civilization, is to be understood in part, at least, as a reaction against tyrannization such as that which began to develop both in the rural religions of Greece and Rome and in the civic faith of the city states. As an illustration of the breach in an opposite direction, we can cite the growing suspicion of mysticism in the Roman Catholic Church as its formal institutions developed. The Roman Catholic expression of faith, in fact, is a classical illustration of the extent to which faith can become objectified as a body of content and practice, wholly divorced from the subjective drives that originate as psychical energy in the human psyche.

It is difficult to carry the analysis of faith as psychic and social energy very far into Christian history because the term 'faith' in Christian literature became frozen into a theological concept which precluded its being readily related to the life-process. In this orientation, faith became simply an attitude toward dogma, a highly self-conscious expression of faith in which the concerns of the *kerygma* crowded out and, in some instances, actually displaced the concerns of culture. Christian faith in this context is at once a psychic force supervenient to the cultural stream, and 'a huge potency of ambiguous meaning' permeating the cultural process. It is for this reason that our culture at once reflects the formative influences of the Christian faith while at the same time it disavows it as a directive. This may be found to be true regardless of the period under consideration. Thus when we undertake to identify the content of the faith with the structure of experience which defines the living tissue of the culture, the identification seems somewhat forced. This is a problem which constantly confounds any analysis involving Christianity and culture.

The tyrannization of the objective expression of faith through institutions over the subjective life of persons should be further analyzed from the point of view of the individual. The identification of faith with dogma immediately intruded a coercive element, compelling the individual intellect to conform to the common mind which had been corporately defined as objective truth. Faith in this context is indistinguishable from intellectual acquiescence. Faith becomes credulity, a willingness to believe what is objectively given, quite independently of a person's private thought processes. Now a distinction must be made here: Credulity comes in various shades and qualities. The coercion of dogma is least disruptive of the human psyche when it is least resisted. That is to say, where credulity in an individual is complete, the full, affirming capacity of the individual is released in an acquiescence to dogma. In such instances, faith as an objective structure and faith as a psychical energy of the subjective life tend to coalesce. Here the intellectual issue recedes to the point of vanishing. The person possessing faith (or credulity), instead of being forced to declare his intellectual allegiance to what has been formulated, is able to relax into habitual acts of devotion in which the human psyche is fused with the social consensus into a total, integrated energy. It is human energy integrated at a low structural level, to be sure; nevertheless, it presents a clear instance of the life of faith completely resolved and fortified for the worst that life can bring to the individual. This is the meaning of 'the unspoiled faith' of the peasant, say of the Mexican peon. The sophisticated American tourist, when he first encounters the seemingly unperturbed life of the villager in the hinterlands of Mexico, is often seized with a kind of nostalgia for the innocent integration of experience which he once knew in his childhood. Some tourists have sought to recover this 'unspoiled' sense of faith by identifying themselves as completely as possible with the villagers and with their routine of work, worship, and festivity. They are able to do so to some degree until a consciousness of the formal institution as an external intruder breaks in upon them; and then the breach reasserts itself. What had appeared to be an ideal condition of faith suddenly looms as an intolerable state of ignorance in which the tyranny of dogma is permitted to prevail. Actually there is more to commend this innocent, communal expression of faith than the disillusioned observer can acknowledge. The tension in his own more critical judgment of the situation obscures the good which is actually operative in the situation to which he was first attracted. For there does rise from such village life a spontaneous zest that reveals a habitual response of taking each moment for what it may offer, whether it be ill or beneficent. The hardship is assumed with equal, spontaneous acceptance, as if it were a fate against which no mortal hand should be raised. And when the good is given, it is received in festive mood. Thus the praise of life persists despite the intermittent events of evil. The praise of life in this situation, to be sure, is of dubious merit. It is childlike, evidencing no discriminatory power to cope with the problem of good and evil. Yet the capacity to see and to accept the good in the very routines of existence so heavily weighted with hardship and even tragedy should not be dismissed lightly. This is a human power of a sort — a technique, if you like — for keeping the balance of good and evil sufficiently to the fore to make life as it comes both bearable and rewarding. What is absent in these simpler cultures, beyond the lack of a power of discrimination, is the accentuated egoism of the more civilized person who is impelled by his egoistic drive to seek an overbalance of the good in existence. The unrestrained yearning for happiness and for well-being and the endless investment of time and energy in their preservation, breeds in a person who lives at the civilized level an anxiety that precludes perception of good. Such a man rarely lives with the good of the moment or with the present evil; rather he fixes upon its consequence, ominous or otherwise. The very act of transcending what is presently given in the hope that something better may be given; or in the fear that what is given will be withdrawn, robs him of the capacity to receive what is given with zest or praise; or, if it is evil, to respond with genuine suffering such that the evil is courageously borne. Mixed as our judgment of this praise of life must be, as it appears in elemental folk, we cannot cancel out completely the genuine expression of human vitality arising in these situations which enable these people to receive their meager good with zest, and the evil with fortitude.

Where credulity is attained at the price of a conscious commitment the cost to the human psyche is greater. It is here that the tension between faith and intellect becomes acute; and the tyrannization of dogma over the subjective experience can be most complete. A psychological study of non-conformity is yet to be made which will adequately assess the interplay of the human psyche and the social energy of faith as it is communally embraced. Non-conformity in its open and explicit form may involve less psychical impairment than the more secretive kind; for the outspoken non-conformist is generally able to rally a following or to find affinity with others who are of a similar turn of mind. Non-conformity then becomes simply a stimulus within the larger, social group to consolidate these deviations from the faith in the form of a concerted protest within a smaller nucleus. The integrity of the person is thus preserved because he is able to retain both the structure of his own inner commitment and a sense of solidarity wherein this commitment can be overtly expressed.

Non-conformity imposes its most serious psychic effects when it exists as a secretive impulse of the personality, compelling a degree of dissociation in the person. The extent to which this condition exists among clergy and lay people alike may be far in excess of what is generally assumed; for the prevalence of a high degree of individuation in personality renders credulity or commitment to a consensus in complete form unlikely. The term 'sick soul,' which William James applied to individuals under serious stress of a consciousness of sin, can properly be extended to include individuals caught in such a tension. Actually the sense of sin, to which they have frequently confessed, carries some implication of being at odds with the consensus of faith. Since the mind of the individual is split in its loyalties — in part conformist, in part non-conformist — the alienation that is experienced leaves him insecure in regard to the ultimate demands to which his conforming self now gives ominous meaning. Undoubtedly this condition of partial non-conformity entered into the spiritual struggle of Luther, accentuating his sense of alienation. It is noteworthy that once his non-conformity became explicit and support of his position was publicly assured, the acute sense of alienation, aggravating his sense of sin, subsided.

It is not always possible for the individual under stress of such dual loyalties to resolve the tension, either in an open stand of non-conformity, or in a reconciled state of compromise. In such cases, the person persists in a state of psychical indecision which periodically must find release in some kind of pathological form, or create a constant condition of insecurity and timidity which continually threatens the person's sanity. The observation by Jung to the effect that in all his years of practice, he never had any serious case of personality disorder which did not, in the last analysis, involve trying to find a religious outlook on life [1] must be taken more discriminatingly than his statement suggests. Actually, it is a problem of integrating the human psyche so that an individual does not become involved in competing value systems; or, to state it conversely, it is a problem of so correlating diverse and even conflicting demands that the human psyche can attain some degree of unification and decisiveness. For it is out of this condition of the psyche that affirmation, zest, and

[1] *Modern Man in Search of a Soul,* Harcourt, Brace, 1933.

joy arise. People will vary in the degree to which they will require these emotions of commitment; but in some sense and to some degree, sanity depends upon their periodic renewal of spirit.

It does not follow that non-conformity must issue either in open rebellion or in a secretive sickness of soul. It is often possible for the quickened intellect to come to terms with the demands of dogma through an arduous experience of intellectual searching in which the individual human psyche becomes fused into a harmonious relation with the objective structure of meaning. Or this can happen through some compromise of the intellect in deference to other values that can be more readily accepted or harmonized. Where neither intellectual integration nor compromise is possible, rebellion in the interest of the inner demands of the psyche is the only recourse.

Western history reveals all of these processes at work. If credulity has persisted at a seemingly non-intellectual level throughout countless villages of Europe and in the Americas, as in the Mexican communities I recently had occasion to observe, integrity in faith in more sophisticated form has been variously sought through rigorous, intellectual effort, or through conscious compromise. But rebellion and a subsequent reorientation of faith has been equally evident. Even as the Roman Church kept strict vigil over every intimation of heresy, there emerged piety groups in Western Christianity, nurturing the inner spiritual life in self-conscious ways which lifted the private possession of faith into visible and articulate rebellion against the pervasive, social expression of faith in the institutional church. To some extent, these piety groups initiated a secondary process of articulating and dramatizing the inward vision of faith; thus there developed a cultus within the cultus with ambiguous relations between the inner and outer aspects of faith.

The tendency implicit in the piety groups became explicit and explosive in the Reformation. Here faith as an inward propulsion dramatically severed connections with many of the institutional expressions of faith. The dissolution was not complete in its initial stages, for the Reformation movement transpired under national auspices and to this extent retained its cultural orientation even though it became increasingly iconoclastic in dissociating the Christian witness from its traditional forms and mediums. Among Protestant groups faith as an objective structure of assurances as given in the seven sacraments, in the authoritative priesthood, and in the Mass, with its rich musical heritage, crumbled away as the acids of individual piety ate away at its formidable supports. With the dissolution of their hold, much of cultural experience itself, which had borne the imagery of the faith and which were its mediums of expression within the culture at large (a vast portion of the arts, literature, music, and learning in general), lost its sustaining force for the human psyche. Thus faith as a cultural energy underwent a serious set back at the time of the Reformation. It is difficult to understand or to assess this fact, for it is so inextricably bound up with the social and religious iconoclasm of the period that the good and the ill of its effects can hardly be disentangled.

In rebelling against Roman Catholicism, therefore, the Reformers and their spiritual contemporaries dissociated themselves, not only from an institution but from vast areas of the culture in which the influence of the institution had been pervasive and controlling. The supports of its society, along with its agencies of salvation, were relinquished. This meant more than the fact that the Reformation had its political and economic aspects; it meant that its iconoclasm reached to the depths of cultural valuations.

Although the Protestant revolt penetrated deep in its reaction against institutions and forms of the Roman Church, it left intact the essential core of the faith. I am speaking now not of its theological structure but of the valuational pattern which was given in the elemental myth of the culture to which the Roman Mass had given extensive aesthetic expression through liturgy, and to which the Schoolmen and theologians before them had given detailed conceptual elaboration within various frames of thought. In the *Divine Comedy,* Dante had fixed its ethical schema and its cosmological imagery in a common medium, preparing through literary form for the popular dramatization of the mythos as it had been philosophically perfected in Thomism. The great

Gothic cathedrals, rising from the labors of dedicated hands as the witness of a folk movement to the pervasiveness of the faith, marked the summit of its demonstration.

The faith in its objective formulation had become a drama of redemption, carrying along with its Christology and its conception of God, implications for a view of history as well as for a conception of the nature and destiny of man. This drama had been in process of emergence for a millennium and a half through Old Testament history. It appeared in summit form in the New Testament narratives; hence these became the primal documents of the culture, providing it with its motifs and its pattern of sensibilities. The assimilation of these motifs and sensibilities within Western culture required another millennium and a half. Thus it may be said that at the time of the Reformation, the structure of experience, bearing in its depths the seminal sensibilities of the formative myth of Western life, had attained the ripe old age of approximately three thousand years.

The Reformation seen against the background of this age-long history of our religious culture, represents a less radical departure or breach within the culture of Christendom than appears to be the case when viewed simply in relation to the medieval synthesis of the three centuries preceding the posting of the ninety-five theses.

The structure of experience exemplifying the formative influences of the elemental drama of faith, the primal document of scripture, theological works, particularly those preceding the Scholastics, the sermons and journals of mystics, a legal tradition, inhibitions, customs, practices, and notions too numerous to mention, carried the heritage of the culture into the Reformation experience despite the relinquishments that we have mentioned.

The faith as a social energy thus persisted in psychical ways to inform the Reformation experience and to give content to it even though, on technical theological grounds, it had ceased to be acknowledged as a medium of access to God. The Reformers themselves were obviously more sensitive to this distinction than were the people who rallied to their support.

It is common to point up the discontinuities between the Roman Catholic and the Protestant expressions of faith by noting their doctrinal divergence at the Reformation. These differences centered chiefly around the conception of the church and the mediation of grace by which redemption was assured. They extended, also, to the nature of man particularly with regard to the condition of the *imago dei* and the consequent condition of the human will and reason. The theological and ecclesiastical implications of these doctrinal differences became vast indeed, altering the course of each, liturgically and culturally. Yet, from the point of view of the deeper concerns of the human psyche, involving the nature and direction of the aspirational outreach, there was more continuity than a comparative study of doctrine would reveal. This is to be explained by the fact that the Reformation movement remained within the valuational orbit of the Christian myth in so far as man's ultimate concerns were involved. The dimension of depth pertaining to man's condition and destiny, to which the energies of faith had relevance, persisted in Reformation Protestantism, giving form to its framework of meaning and a feeling tone in which the elemental sensibilities of the Christian faith continued to inform personality and culture.

We should not, however, allow this deep continuity at the level of the human psyche to obscure the real differences which arose within the Protestant psyche itself as a result of institutional changes to which the analysis of doctrine has reference. These point to an altering of conditions within the realm of psychical resources, affecting the security of the human spirit and its capacity for spiritual expression. The human psyche, which remained secure within the impregnable fortress of an authoritarian sacramental system, was insulated from the shock of ultimate issues bearing upon the frailties of man and his dependence upon the Infinite Will. The psyche of the Protestant convert, on the other hand, being stripped bare of these institutional defenses, stood naked and insecure before the final court of judgment. Its precarious plight was heightened by the Protestant being acutely conscious of his human frailty. In this reorientation of the human psyche, the energy of faith underwent a radical change at the Reformation. From a superficial point of view, we could conclude that faith as a social energy was altogether dissipated. We might go farther to conclude that in this process of rebellion, carrying with it, as it did, such far-reaching iconoclasm, the support of the psychical energy arising from the structure of experience as an inward vision, was similarly lost to the early Protestants. Thus faith, both as a personal and as a social energy, in so far as these were derived from the structure of experience which had been formed within Christendom through centuries of influence, was wholly dissipated among followers of the Reformers. Following this line of analysis, we should have to conclude that the real motivating mood of the Reformation experience was not faith, but despair. Despair, it would seem, came to be looked upon as the psychical condition in the individual that marked an emptying of sensitivities and affections which might seem, in any way, to mediate psychical support, giving assurance of redemption. Thus faith, it would be argued, could no longer be equated with structures of events, but with an individual attitude, a venture of belief unsupported by events, generated out of an individual experience of despair.

This appraisal of the Protestant condition of faith may not be altogether set aside. In fact, we could claim that it describes precisely one strand of reaction which remained a condition of despair, except as it could be relieved by a desperate venture of faith. The difficulty, however, with letting such an analysis stand as a general description of the Reformation situation is that it overlooks the constructive mood that was exemplified both by Luther and Calvin, although Calvin seems to express it more explicitly and confidently than Luther.

Faith, as defined by the Reformers, assumed an explicitly individual status, though we should not overlook its communal expression when the company of the elect became self-consciously identified as the community of believers. In origin, however, and in its operations, faith was clearly the inward vision responding to the witness of the Word as it declared *to the individual heart* what Christ had revealed of God, the Father. But the inward vision was no longer simply the human consciousness asserting its own resources of psychical energy. These, according to Reformation doctrine, had been spent. The interim of despair, in this sense, was real. The act of faith could then occur only through an operation of grace wherein a new awareness, a *knowledge* of God's will for the individual person *through acquaintance* with a goodness discerned in the Christ possessed the person's heart as an affection, informing both mind and will.

In this act of faith, no uncertainty was implied. The despair of the human psyche had been routed and the sense of alienation dispelled as the benevolent will of God became assured. Thus Calvin wrote concerning the nature of faith,

It is a steady and certain knowledge of the Divine benevolence towards us, which being founded on the' truth of the gratuitous promise in Christ, is both revealed to our minds, and confirmed to our hearts by the Holy Spirit.[2]

It is not clear whether this solitary act of faith, made possible by a good not our own, meant a renewal of the inward vision in which faith as a psychical energy is restored. It is even less clear whether it implied a recovery of orientation within the structure of experience such that the appeal of concrete events can, in any sense, become restorative as a bearer of the seminal motif of the culture, and a wider witness to the sensibilities of the myth. The conclusion on either point is decisive in the minds of many who emulate the Reformers' position. On the first point, they would hold rigidly to an insistence upon viewing faith as a work of supernatural grace, having no important relation to the natural health of the human psyche. Yet this appears arbitrary and formalistic when it is realized that in both Luther's and Calvin's interpretation of human nature, following the act of faith, a restorative process ensues that transforms and fortifies the human will, and releases the human spirit from anguish and despair. Calvin is particularly insistent that the man of faith is possessed of a new confidence which, at the level of spiritual man, is steady and secure. Holding to a dualistic metaphysics of man, he acknowledges that there are rising and falling moods within the

[2] *Institutes of the Christian Religion*, III, Chap. II, vii, p. 496.

man of faith due to his physical nature; but where faith obtains, the confident mood of the spiritual self invariably prevails. Luther also looked to the man of faith to be delivered from the insecurity and anguish of soul which kept man focused upon himself, and released him to be attentive to the needs of his neighbor. The psychic energy which actually empowered these Protestant men of faith who had availed themselves of this individual medium of access to God would argue even more strongly than these venerable formulations that the subjective life of the individual, following the act of faith, was powerfully motivated with confidence and purpose.

Where such renewal of the total personality, following the act of faith, is not acknowledged, as in certain expressions of Reformation thought, faith as a gift of grace would seem to be held to be a form of hypnosis, evincing disturbing symptoms of disorientation in the convert; thus making the Christian assurance border constantly upon a deep and tragic sense of misgiving. After all, as it was later expressed, the wager of faith might be lost in the end.

On the second point, they who make the Reformation view of faith decisive in its relinquishment of empirical supports, argue that the act of faith implies a turning away from the valuations of the culture in a way that the man who chooses the one God casts aside all idols. Protestantism, in so far as it emulates the single-mindedness of the Hebraic moralist, presses this imagery to its extreme, thus carrying the iconoclasm and the literalizing tendency of Protestantism to its farthest extreme, excluding not only the natural events as a possible resource of the spirit; but crowding out as well every imaginative expression as being a vane and veiled form of idolatry.

In so far as the Reformation made faith discontinuous with any structure of events which define the common life, as well as with the formal organization of the cultus, it rests with fierce dependence on revelation as a stark and isolated event. The question in regard to whether or not this dissolution and discontinuity are to be relieved relates not only to our estimate of the cultural iconoclasm which occurred in the Reformation; but to the deeper problem of God and nature, God and the structure of events which stand over against our human emergence even as they contain it as the ground and cradle of our being.

The more radical departures within the Protestant movement which issued in doctrines of the *inner light* and later, the inward witness to the work of the Holy Spirit, as in Pietism and the evangelical awakening, may be regarded as a partial recovery of the subjective dimension of faith which had waned under the over-dominance of the institutional expression of faith. Here the reverse process occurred. The inner witness tended to tyrannize over the outer, objective expression of faith. Among the Quakers, the institutional expression of faith tended to crumble away altogether, or at least to approach the vanishing point. Quakerism, in this sense, is the antithesis of Roman Catholicism. It represents an absolutization of the individual report of experience; and a corresponding suspicion of every attempt to give this inward vision outer form or dramatization. Other radical Protestant groups such as the Baptists and, later, the Disciples of Christ, have shared this preference for an exaggerated individualized expression of faith.

The Quakers and the Pietists have stressed an aspect that relieves this ardent individualistic faith: namely, the religious community (the fellowship of the concerned). In many ways this correlation of the individual witness and the confessing community has restored a condition of faith comparable to that of elemental groups before the inner and the outer dimensions of faith had been rent asunder. The sect, of course, lacks the full communal dimension of the primitive group or of the civic community. Thus it does not recover the total cultural expression of faith which earlier communal groups exemplified; though in some instances, as in certain German villages where pietism has been pervasive, and among early communities in Pennsylvania where quakerism has been dominant, a remarkable degree of cultural integration of faith has developed. To be sure, it remains a restricted expression both of culture and of faith.

This account of the historic contours of faith conveys a greater degree of disunity, dissipation, and hence disorientation than has actually occurred from within one perspective; though from within another perspective, it hardly hints at the real condition of disunity, dissipation, and deep disorientation within the culture at large.

Concerning the first perspective, we can say that despite the cleavages of faith to which we have pointed, there has been a persisting Christian faith within Western culture. This has been as pervasive and formative as any cultural faith to which we can point. However much divergence or rebellion may have occurred within the area of belief where faith has been allied with dogma, there has been no lack of a deep-forming ethic and an aspirational thrust or outreach, where faith has been inextricably bound up with sentiments, valuations, and hopes. Thus our culture, despite all of its historic cleavages within the area of faith, and despite all of its dissolution of Christian commitment, stands within a common psychical structure of experience which can only be explicated in terms of the Christian mythos, assuming that the mythos will be thought of as being inclusive of Hellenic and Judaic motivations as well.

Concerning the second perspective, it must be said that despite this pervasive hold of the Christian mythos over Western culture, the degree of disorientation in the human psyche of Western people, resulting from a dissipation of faith, is beyond calculation. The modern era is a continuous story of the progressive advance of this disorientation. Within certain periods this fact has been wholly obscured. For example, in the first flush of the Enlightenment, the triumph of reason was widely acknowledged as a spiritual victory over a decadent age of faith. And at the height of the Romanticist era, the recovery of a sense of the whole man in terms of his profoundest feelings was hailed as a spiritual victory over the anemic age of rationalism which had passed. With the rise of the scientific mind to a position of dominance over the thinking of Western man, the emergence of what has been called the *technical reason,* with its greater precision and clarity, was announced as the human triumph over an age of indiscriminate emotion and elemental force. Today the acknowledged peril of the ambiguous power released by our technical reason, which is uninformed by an ethical or spiritual sense, leaves us bewildered and baffled by the very resources which gave promise of cultural deliverance from our irrational plight. What this might mean, we are almost afraid to contemplate. One clue to sanity seems to be a reappraisal of this drift toward modernity and a more sober look at the cultural meaning of the psychical forces which are generated by faith and myth.

What the historic faiths sought to impose upon enlightened minds may have demanded an excess of credulity to the peril and indignity of the human mind; but what the enlightened mind rejected in these faiths may have resulted in a spiritual impoverishment of such proportions that no amount of reconstruction or reorientation can restore our cultural loss. The problem, however, remains to be explored. It is to one important aspect of this problem that we must now turn.

V

Faith, Myth, and Culture

CULTURAL ANTHROPOLOGY, by its persistent attempt to penetrate the façade of ritual and symbolic utterance among elemental people, has achieved an understanding of the mythical consciousness which can illumine all religious language and acts of worship. The anthropologist's grasp of the meaning of faith and worship has not always been so rewarding. Being insensitive to the complexity of the response to which he was trying to give interpretation, he was content to find plausible explanations for these acts and expressions by applying in direct fashion, methods of rational inquiry which often prejudged these events as having a certain kind of meaning or no meaning at all. The primitive was compelled to be some kind of philosopher; and in this role the simple religious man did not always fare very well. In fact, whenever the demands of rational inquiry have been imposed upon religious utterances without regard for the subtle and indirect qualities of their meaning, the religious mind has suffered by analysis. The prodigious labors of psychologists of religion, anthropologists, and sociologists of religion who, over the years, have sought to wrest from the enigmas of faith some intelligible explanation of religious conduct, have served largely to discount the importance of faith in civilized cultures. The attempt of anthropologists such as Frazer and Tylor to localize the irrationality of faith in the religions of early man by distinguishing between magic and religion, reserving the more respected word for the civilized faiths, was of short duration. In time, implications of superstition spread to religion in every form where the overtones of a living faith remained. Nothing short of a complete reductionism, leveling the poetic language of faith down to its lowest rational denominator, would suffice. Little wonder that one culture after another, in so far as its leadership succumbed to the pleas for modernity, sought to cast out the ancient myths and to establish society upon a purely rational basis. Religion reduced to its rational minimum was no match for logic or science.

A more moderate view of the role of myth and religious ritual appeared when the anthropologist abandoned his effort to find purely rational motives behind these expressions and sought, instead, to understand their function in the life of the community. Here the social scientist was able to point out the unifying force of myth in giving, as it were, some direction to the life of the people. Ritual, in repeatedly re-enacting the themes of the myth, could be accounted a stabilizing influence in society, conserving the cherished values by infusing them into the sensibilities of the people. Put in this form, the rationalization was tantamount to damning religion as a reactionary social force. The mixture of truth and error in this explanation made the judgment at least plausible to many and convincing to some.

The return of the philosopher to sociological and psychological concerns, and ultimately to the problems of anthropology, has probably been one of the genuinely scholarly advances in our day. This advance occurred quite accidentally. For generations the philosopher remained bogged down in epistemological inquiries, seeking to find a suitable answer to the question, How do we know? The query, What do we know? was an irrelevant question as long as the possibility of knowledge remained in doubt. Quite fortuitously, possibly by way of uttering a word of despair in the midst of this philosophical maze, some soul in distress asked, 'What do we mean when we ask, How do we know? How can we determine whether or not we know until we can be sure what meaning is?'

The effort to determine the meaning of meaning has led philosophers into labyrinths of technical inquiry which would seem to have bogged down the modern philosopher even more deeply than his predecessors who were obsessed with epistemology. However, two happy outcomes have resulted from the inquiry into meaning: (1) the philosopher has been pressed into explorations that have taken him into new fields of human thought and experience; and (2) the more discerning among the philosophers have discovered, as a result of these wanderings, that thought itself is a multidimensional happening. Its mysteries cannot be opened with one key; for thought is attended by a depth of feeling, signs, and symbolic utterances which exemplify resources of meaningfulness even when they cannot, on technical grounds, be said to have meaning. In the effort to fathom this complex occurrent, the efforts of philosopher and anthropologist have converged. For, like the anthropologist, the philosopher in search of an understanding of language and signs has turned to elemental communities where meaning has remained undifferentiated. Language, he has discovered in this context, is more than direct discourse. Even for practical purposes language is ceremoniously lived.

Out of this pursuit of the meaning of language and the use of symbols in action and in speech has come fresh insight into the meaning of myth both as a language and as a function of the culture in conveying to conscious experience something of the depth of awareness which would otherwise remain at the level of bodily feeling. It shall be my purpose in this chapter to recount important contributions to the understanding of myth, and to assess the significance of myth as a theological resource in the constructive task of conveying the meaning of the Christian faith to the present age. In pursuing this general problem, we shall be taking a step toward illumining the predicament of the liberal Protestant church; for a reconstructed liberalism awaits some grasp of the deeper dimension of faith which was relinquished in its zeal for clarification. The problems here, as I view them, are not simply apologetic inquiries. That is to say, they direct us, not simply to questions concerning the fashioning of tools by which to formulate some justification for the Christian faith in our time; but to such basic problems as the interpenetration of faith and culture, and the nature of the religious response as a creative act within history wherein man's inner life, the private world of thought and emotions, is brought into vital, serious play with what is ultimate and other than man. They press us further to consider the nature of religious discourse, both as symbolic expression in the wider, emotive sense, and as a form of communicating knowledge in the more definitive sense of reasoned understanding. In so brief an analysis we cannot hope to deal with all of these problems. Perhaps the best we can do is to summarize some of the findings of recent studies of myth and to show how they bear upon these three areas of problems. On the basis of these observations, we will be able to draw some conclusions about the constructive importance of myth in any theological formulation.

I

FAITH AND CULTURE

Without exception, I should say, recent studies of faith and myth see the problem as being, in some sense, involved in the issue of faith and culture. Among anthropologically minded philosophers such as Cassirer [1] and Langer,[2] this issue is given prominence; for it is clear to them that religious expression is, itself, a cultural occurrence, not only in the sense of partaking of a cultural coloring but in the deeper sense of giving voice to human hungers, anxieties, and appreciations which, in turn, exemplify and articulate the cultural psyche in so far as religious utterances achieve a consensus. Even theological interpreters such as Brunner [3] are compelled to acknowledge the relevance of the cultural issue in dealing with the total content of the myth and its corporate witness; although Brunner's insistence upon restricting the Christian meaning of myth to revelation in the decisive, Christological sense, causes him to take the problem out of its cultural context and to treat it as a concern to go beyond history and to speak with

[1] Cf. his *Language and Myth,* Harper, 1946; *An Essay on Man,* Yale University Press, 1944; and *The Myth of the State,* Yale University Press, 1946.

[2] Cf. her *The Practice of Philosophy* (1930); *Introduction to Symbolic Logic* (1937), and *Philosophy in a New Key* (1942).

[3] See esp. his chapter on 'Christian Mythology' in *The Mediator.*

dogmatic assurance from a point outside history. From such a vantage point, Brunner is able to dissociate Christian myth in its decisive sense from all non-Christian (what he calls pagan) myths. For the latter, from his point of view, are clearly immersed in the stream of history and thus bear all the limitations of the human mind and the human psyche. They are, in the last analysis, according to Brunner, the precursors of metaphysics.[4]

This distinction bears analysis because, upon its issue, both the meaning and the relevance of myth as a theological tool turns. If myth in the Christian sense is so wholly different from myth in the long range of human response to mystery, then the literature in cultural anthropology has no contribution to make to the theological use of myth. And if myth is to be equated with revelation in the radically super-historical sense in which Brunner uses the term, the bearing of the cultural context or of cultural history in general, to say nothing of the cultural pattern of response, is of no consequence to theological inquiry. I should argue, however, contrary to Brunner, that we have no choice but to acknowledge some continuity between mythical thinking within a Christian context and mythical thinking as it has occurred in non-Christian cultures. This is not to equate Christian and non-Christian myths; nor to relate them in any serial sense. It is simply to recognize that comparable human responses in the way of being expressive and creative lie back of the cultural motifs to which the various myths have given form.

Such an observation places myth at the psychical core of culture and generalizes it as a common feature of every historical experience within a geographical and ethnical frame. It makes of myth a characteristic, human response in any situation where the human psyche is awakened to a disturbing realization of an *otherness,* either in the form of a single object or power, or in the form of a total datum, affecting or determining man's present existence as well as his future destiny.

The cultural conditioning of the mythical response, however,

---

[4] The conception of myth as a precursor of metaphysics was developed by Hegel. A restatement of this point of view has been given with extensive elaboration by W. M. Urban in *Language and Reality.*

is inescapable. That is to say, the human psyche, being inwardly formed by the valuational responses arising from numerous events within experience, assumes a characteristic probability of response in keeping with these serial events. Psychic life, like vegetable life, thus partakes of a regional character which can never be completely obscured or canceled out.

This observation would suggest that the culture is always an exemplification of the structures of consciousness which are available within the region to initiate psychical responses as well as to express and to assimilate meanings. Sensitivity evidenced in creative imagination, in concern over human relations, or in the qualitative attainment of individual lives and in the group life, reflects the operation of processes within these human structures. The culture can rise to heights of sensitive creation and to sensibility in relations only to the degree that there are structures of consciousness available to carry and exemplify these happenings. Culture, I should say, is the creative work of God, made possible through his prior creation of these structures of consciousness, articulating the full psycho-physical organism.

Given these cultural determinants, we shall see that the character of the psychical response, its quality, its degree of sensitivity, both in the realm of feeling and in the area of expression, varies from region to region; from culture to culture. There is no universal human psyche; hence no universal human mythos. There is no common level of human, psychical response; hence no common level of mythical thinking; any more than there is a common level of creative expression. All cultures have historically manifested some capacity to be expressive in sensitive and creative ways; but there are marked variations among them, and in some instances the range of variation is vast indeed. It follows that no culture deserves to be neglected in the search for a full grasp of the psychical depth and outreach of the human spirit; for each culture exemplifies the concrete nature of God's working within the range of its available structures. But it is clear that some cultures deserve more serious attention than others when the concern is to focus upon the fullness of God's working within human structures.

Without attempting to appraise the degree of psychical superiority which can be ascribed to the Christian culture of the West, it can certainly be said that it reveals a range and reach of sensitivity and of creative imagination which must place it high in the human venture wherein God's creative working is exemplified. The pivotal point, or the summit of this cultural creation of the West is Jesus Christ. But Jesus Christ as a structure of consciousness in which God's intent and creative working are concretely exemplified is not an isolated datum. Behind the Christ lies the long history of the Jewish people. Their moral consciousness which had been processed and refined throughout the centuries of devotion to the Law became as a seed bed for a more sensitive and appreciative consciousness in response to the working of God. The prophets, we might say, were intimations of this emergent in so far as they were in some sense sporadic efforts to transcend the rigid mechanisms of the legal tradition. Yet, the prophets were in a very real sense the fruition of the legal tradition; and must ultimately be interpreted in the light of its claim upon the Jewish people.

Christ stands to the moral culture of the Jews as love transcends the law. As over against the moral and the rational consciousness, the Christ exemplifies the appreciative consciousness in which love is regulative. His structure of consciousness is the ground from which spirit emerges as a novel event. The Christ is at once the exemplar of the human consciousness at the level of spirit and the innovation of spirit within the conscious structure of man. He is the clear exemplification of the concrete work of God in history, possibly the clearest; the clearest within Western history without any doubt. Christ as the innovation of spirit and the exemplar of man at the level of spirit constitutes a redemptive consciousness among the structures of human consciousness which are motivated and, in large measure, bound by the moral and the rational consciousness.

Christ as the summit of the cultural creation of the West is the focal point of the Christian myth. This should not be interpreted to mean that the Christian myth is to be equated with revelation in the trans-historical sense described by Brunner. On the contrary, I should say, this summit vision points not beyond history but back to the formative events of history which have issued in this redemptive act; and to a further range of history which is to be seen, understood, and judged in the light of this redemptive act.

The Christian myth, then, is not one, decisive, isolated event; it is a pattern of events which has its luminous center in the Christ, but which begins in the earliest vivid awareness of God's creative work in history. The full pattern of the myth is to be found in the Biblical account wherein the drama of creation and redemption is delineated. This drama conveys the feeling tone of the culture with regard to its ultimate dimensions. Its details consist of apprehensions concerning God's intent for creation, the nature of God's creative activity in history, the nature and destiny of man, the interplay of tragedy and hope in human history, the facts of good and evil, and the attending operations of judgment, grace, forgiveness, and redemption.

These details of the myth have been variously analyzed and elaborated into Christian doctrine. They have been applied in liturgy, Christian art and architecture. They have been subtly woven into the literature and musical epics of the West. To some extent, their motifs have shaped the philosophy and ethic of the West. To a degree not commonly recognized they have influenced the political expressions of Western man. Deeper than we can discern, these primal notions permeate the feeling context of the culture in this present moment of history, giving the structure of Western experience its distinctive character.

II

THE NATURE OF THE RELIGIOUS RESPONSE OUT OF WHICH THE MYTH OF THE CULTURE TAKES FORM

The myth of a culture is a symbolic utterance of long standing, attesting to a persistent outreach in man toward what is ultimate in that which is other than man. This outreach varies in depth and in clarity of procedure. The clarity of the response is often in reverse proportion to the degree of depth which is achieved.

It is possible to detect certain periods in Western history when clarity and control have been sought in preference to every other form of orientation. Thus expressions of the religious response which early anthropologists were inclined to call magic conveyed a singular concern to bring the uncertain powers of this numinous experience within manageable bounds. The religious response in this context became a carefully developed technique of cursing and blessing, highly ritualized and corporately controlled.[5] In formalized and conventionalized periods of religious history, we see religious expression being reduced similarly to a minimum ritualistic response as a saving technique. In highly rationalistic periods the religious expression has been defined rather restrictively as ethical demands or agreements. In recent years we have seen the religious response narrowed down to a practical concern with religious energies comparable to the practical products of scientific research. We may say with some accuracy that in such efforts at clarification and control in religion, myth tends to lose its relevance and force. In its place, more precise and literal methods of thought and practice are sought.

Myth gains ascendancy where the appreciative moods of wonder, adoration, or praise are in dominance in recognition of an unmanageable datum in the objective event. Here the religious response is less a direct effort to use or to control the ultimate power discerned in the Reality not oneself, and more a readiness to encounter the fullness of the mystery as an Event of Grace and Beneficence, or as Judgment. The initial response in the mood of wonder or adoration may assume varying degrees of articulate form. In its lowest degree of conscious awareness it becomes a pervasive sense of unity with all being, as in certain forms of animism, and later, in nature mysticism. In its most articulate stage it becomes worship, or perhaps lyrical utterance such as we find in the songs of the Psalmist.

The mythical orientation is always one in which feeling takes priority over conscious attention or cognitive action. The feeling

---

[5] I have summarized and illustrated some of the features of this tendency in an article, 'The Development of Cursing,' in *The Open Court*, October, 1934.

orientation may be one of apprehensiveness, a shuddering before what is alien or unknown, as Rudolf Otto has indicated by his phrase, *the sense of the numinous;* [6] or it may be one of identity, an immersion in the deep ocean of reality, as the modern mystic has often described it. It may be of a third character: more dialectic in character, either in the sense of the encounter as Brunner describes it in a radically dualistic setting; [7] or in the sense of partial identity and partial discontinuity, as might be experienced in a situation which Whitehead has described as the *individual in community,* [8] wherein the bounds of individuality are noted and accepted in a cosmic situation which is dominantly social.

The religious response in this mythical orientation is thus a form of undefined awareness, a sense of knowing which must be taken to be a knowledge of orientation, or a knowledge by acquaintance — an inward assurance of having felt one's way into a situation. [9] Bergson defined this orientation in a way that appeared to have made it coalescent with instinct; so that creatures moving within a familiar environment without conscious awareness and without need of intellection appeared to be the most perfect mystics. Actually this was not his intention, though his formulation had difficulty guarding against this impression at times.

Suzanne Langer has helped to correct such an excess of animality in evolutionism by suggesting that what occurs in the mythical consciousness is not just an extension of this instinctual behavior, but a distinctively human response; continuous, to be sure, with the instinctive feeling of orientation, but having a creative and imaginative character which marks it as a distinctly human dimension. [10] Miss Langer has established that myth is a serious enterprise of people who are sensitive to the depth of their experience. Particular myths, she insists, can have symbolic force in a culture only as long as they persist as truth-bearers, undisturbed

[6] Cf. *The Idea of the Holy,* Oxford, 1923.
[7] Cf. *The Divine-Human Encounter,* Scribner, 1943.
[8] *Religion in the Making,* Macmillan, 1926.
[9] See James, *Psychology.*
[10] Cf. *Philosophy in a New Key,* pp. 138ff.

by literal inquiry. The moment the literalizing of their meaning is begun, their mythical force is dispelled; henceforth such meaning as their symbolizations support can persist only as metaphysical generalizations, on the one hand; and as epic poetry, or similar aesthetic expressions, on the other. This, however, is not her whole story. Langer has established also that the dimension of feeling which myth expresses and to which its symbols constantly refer, is not only a valid structure of meaning for the human consciousness, but an indispensable one if the distinctively human dimension is to be expressive in man. Relinquishing this reach toward symbolization at the level of feeling means literalizing experience in a way that lapses into pre-human or animal responses; which is to employ signs for direct, functional activity in the satisfaction of needs arising from a physical orientation in environment. Thus the effort to clarify experience by ridding it of non-functional signs or modes of expression which cannot be justified on the basis of direct discourse or communication of meaning, is judged by Langer to be a relinquishment of the humanizing dimension itself.[11]

Can metaphysics and epic poetry, then, succeed the appeal to myth? In a sense we can say that this is what happens in a civilization such as our own where the self-conscious attitude and habit have begun their work. The myths themselves cannot be revived as myths. They can be retained, on the one hand, in the form of poetic insights or parables to convey, within a disciplined emotional context, the valuations implicit in the feeling tone out of which these symbols have emerged. In this sense they remain motifs at the level of feeling, though in refined, and possibly, remote form. On the other hand, they can be retained in the form of abstract generalizations which a metaphysics might provide. The metaphysics, in this case, becomes a source of authentication in the way in which the feeling context initially gave authenticity in direct form to the valuations. The authentication is of a different order, being of a discursive nature. As such it cannot replace the emotional force of the original impact of the myth. Nevertheless, the metaphysics in combination with epic poetry or the musical

[11] Ibid. pp. 20ff.

epic may provide a civilized equivalent of the aboriginal orientation such that the mind will be both tempered and deepened by feeling, and the feelings structured and disciplined as a directive of human drives and impulses.

The retention of myth in this sophisticated form is not wholly secondary in its effects; for it can be the nurturing matrix of fresh and original mythical impulses. This simply means that the feeling context of culture, being active and continually formative, generates deep emotions of a direct and spontaneous sort, authenticating the valuational responses of modern man at the level of sensibility where judgment is immediate and unrationalized. In this awakened state of sensitivity, human consciousness may reach a depth of feeling which will enable it to appropriate the valuations of the myth as an original impulse, thus giving these valuations the force and authenticity within the modern consciousness of knowledge by acquaintance.

The process here is comparable to the emergence of creative art in the matrix of a disciplining tradition. The retention of the cultural myth, through a fusion of metaphysical and poetic, or aesthetic, effort, is similar to the retention of art forms as a nurturing and accrediting medium. Through this medium, the valuations of the persisting structure of experience are carried forward into the emerging moment, thus bequeathing to it the promise of character. Character, whether in art or religion, in individual or in culture, is a qualitative attainment that issues from the creative happening wherein past attainment and the novel event are somehow made to coalesce, or in some sense to achieve an integration. Character is always threatened from two sources: one, from the pressure of tradition which threatens to suppress or to frustrate creativity; second, from the insurgence of the passage into novelty which threatens to dissociate itself from the nurturing matrix. Qualitative attainment results to some degree, however, in spite of these overreaching or rebellious tendencies; and the metaphysical explanation of this occurrence is the creative work of God which presses upon every emergent event the possibilities of past attainment; or bends the persisting valuations to the opportunity of creative emergence. The work of God in this creative passage is always either enhanced or obstructed by the facilities of structure and response which include both the habits of individuals and the corporate barriers in policies of institutions available in any period of creativity. God does not work in a vacuum. He works through the available structures of the culture. Thus the beneficence and wisdom of man are not in vain. Neither is his evil working and folly without irreparable loss.

Although Reinhold Niebuhr's characterization of myth presupposes a dualistic imagery comparable to that of Brunner's thinking, his insights into the truth of myth help to convey the indispensable character of myth as a primary mode of the religious response.[12] What is Niebuhr's view of the truth of myth? Niebuhr insists that myth is a mode of apprehension which grasps the depth dimension of experience as it is given in the inner nature of any organic form of existence and pre-eminently in the existence of man. Description, he points out, is able to delineate the external, visible features; and the full account of any living organism from within this perspective can depict it only as mechanism. The essential unity of the event or being can only be discerned and articulated through an imaginative form of cognition which is the mythical method.

In man's experience this inner core of being which resists ready comprehension is to be understood best in the exemplification of freedom and transcendence. These two facets of man's depth dimension exemplify man's spiritual capacity to go beyond the sheer mechanistic level of cause and effect and to participate in a world of decision, choice, sin, and responsibility; and ultimately in redemption. Freedom is man's capacity to break free of the causal chain within history; transcendence is his capacity even to go beyond historical experience itself and to participate in super-historical dimensions of living. Because this dimension of depth is at all times present and operative in man's experience, and forever interpenetrating the events of history, it is a dimension of historical existence in the most realistic sense; not simply an imaginative perspective for contemplation. Time, man's days,

[12] 'The Truth in Myth' in *The Nature of Religious Experience,* J. S. Bixler, ed., Harper, 1937, Chap. VI.

the cultural process, rise and fall within a rhythm that partakes of this total actuality, even though the describable events cannot convey the full importance of its momentous passage.

Myth, that is, permanent myth, myth that is as true today as in the primitive world, is the mode of apprehension by which this total actuality is seriously envisaged and encountered. Christian myth (the drama of creation and redemption evincing man's relation to a Creator and to a Redeemer, and the ambiguities of man's nature, held in tension between good and evil) is such an effort through dramatic imagery to glimpse and to probe man's total actuality. In Niebuhr's judgment, it is the most adequate and the most expressive myth for achieving this orientation within existence.

In my judgment, Dorothy Emmet brings us nearer than any of the writers we have considered to a contemporary understanding of this feeling orientation in which mythical thinking takes place. Because she sees it as an elemental condition of the perceptive act whenever consciousness is confronted with events of import which are at once intelligible, yet beyond immediate comprehension, her conclusions seem less inclined to make of myth thinking an outmoded response which must now be replaced by metaphysics or some other form of sophisticated symbolization. Her view of perception in what she terms 'the adverbial mode,' a pre-animistic orientation in which we meet environing reality with a full, bodily response ('a responsive state of the organism in *rapport* with or receiving shocks from its environment' [13]) prepares the ground for conceiving of mythical thinking as following from a condition of responsive awareness, as she calls it. Responsive awareness, as Miss Emmet uses the term, I understand to imply in part what I would mean by appreciative awareness. Hers is a more active term and thus in some instances expresses better the nature of the religious response in such an encounter. Appreciative awareness means a reaching out toward reality beyond the self and thus is never as passive as the term would seem to imply; but it strongly inclines toward receptiveness

[13] *The Nature of Metaphysical Thinking,* London: Macmillan & Co. Ltd., 1946, p. 61.

to that to which it attends. Yet this act is not passive either — not sheer acquiescence to what is encountered; but a creative act of acquiring unto oneself real meaning of another self or of another object through a process of exercising empathy and identification in a circular movement which returns this feeling-into-another-center-of-existence to one's own self-orientation.

With the conception of perceptual experience to which Miss Emmet holds, such responsive awareness takes place in a context of depth or of relations which makes its rise less a cognitive act, in the usual sense of a subject attending to an object outside of itself in which all the hazards of isolation and the means of communication enter in, and more a matter of the organism, deeply involved in this nexus of interpenetrating relations, rising toward a self-conscious status. Responsive awareness marks a sort of threshold between the deeper levels of communal existence, to which the bodily feelings give fuller report, and the towers of the mind that rise from this nexus of relations in more solitary, reflective awareness. Thus Miss Emmet writes,

> If something like a 'pre-animistic' stage underlies experience, we do not start from projective modes of our consciousness, or analogies of our own activities, on to a world beyond us. We start from consciousness of ourselves as arising out of a *rapport,* interconnection and participation in processes reaching beyond ourselves. Such feeling is a pre-condition of self-conscious experience . . .
>
> Knowledge is only possible where there is some actual situation of relatedness together with conscious awareness of relationship.[14]

It will be seen then that the situation in which myth-thinking takes place is thus a perceptive horizon of consciousness in which bodily feelings, conveying the nexus of relationships, and conscious awareness, attentive to solitary concerns, merge; and, in fact, interpenetrate. The religious response is thus bi-polar, involving, on the one hand, a genuine concern for individual destiny; and, on the other hand, a responsive awareness to that which is more than the self, out of which ultimate demands arise.

[14] Ibid. p. 65.

III

THE NATURE OF RELIGIOUS DISCOURSE

It remains for us now to inquire into the third area of problems concerning the nature of religious discourse. Here the concern is to understand (a) the function of symbolic expression as a language of myth; and (b) the nature of theological discourse as an intellectual interpretation of myth.

By symbolic expression in this instance I mean the use of religious symbols through the media of the dramatic arts, poetry, and music for expressing or conveying especially the depth of feeling through which the ultimate demands of being are mediated. Such symbolic mediation will vary in the degree to which it holds feeling and awareness of meaning in a creative unity. Where feeling predominates to the neglect of a concern for meaning, symbolic expression lapses into sentimentalism. Where the concern for meaning is over-stressed to the neglect of feeling, the result may be an arid formalism. Here the relevance of the aesthetic discipline to religious expression is made evident. It is the indispensable source of control and discrimination in the blending of feeling and meaning, giving both power and pointedness to religious expression. Such symbolic expression is, in Suzanne Langer's sense, the highest form of humanizing activity; for it addresses both mind and the bodily feelings to demands which extend the human reach toward symbolization.

Theological discourse as an intellectual interpretation of myth must be differentiated from theological inquiry which is addressed to discursive problems. The latter is pre-eminently analytical in nature. It would include, for example, thinking upon the relation of theology to philosophy or to cultural issues arising from political, educational, or economical situations within the perspective provided by the valuations of the myth. Here the theological perspective or, we might say, the religious vision in the form of theoretical affirmations, is brought to bear upon various issues as a criterion of criticism. The witness of the faith is made to speak as a directive of culture in terms of possibilities of good or evil; in terms of motivation with reference to choice or decision in relation to good or evil; in terms of judgment bearing upon conditions within such areas arising from choices and decisions in regard to good or evil.

Theological discourse as a mode of inquiry into the meaning of myth, on the other hand, partakes of a more subtle and indirect use of language. Theology under this aspect should be conceived of as being midway between art and philosophy. If worship is viewed as a form of the fine arts, theology as an interpretation of myth should be seen as having direct affinity with the arts. It should, in fact, be allied, as a mode of disciplined criticism, with art criticism and with literary criticism in so far as these are conceived to be directly responsible for illumining creative effort, disciplining its expression, and thus enhancing its communicable force.

The theologian in his attempt to lift the themes of the myth, or the full drama of redemption, to a more explicit, cognitive expression, is constantly caught between two demands which tend to be antithetical in purpose. The one is discriminating thinking of a more direct sort, requiring analysis and the searching out of implications; the other is relational thinking of a perceptive sort, requiring the use of analogy, metaphor, and parable. The theologian is constantly seeking to achieve penetration of meaning in relation to a vast orbit of related meaning. His language, if analytical, is never simply scientific. He must use the sciences in a way in which the scientist cannot be expected to employ them: namely, in a context which shocks the understanding with surprise implications because of the juxtaposition of scientific fact and poetic vision. His language, if relational, is never simply metaphysical; for he operates at a level of imaginative thought which, as yet, has not yielded to extensive abstraction. He must use metaphysical concepts in a way that enlivens these bloodless abstractions with the vitality of concrete existence. His language, if aesthetic or poetic, is never simply poetry; for he seeks to interpret and to communicate mythical meaning with more direct, cognitive concern than the poet can exemplify. He must make use of poetic imagination and poetic expression in a way that turns the indirect assertion into immediate alliance with direct inquiry. Theology, in its function of interpreting myth, thus carries forward two seemingly contradictory modes of inquiry: the one, definitive with a view to explicit clarification; the other, imaginative, with a view to insinuating the fuller range of meaning implicit in the adumbrations of experience which can never be fully borne by explicit language.

IV

From our analysis of these three areas of problems, we can see that myth, both as a concept and as a content of seminal meaning, is a constructive tool by which the depth of the cultural experience can be theologically envisaged and organically related to worship and to religious inquiry. Within an emergent perspective, myth is seen to be a symbolic method for seizing upon the tenuous intrusions of the psychical thrust within history and within the cultural experience, wherein the creative movement of the life process toward the new order of events can be discerned. But myth, being the symbolic carrier of the deeper sentiments of the culture, pointing at once in a mood of judgment to the current, creatural limitations of man, and in a mood of grace and forgiveness to the redemptive activities of God in history, is also the source and the nurturing matrix of the most profound sensibilities of man. Without its resources, and without its nurture, the heart may literally be *hardened,* the mind made arrogant, and the spiritual outreach of man altogether atrophied. Myth, therefore, is indispensable to a profound orientation of the human psyche in our culture, and the source of our most discerning theological insight.

VI

Structure of Experience

THE MYTH of a culture, which rises to the surface in song and poetry, and is retained from age to age through these mediums, always points to a deeper, less articulate, emotional context. We might speak of it as a *feeling context*. We can speak of it also as a structure of experience, even though this term attributes too much form and definitiveness to the cohesion of feeling.

The structure of experience, or feeling context, is the most elemental level of meaning in any culture. I hesitate to call it a level of meaning because immediately it assumes a cognitive character. Obviously there is awareness of some sort, but it is an awareness comparable to that of nature's mindless creatures, moving in a familiar environment.

The structure of experience gives form to our repeated valuations. It is impossible to get at the details of this accumulative valuation response, though of course certain memorable events or observations stand out in any period. And the history of events presumes to tell the story of this growth of the psychical structure. But compared with the actual process of an evolving structure of experience, recorded history is a relatively superficial account.

It must be said, too, that the evolving structure of experience is not to be equated with the passage of events. Somehow all events enter into this emerging structure of experience; but something of all events partakes of a perpetual perishing that accompanies emergence.

The structure of experience is not just accumulative. That is, it is not just a blind appropriation of heterogeneous valuations; rather, it simulates an organic unity at every stage of history. The struggles and crises of concrete events, the dedications and betrayals, the discoveries, creations, and intellectual triumphs, become the formative stuff out of which rises the persisting structure of experience. Great insight at any one point becomes creative in its influence beyond calculation. Stretches of insensitivity, with its consequent brutality and evil, likewise affect the accumulative valuations, not only in an additive sense but in a transformative one. Within any given geographical environment, then, where human history has been in process, the present movement of time is laden with qualitative meaning so complex in character (being the accumulative decisions and resolutions of ages), so profound in implication for all existence and for all present events, that no living consciousness is equal to discerning its burden and its opportunity.

Now generations come into an organic inheritance that is greater in depth and range than the perceptions of any living persons. Thus they live in a context of feeling and awareness that is always beyond their grasp, emotionally or cognitively. They are not automatically bound by this inheritance; for they, too, are creative of its yet emerging structure in the way that all concrete events have influenced it. Nevertheless, all living persons carry within their conscious existence and in their perceptual nature something of the hidden drives and aspirations which rise out of this accumulative structure of experience.

Within our culture, the Christian faith is mediated in this structure of experience, rising out of the accumulative valuations of the culture in which its prophets and poets, its hopes and aspirations, its destructive and redemptive forces, have been persuasively at work. It is an oversimplification to say that this is the structure of experience that has arisen out of the dedications and betrayals of Jesus Christ, but this is one way of saying it. The process is much more complex, but clearly, Christ is the focal point of the pattern.

I have been using the term structure of experience in a rather singular fashion but I should now point up some of its nuances.

Whether one should speak of structure of experience as a compound term containing the implications of faith and tradition, or conceive of structure of experience as more elemental than either of these, giving rise to them, I confess I am not as yet quite clear. And how we are to distinguish faith and tradition in this context may not be as obvious as first appears. Tradition certainly carries the burden of past assent. It is the accumulative element of form, authorizing the proprieties within the present on the basis of this past assent. Faith is a more mobile term. It might be merged with the structure of experience so that we should say it is this feeling context in so far as it relates to that something in experience which connects our lives with all life that has been lived in our culture. Our faithfulness to them, meaning the predecessors whose valuations we bear as our burden, unites us contextually. But faith is more distinctively a psychic force that arises from this sense of continuity, giving assurance to conscious experience and a sense of direction in the way that a feeling orientation can provide.

Any dissociation from the structure of experience, in the sense of distrust in its valuations or revelations of the enduring good, places faith on an individual basis. When this occurs there is a loss of cultural orientation or such conscious extrication from the feeling context of the culture as to lose the sense of a saving continuity with it. We may then arbitrarily select out of the cultural history some event in history or some record of events, as an alternative norm or authority, thus placing some one element of the culture awkwardly in opposition to the structure of experience.

The conflict in thought which arises from this dissociation is on the level of intellection, making for confusion in symbols and ideology; since obviously, no one by dissociating himself from the structure of experience as a mental act actually succeeds in doing so at the level of feeling where his perceptual nature roots down in the pervasive context of feeling that defines each present moment.

Sectarianism tends toward such dissociation, generally becoming an insulated faith that bears no conscious relation to the context of culture. Something of this dissociation occurred in the rise of Protestantism, resulting in a distortion from which Protestant ideology has never recovered. The Reformers reflected varying degrees of it; but in their followers, the tendency was accentuated. Dissociation took the form of anguish over original sin such that a special degree of assurance was sought. The Gospel was lifted up as containing singularly the reassuring word, Christ as Lord being the medium of communication. This meant an extrication of the Word and of Christ, and of God as well, from the structure of experience. Henceforth these were represented as being antithetical to it. Faith was represented as an individual attitude of trust that led to an individual encounter with God.

Now I am not inferring here that the Protestant criticism of culture in the name of an objective criterion implies in itself dissociation. The current culture and the structure of experience are not to be so equated. The distortion, as we have noted, arose in the Protestant tendency to oversimplify the religious norm by individualizing the religious relationship, on the one hand, and by particularizing the norm itself, on the other. The current culture in any period of history in the form of men's acts, their desires, institutions, and policies, may be a betrayal of what is deepest in the cultural inheritance. Wherever this betrayal occurs, the sensitive consciousness that bears witness to the enduring good may rise in protest or suffer silently, awaiting an opportune time of renewal. But the enduring good in this case, the good that was in Christ, as our culture would word it, would not be an alien structure of meaning, nor a particularized norm outside of the culture; but rather the creative source of its intended value, forever judging its betrayals, its denials and failures, yet holding before it, as well, grace and forgiveness where there is penitence and humility to receive the redemptive good.

Protestantism, it must be said, opened the way for a presentation of the Christian faith as a formula isolated from the structure of experience. Transcendence thus came to mean more than a valuational corrective of the autonomous tendencies within the culture; it meant discontinuity with the structure of experience itself. The Protestant corrective of Roman Catholic institutionalism, together with the persisting acidual cleansing which it provided, and its recognition of the illusion of rationality, justify it as a re-creative force in Christianity. In so far as it fostered a particularistic and schismatic faith, however, in rivalry with the structure of experience which communicates the living faith as a context of feeling, Protestantism precipitated two tragedies: a venture in faith that tends to be culturally impotent, and a culture, wherever Protestant influence prevails, that is meagerly nurtured in its spiritual aim.

Since the emerging structure of experience is the work of a creative happening in which the events of men become the focal point of brute force and God's sensitive working, this structure of experience, bearing its present fulfillments, can no more be dissociated from God's working than it can be dissociated from man's working. The creative process in which this structure of experience emerges is a highly complex pattern of events, accompanied by this undefinable, even undesignable, something which is not actuality and which is therefore not event, hovering over existence as possibility and as yet unrealized meaning. It will be seen from this characterization that no easy contrasting of God and culture is possible. What is possible is the designation of those events within the cultural process that pyramid in power when unrestrained by God's sensitive working, and which thus imperil the creative good that is in God. This is often so enormous in proportion to the sensitivities in men that carry the working of God in concrete form that it is readily identified with culture as a whole; hence the culture is seen as being antithetical to God.

We may be able to convey the meaning of the structure of experience more adequately if we attend to its concrete character. We have said that structure of experience is a static characterization of the persisting valuations of the culture which carry the net result of the cultural history into the present. The cultural history I am speaking of here is the continuity of human events that is represented by the generations that move in upon one another. Every contemporary period, every present, embraces at the most four generations: great-grandparents, grandparents, parents, and children. These are strands of experience meshing into one another to form a social fabric. The nature of the process by which the valuations within these several strands interpenetrate is too subtle to describe. And the rhythm of interpenetration, being intermittent, does not permit of easy generalization. At a certain stage of the grandparents' lives, the full impact of history, as it was carried by the great-grandparents, intrudes itself upon their consciousness and their feeling responses of the grandparents. In the same way, the net result of the fusion of experience penetrates the lives of the parents; and, through them, in part at least, the diverse and the correlated valuations of the whole network of meanings subtly become integral with the child's emerging consciousness.

In addition to this progressive transmission of meanings by stages, there is the simultaneous interchange of valuations in that span of present experience when, and in so far as, these generations become contemporaries. The living together in filial relationship sets the sequences of historic valuations represented by each of the generations in a live, creative context by which new historic meanings are made to emerge. Multiply this filial process of interchange in valuations and one has an impression at least of how history and a structure of experience move into the present.

The radiation of meanings within the filial groups is, of course, but one aspect of the total process of interchange within any given period of time. Where the filial group is dominant in a culture, it becomes the chief carrier of inherited meanings. In our modern Western culture it is but one of many. To trace the routes by which the valuations of the culture are mediated to each emerging generation would be an enormous undertaking; but it could be done with some success. The full delineation of these routes, however, would be only a partial portrayal of the emerging structure of experience; for there is much that is gathered into the depths of the moving moment of history that cannot be brought to light or designated.

What the historian cannot bring to light is the accumulative wisdom and concern that works at the feeling level of men's consciousness, unbeknown to them, but with a shaping that is unmistakable in retrospect. The historian, looking back, can recount the visible features in contrast to other moving edges of history;

thus he can know that this deeper shaping was at work. But this internal wisdom of existence, by which the structure of experience is communicated to each living person, can only be appropriated; and, as it were, unwittingly disclosed. This contrast may appear more vividly in the more intimate, personal histories of people.

Every family group discloses two levels of history: the one they talk about, and the one they possess more hiddenly. Letters, family albums, journals, and the like provide the tangible evidence of events now held in memory. Except for these momentos that fix a few fragments of the past, the personal history of individuals would indeed seem but a perpetual perishing. Yet this is not altogether true (and this points to the second level of history); for events live on in the sufferings and joys of those who, in ways remote or immediate, have been shaped by them. The past events of the family, those consciously cherished and those but dimly perceived, perhaps forgotten, live on in the character and disposition of the children now emerging; and in the anguish or rising hopes of the parents for whom the past is now a living burden or a foretaste of joy.

The family history is one thing. This may be recaptured in festive moods that celebrate the passing of the years. The family character — this may be more; for it preserves as a present structure, subtly made manifest in a look of anguish or in a mood of expectancy, the uncommon workings of destiny which no celebration or historical review can apprehend. Thus actuality presents history in its stark, creative residue. It is here with the blessings and benedictions of God and with his wrath as well. Every community, likewise, carries as a living burden this survival character as a structure of experience which cannot easily be explicated or described.

We may pause at this juncture to ask, What is history? History, I should say, is not identical with the creative process, unless we are to ignore the degrees of depth in observation. The philosophy of history may penetrate to the substratum of causal connections and thus, perchance, come to understand something of the mystery that gathers in the emerging structure of experience; but history is at the level of conscious awareness. It is the descriptive course of events; a record of men's decisions and their consequences.

The narration of history serves the purpose of recovering the past as a present act of consciousness. Through the study of history, man recaptures as an intellectual experience what he possesses in immediate feeling as a formative structure of experience. The intellectual grasp of historical events is itself a formative factor in the sense that intellect modifies attachment to life. History that illumines human decisions, acts, and their consequences — where these have been consequential for the psychical thrust in man — provides a technical aid to faith; i.e. it serves to provide an intellectual horizon of understanding by which the feeling context can assume sharper, conscious awareness and be given clearer discrimination and judgmental bases than the feeling orientation affords. Furthermore, history is the only source from which insight into the cognitive character of the structure of experience can be gained. It is never more than fragmentary; but it serves periodically to light up, in a momentary flash, this mystery that forms the depth of our present experience.

History is seemingly inexhaustible in gaining perspective upon the present; for not only may new facts be discovered, but new perspectives may be achieved in any particular age, enabling one to recapture the past in a new light and with new significance.

While history is thus an indispensable source of illumination about the content of meanings and valuations that now sustain existence, the study of history may prove to be desultory in its effect upon the feeling orientation of a people. For the past may become so absorbing to the historian that he seems to be detached from all existential concern and thus is placed wholly in the role of a spectator. History then becomes a critical discipline of the intellect only, with incidental relevance to the contemporary moment of existence. The fact that the historian lives in a medium of influence that is sustained by a structure of experience which carries this history into the present moment of time may have no conscious meaning for him. He will think history on one level — the level of conscious awareness — and he will yield to history on another level — that of subconscious feeling.

Much narration of history bears little relevance to the existential structure of experience by which the historic valuations are borne. It is the delineation of data that serves to reconstruct in imagination the pattern of events which has become dissolved in fact. Except as these events might once have issued in some vital, historic decision such that the habits, hopes, and psychical orientation of men were altered, affecting the structure of experience, they have relatively no faith value. They are incidents for only the intellect to contemplate and to enjoy in retrospect.

Preoccupation with history may have the further danger of isolating the past from the present in a normative sense, setting up some formal authority of the past as controlling, thus dissipating trust in the attachment to life. All forms of orthodoxies commit this folly. If none of these authorities can be accepted as sovereign by some individuals, then these individuals, uprooted from the existential faith, are thrown back solely upon intellectual resources. The fate of the modernist has been precisely this. His intellectual formulation, either as an historical analysis or as a philosophical construction, has been made an alternative to a faith now become impotent. That this is inevitable where the critical concern is pursued with indifference to the existential structure of experience, has been amply demonstrated within the years that anyone of our time can recollect.

The substitution of historical perspective for faith, or philosophy for faith, or ethics for faith, or art for faith, or sensuality for faith, attests to the widespread dissolution of faith itself for the modern mentality. When a person asks how this has come about he has opened up a problem that literally bursts with plausible answers. Before you can stop him, the sociologist will have laid it to the dissolution of the home. Educators will find an answer in the unprecedented spread of education. Some people will be sure to cite industrialization. And the theologian will pack up all of the world's troubles in the one bag — secularization. I am of the opinion that none of these is a basic cause. They are simply prominent features of the modern era that can somehow be related to this condition. To be sure they changed the circumstances under which faith was normally nurtured; but had they been accompanied by a corresponding wisdom that took account of the psychical life of man, all of these features could have arisen, and the sense of faith would have persisted.

The truth is that modernism in every one of its manifestations gave evidence of a faulty perspective upon man as regards the feeling orientation of his existence — that is, the orientation in which depths of past valuations persist in present experience. Henry Ford's much-quoted remark, 'History is bunk!' gives one clue to its defect. Ford represented modernism in its industrial role. Industry is radically modernistic. The past, we might say, literally has no meaning for it, except as a realm of spent ideas and processes. Technologically, industry rests back upon invention and scientific discovery, for science and invention the past is purely antiquarian. The present model is the superior one. The present process automatically displaces all previous ones. *Time marches on!* Science and industry are predisposed to modernity both by the nature of the value that is embraced and by the knowledge that is sought.

Before the turn of the century, the modernism of science and industry provided a climate of thought in which philosophy, education, and religion found orientation toward the future event. It may be said, I think, that this development in our history during the late nineteenth century was something of a direct outcome of the concern with the *American experience,* as Emerson had defined it, and as Thoreau and Whitman extolled it, which, in turn, had been the fruition of the pioneer. The nineteenth-century understanding of evolution provided this mood of thought with a world-view. Evolution in this sense implied that all relevant meaning lay in the future. It followed that history as a spiritual force was non-existent. In this understanding of existence, spirituality implied acquiescence to the momentum of change.

In acquiescing to change as a spiritual principle, the modernist was to overlook the basic idea of relationship, particularly the relationship between the past as recourse and the present as act. He was not unaware of a relationship between the present and the future occurrent. In any case, he showed a concern here. For example, Dewey, in defining God as 'the active relation between ideal and actual,' gave indication that the latter relationship was a live problem with him and a focal point of concern in his thought. Wieman was to sharpen his thinking upon God in a more explicit preoccupation with the future occurrent, identifying his process thinking more exclusively with the modernist motif that took emergence more seriously than persistence. To a certain extent, both to Dewey and Wieman, history was 'bunk.' This must be understood as an oversimplification. It can only be partially defended; and it can be partially refuted. But a direction of thinking is indicated by this characterization. Wieman's more recent use of the term 'Creativity' has significance here. Creativity, in Whitehead's thought, is equivalent, in process thinking, to the Aristotelian term 'matter.' [1] It is the basic on-goingness of bare, brute force. The ordering, creative activity of God, with the aid of ideal forms, constantly presses this aimless Creativity into actualized, meaningful events. Wieman has fused these three concepts into one. Creativity, for him, carries the complex meaning of on-goingness, integration, appreciative awareness of possibilities, and the consequent of all these, deepened community. Now it is impossible to hold these diversified meanings together in a single concept; though Wieman struggles hard to do so, itemizing the four-fold event, and then adding, that 'these must happen simultaneously if creativity is to occur.' [2] But a person does not succeed in thinking these diverse happenings simultaneously in one concept in a way that gives adequate stress to each one. Thus one process becomes primary, despite all he might do, and the others attend it as overtones or as secondary qualifications, perhaps concessions. Here Wieman's modernism again comes to the fore: Creativity emerges from this fusion of terms with more of the character of Whitehead's 'Creativity' than of the principle of concretion; yet it bears the name 'God.' Wieman thereby lifts the modernist principle to a dominance it had not hitherto had in his thought, making it normative, not only for history but for con-

[1] *Process and Reality*, Macmillan, 1929.
[2] *The Source of Human Good*, The University of Chicago Press, 1946, pp. 58f.

temporary value as well. Wieman's interpretation of history becomes a selective rereading of events in the light of this norm, namely: *the advance into novelty* with its creative accompaniments as given in his four-fold conception of creative event.

To equate the meaning of God so closely with Creativity as reproductive process is to lift the modernist principle to such dominance as to seem to abandon, or seriously ignore, concern for qualitative attainment.

Creativity is, on the one hand, the tragic process of dissolution. It is made good only as its perishings are transmuted into meaningful events. Our devotion is not to Creativity, the process of perpetual perishing. This we may accept as a tragic fact about existence; but we do so with lament, knowing this is an evil no man can allay. Our devotion is to the creative working that wrests from the tragic dissolution of concrete goods some quality of attainment that will transmute the evil into good. On the other hand, bare Creativity is advance into novelty. It is the reproductive capacity seen in its cosmic context. Now to say that our end is devotion to the maximum possibility of value is again to lift the modernist principle to such dominance that concern for qualitative attainment in any actualized sense is relinquished. This is to set the future event *per se* in a place of preference over persistent, existent value.

Creativeness does not imply that the future event is necessarily a preferred value. It implies, to be sure, that on-goingness is a basic feature of reality; and the advance into novelty is the inevitable consequence of this on-goingness. Yet there is no need to do homage to the reproductive process, saying this is the chief value in events; nor is there any point in saying that this process must be preserved above all else. It is the most assured of all processes. It is also the most basic in a non-valuational sense. Yet, as Edna St. Vincent Millay writes,

> It is not enough that yearly, down this hill,
> April
> Comes like an idiot, babbling and strewing flowers.[3]

[3] *Second April,* M. Kennerley, 1921.

Creativeness, or the creative act, issuing in event, implies turning the reproductive process toward meaningful ends by transmitting to each event the burden of actuality, which is to make it, in some sense, the bearer of attained value. God is on the side of qualitative attainment, pressing its demands upon the impulse toward novelty.

That the burden of past attainment shall be transmitted to emerging events is a far more precarious matter than that this on-goingness shall be kept operative. The latter is not a matter for concern since it is *given.* The former is never assured because of the perpetual perishing on the one hand, and the impulse toward novelty on the other. It is assured in the sense that it is God's working that fulfills such qualitative attainment; but it is not assured in the sense that God works through the structures of events in which emergence and qualitative attainment must simultaneously take place. God's fulfillment of actualized good clearly depends upon the opportunities of history.

The concern for the transmission of qualitative attainment is not to be confused with sheer traditionalism, or with conservatism as a reactionary force. The latter has to do with what T. S. Eliot terms 'adjustment to our fixed relations with the world.' [4] This points to a different objective. Creativeness in the sense of pressing the burden of past attainment upon emerging events is attentive to the forward moving rhythm of life. It is not resistant to the emerging event. On the contrary, God is conceived as being eagerly receptive to it, but with a concern that arises out of his responsible relation to the achieved values of existence; concern that, from the advance into novelty, meaningfulness, which implies continuity with a cultural character, shall result.

Now it is my concern to say that God's work is of a structurizing nature at the level of feeling, achieving the creative act of transmitting past attainment to every moment of advance into novelty. You cannot say that this is simply a conserving of values, as Höffding, for example, viewed it.[5] It is rather putting attained values to active use in the shaping of novel events. The creative

[4] *After Strange Gods,* London, Faber and Faber, Ltd., 1934.
[5] *Philosophy of Religion,* Macmillan, 1906.

result is not a simple preservation of the past, but the past, as a feeling context, infused into new meaningful events.

It can be said, then, that the structure of experience in any age is the context of feeling in which past valuations persist by reason of God's creative working. It is, as it were, the reservoir of inherited wisdom, awaiting renewal in cognitive form whenever the impulse toward qualitative attainment shall motivate experience.

I am not implying that there is a static, inherited wisdom that can rise up as an authoritative good to coerce experience. Every present moment is adding to and transforming this inherited wisdom. I am suggesting that all experience, within a given culture, is of a piece; but that the totality is constantly undergoing creative change. This follows, on the one hand, from the basic fact of ongoingness, brute force, creativity, or the advance into novelty. It follows, on the other hand, from the nature of the creative act of God which transmutes every novel event into a qualitative event by transmitting to it, infusing into it, such past attainment as the structure of experience at any time in any group life will permit.

This does not pose any necessary problem between inherited good and newly created good at the level of actuality; for here past and present are fused into a novel unity. At the level of intellection, this fusion is overlooked, possibly not perceived; so that there is a tendency, at the intellectual level, to abstract an illusory present good and to place it, in one's mind, antithetically to an abstract, illusory good of the past. Where past and present become integral in the creative moment of an emerging event, this battle of words and abstract concepts is seen to be a sort of movie dramatization that essentially falsifies the actual events.

The full, actual valuational content of the structure of experience, which is our immediate possession, no human consciousness can know. It is a depth in our natures that connects all that we are with all that has been within the context of actuality that defines our culture. It is a depth in our nature that relates us as events to all existent events. It is a depth that relates us to God, a sensitive nature within the vast context of nature, winning the creative passage for qualitative attainment. The actual content of all this, I say, we cannot know. Each man lives within his limitations. All men as a total system of conscious events live within limitations that characterize the human emergent. Beyond the perceptual powers of the human creature, vast, meaningful processes of creativity and qualitative creation transpire. Man picks up intimations of this vast working with such instruments of perception, conscious awareness, imagination and feeling, as he may be able to employ. The degree to which men apprehend this vast working depends greatly upon the sensibilities with which they are able to receive what is more than their self-conscious, self-attentive person.

The actual content of this we do not know. Yet, like the faint glimmerings of distant stars, there comes to us a perennial witness to the valuations that have been of the stuff of experience in this creative process out of which we have come. Such a witness comes to us through the mediums of access which we possess in memory, in recorded history, in the surviving creations of other days, in music, poetry and prose, in architecture, in numerous evidences of actual events long since gone into oblivion, except as they survive in the motivating structure of experience.

Of this witness there are many levels, reflecting the variegated coloring of life itself. In the continuing account of costume design, recreation, music, the dance, architecture; in the wealth of detail describing the customs of diet and dress, in all these we have one level of witness. One may call it a superficial level. It is nevertheless part of the concrete fullness of human existence, exhibiting men's valuations. At the deepest level of witness we encounter the themes of the myth, wherever they occur: in the written Word, in the stained glass window, in poetry and drama, in chorale and cantata, the Mass; in the symphony, in sermon and prayer, song and litany; in theology and in conversation that discusses its problems, in all of the numerous occasions where the myth or some theme of the myth is articulated, a witness is borne to what is deepest in our natures, and in the structure of experience which sustains us.

What is deepest in our natures and in actuality itself is defined by the creative act of God — a sensitive working that transmutes sheer process into qualitative attainment. The Christian myth is the drama of redemption that portrays this creative act of God in the destiny of human nature. Thus every communication of this tender regard — what Whitehead characterized as 'the tendernesses of life' — bears witness to this work of God in human history and in the world.

It is the testimony of our culture at its deepest level that the basic event of our history, giving witness to this perception of good as sovereign for all existence, is the person, Jesus Christ. This is the implication of the myth; it is also the accepted judgment of metaphysics whenever it seeks to give cognitive explanation of the 'tendernesses of life' to which the myth bears witness.

Nothing out of history, we may say, is lost to the persisting structure of experience in which God fashions the creatrix of every emergent moment. What is here to shape us in this structure of experience is as trivial as the costume influence of Greece and Rome; it is as significant as the sacrificial love of Christ on the cross, evidencing the creative love of God Himself.

The meaning of the Christian faith, then, is clear: It is the present affirmation of living Christians, attesting to this formative myth that bears witness to the creative good of existence. It is inclusive of all groups who, in any way, lift up this cultural myth. But we shall readily see that there are all grades of articulation, ranging from the most literalistic caricature, capable of informing only the most illiterate of Christians, to the most sensitive affirmation, taking account, not only of the appreciative range of meaning that is implied in the creative works of Christian art and poetry, but of the cognitive concern made explicit in theology and metaphysics.

The theme running through the pages of this book like a binding thread, weaving its discussion into a single affirmation, is that faith is the fruition of an age-long venture of dedication and inquiry among any people in response to a persisting concern about their creatural destiny. More than a set of beliefs, the faith is a set of the mind and an orientation of the human psyche which have emerged within the structure of experience of the Western culture, availing man of resources that are deeper and more enduring than his own creations, for they arise from the creative source of life itself: the work of God in history.

The faith of a people is not to be identified wholly with any specific formulation in theology which seeks to elaborate or to illumine its cognitive meaning; for the faith is a cultural force, or better, a resource of real energy and incentive for the whole of human life which has been shaped in its psychical depths by the valuations arising from its seminal motifs. This is an insight which cultural anthropology in our time has helped us to grasp. The themes of the faith sing through these formulations like a line of melody, as they sing through the great musical and poetic epics of a people's history.

Faith implies valuations and the thrust of the human psyche toward ends and expectations that have been distilled from the summit experiences of successive generations as perceptions of ultimate import. Valuations are to be understood as the accumulative sequence of meanings attributed by a people to objects, events, and circumstances within a common cultural history which, within these bounds, has channeled and shaped the human psyche. Faith, then, in its most elemental form, is the psychical orientation of an individual or of a people under circumstances that generate incentive for living and a zestful attachment to life conceived in its ultimate significance.

Now the Christian faith, as it operates through the human psyche in the overt actions of people and institutions within Western culture, is the articulation of this shaping in conscious experience. Deeper than the faith, serving as a spatial medium for all that occurs under its motivation, is the structure of experience. And within the structure of experience, persisting like a protoplasm to shape the valuations and hopes which give rise to expressions of faith, are the seminal ideas of the mythos, articulating, as in a parable, the perceptions which point to the re-creative and redemptive resources of living.

In these pages I have tried to state in as untechnical language as possible the ground and the appeal of the Christian faith as these have become fortified and illumined by new resources of insight touching upon faith and culture. I have not succeeded altogether in avoiding technical talk, for the issues at times have become too difficult to resolve by anything short of an attempt at discriminating inquiry of the most disciplined sort. Yet the message of this work is simple enough. It is that the Christian faith continues to speak through the tragic and triumphant events of our history, bearing witness to a good discerned in Christ which is both revelatory of God's meaning and redemptive of man.

Faith assumes vast proportions as a psychic and social energy. It is intimate in nature, being, in its most elemental form, a welling up of a profound, inward sense of assurance and incentive out of the depths of human living. Yet it is capable of objectification and of elaborate organization into formal institutions of great power within the culture where a consensus of assurances is attained, attesting to the deeper and ultimate claims of the sensibilities of the mythos which are the seminal perceptions, born of a primordial response to issues of death and existence. Thus faith, however conceived, and in whatever degree of discrimination, points to a dimension of experience within the culture which relates all living to what is of ultimate import, both in regard to ends and to resources for pursuing those ends. On this point I have taken my stand on the side of every religious and Christian movement within our culture which, in any way, bears witness to this persisting depth of experience as over against every tendency in modern life which threatens to dissipate the appeal to faith.

Yet faith, I have insisted, can be made intelligible and discerning, and, to an increasing degree, relevant to the processes of culture. Not everyone will be impelled to relate faith to this wider context of living, or to the deeper and more technical issues of our cultural experience. To one for whom faith is of vast proportions, as we have said, this will not wholly discount their claim to faith. Faith in its simplest expressions remains a bona fide act within culture, bearing its limitations, but bearing also its own form of beneficence. On the other hand, a person who accepts the burden of communicating the Christian faith to the current culture has no choice but to inquire and to deliberate upon the meaning of the Christian faith, both as a directive of history within our culture, and as a resource and constant renewal of incentive for the individual. His concern must be to render the faith intelligible as well as persuasive to responsible and strategic centers of culture.

Faith pursued as an act of inquiry, in which the sentiments and perceptions of the mythos may be given more orderly and disciplined cognitive expression, will yield, not only a more intelligible grasp of the meaning of faith but more discerning insight into the concrete operations of the living God in history to which the faith has persistently pointed.

Faith as a perspective within living will open up to a man the depth of his own experience and of his own nature, setting the problem of human fulfillment in a light which is at once more urgent and prescient of good. Faith does not cancel out the fact of evil or preclude visitations of tragedy. It discloses within these sobering and defeating events of our existence the redemptive good which can transmute evil and tragedy into an emergence of good, thus bending the threat of dissolution toward the creative intent. The fulfillment of life, amidst repeated and often disillusioning experiences of unfulfilled hopes, is to be sought and found in an abiding affection for this redemptive good, the source of our very life and the hope of our renewal when our worlds crumble.

VII

The Discernment of Faith

IT MAY NOT have escaped attention that in this discussion of myth and the structure of experience I have not mentioned the word truth. Truth and myth! How can they be kept apart? If the question inferred is, 'How do I know that the myth is true? And if I do not know whether or not it is true, how may I as a critical intellect be expected to accept it?' I should answer that, in the sense in which this question is generally raised, the question is not really relevant. It is, in fact, on a par with the misgivings of Carlyle's woman friend who, for a time at least, questioned whether or not she should accept the universe. Actuality asks no rational confirmation. It does not wait for the intellect to settle its problems. It literally creates and cradles the mind that questions it.

Truth involves the satisfying of specific canons by which a person presumes to know a thing to be true. This implies accommodating actuality to the intellect: presenting existence in a form and upon a level of symbolization which the mind can recognize as meaningful. The truth aspect of anything depends upon the degree to which it can be made to accommodate itself to the intellect. Objects lying visibly before us present a fairly easy problem of truth. The observations and conclusions can be accurate; and they probably will be relatively insignificant. To the degree that visibility fades, or detectability lessens, the problem of truth must assume an abstract character. Suppositions will be made and upon their bases specific lines of reasoning will be projected. The force of the structure of truth which will rise from this mode of abstract reasoning depends as much upon the receptivity of the mind seeking verification to the symbols and suppositions thus used as upon the inaccessible reality, about which truth is being sought. But it also follows that the abstract procedure, by which truth is sought, tends to construct a fabric of meaning which may have only an incidental relation to actuality. Conceivably a vast structure of symbolization can rise, presuming to be intelligible meaning about something, the concrete counterpart of which is negligible, often non-existent. Elaborations within mathematics and physics tend to be just such constructions.

Conversely, depths of actuality, inaccessible to conscious experience, will escape awareness and intelligibility, and thus be beyond demonstration of truth; yet be able to determine or destroy intelligibility itself. That such depths *may* exist and *can* exist, can be established as true. *That* they exist, cannot be established so long as they remain imperceptible.

Truth as applied to myth or to the structure of experience can have only the force of intelligibility. That they exist and what they convey, can be made consistent with a given structure of thought resting upon intelligible categories. Perhaps they can have one more kind of truth: a practical, functional truth — namely, that what they portray of man illumines experience and provides conditions in the sense of an orientation of the human psyche which actually redeems man.

The alternatives to verification seem to me to be of two sorts. Perhaps they are not two alternatives, but two phases or stages of one alternative. At present, however, they seem to me to be distinguishable. The one is the faith-attitude of trust as developed by the Reformers. The other is appreciative awareness which offers a counter-movement in the mind to temper or to restrain the egoistic element in all intellectual effort.

I have never felt satisfied with the way in which the attitude of faith is characterized, for there seems to be more implied than is conveyed. Usually it is represented as a desperate venture of belief to make up for lack of knowledge. *I cannot know; there-*

fore I must believe! In so far as this is an acknowledgment of realities beyond the possibilities of my knowledge, it carries force. Any analysis of how I came to be the kind of knower that I am would make clear by inference and implication that I am shut out from perceiving, as well as from knowing, a vast amount which is and which occurs in my presence. While together human minds may know a great deal more than any single human mind could conceivably know, every human mind stands limited by the kind of restriction which the thinking situation itself imposes.

To be sure, the attitude of faith as trust has generally been made to imply an act of will rather than a cognitive act. It is an act of choice or decision in the existentialist's sense, wresting from a situation of despair an opportunity to transcend the impasse and to turn it into a situation of hope. Yet, as an act of will, it involves some cognitive transformation. For the mind, in being released from the dissipating tensions of anxiety, is set upon a different plane of reflection. Such renewal of vision as may come to it in this new orientation is due as much to the re-creation of the mind itself as to the spontaneous functioning of will in the act of faith or to its persistent functioning.

To return, however, to the point we were making concerning the restrictive nature of our knowing, we have the choice of living within our common enclosures of mind, viewing the world as if it existed precisely as our restricted vision presented it; or of living with some sensibility to what is beyond our comprehension. This is not what the Reformers meant by faith; but what they meant takes on fuller justification when given this direction. To be sure this opens the door to all the possibilities of illusion. Yet to close the door is to succumb to illusions which rationality itself imposes.

I see a way by which possibilities of illusion can be lessened in the emphasis upon appreciative awareness. Appreciative awareness is that kind of attentiveness toward what is beyond comprehension which assures some nurture of our perceptual powers. It is, on the other hand, that kind of receptivity which assures some removal of the restrictions that normally attend all processes of thought. Appreciative awareness, we might say, is the attitude of trust assuming an explicit cognitive concern.

The intrinsic importance of this wider awareness which faith connotes lies in the peculiar orientation of consciousness, turning it receptively toward data or toward a datum that may be only partially apprehensible. What is reducible to knowledge may be of less significance than the fullness of meaning which resists particularization. Faith as appreciative awareness, unattended by critical intrusions, is the art of human response to the abundance of meaning in the datum that is of ultimate concern to the creatural experience and to all existence. It is the thrust of the creature toward the source of his creaturehood in an effort to nullify as far as possible the limiting effects of his own creatureliness. This he cannot do completely. He can only seek to do it by achieving such abandon as he is capable of accomplishing when, mindful of the source of life, he takes leave of his creatural self-interest.

I shall try to illustrate the contrast between the discernment of faith, understood as appreciative awareness, and rational inquiry or interpretation which remains indifferent to this dimension of faith by citing two different approaches to understanding alien cultures. One procedure is to come to a decision in one's own mind about what constitutes a sound, human culture, suitable for promoting our human well-being. A sound culture, we might then propose, is: (a) democratic in its organization of life; (b) concern for the well-being of its citizens, that is, attentive to the standard of living particularly as this applies to health, comfort, and security; (c) and adequately industrialized to facilitate the production and distribution of goods so that both democracy and human well-being might be assured.

As a criterion of culture, this formula meets the basic requirements as many of our people would see the problem. Presumably we might then follow the suggestion of the late Wendell Willkie and others of how to bring to the world the incentive for attaining such a standard of living, thus establishing a sound culture the world around. Yet a moment's thought will reveal how American this criterion is. It is, in fact, envisaging the ideal possibilities of the world culture through the restricted purview of the American experience.

A second procedure would begin with the recognition that a world culture, even in terms of conception, is as yet unexplored and unknown territory. We stand within our several fragmented cultures, looking out upon one another in a new relationship: that of critical interdependence and compulsory co-operation. Not only are we unacquainted with the possibilities of such a world experience, but we have only a meager amount of knowledge about the immediate and present facts of experience within one another's culture. Our statistical knowledge will aid us in understanding certain physical facts bearing upon each of us individually and upon the conditions that connect us as one people. But the emerging world culture as a qualitative meaning, if this should come to pass, involving associated values, appreciations, aspirations, the things which sustain man and which nurture the human spirit, which would shape men into a world community — these are as yet unformulated in any single culture on a world pattern. The concern with physical well-being is a major motif of our American society. Yet, in any adequate view of culture, it must be clear that sheer well-being is of secondary importance as compared with the zest for life which may arise from simple human joys where life has become an art, as is often evident in cultures where handicraft and the communal sharing of creative experience is as indispensable to the human spirit as the assurance of bread.

The qualitative meaning of whatever is emerging as a world community waits upon: (a) receptiveness to values yet unanticipated or unknown because they are beyond the scope of social experience as it is now known within any one culture; (b) readiness to receive the stimulus of this larger, more diversified reality into our own social experience and to be shaped by new meaning so derived; (c) willingness to let the conflict of cultural values have right of way without undue insistence upon any criterion of cultural good. This will mean some relinquishment of the cultural ego in the effort to be receptive to meaning and value beyond the range of our own restricted social experience.

Now the life of faith in contrast to the restrictively reasoned life is comparable to this second procedure. And the rational effort, bound to the demands of a given criterion, must always bear some resemblance to the first one. The importance of this attitude of faith or appreciative awareness to thinking lies in the humility that it gives to the act of thinking. And this is especially important in all religious thinking. By giving humility to the act of thinking, the process of thinking assumes that orientation for which Christian thinkers have always pleaded; namely, one in which sensitivity to God routs the arrogance of man's reason, or counters the readiness to enclose the mind within the bounds of limited data available to the human situation at any given time or place.

The devices of exact thought to counteract the failings of inexact thought breed their own form of deception; just as recourse to inexactness to counteract an oppressive concern with accuracy degenerates into error and indulgent sentiment. Faith stands to reason as love transcends the law. But faith can be made to betray all truth in unreason just as love can be made sordid and sentimental without the restraint of observing law.

I am simply trying to lift up the intent of Protestant thinking in its classical form to show that, despite its failure to carry Christian thought forward in its revolt against scholastic rationalism, it seized upon an attitude of mind which is indispensable to the religious mind and to the full effort to apprehend religious truth.

Now when a person asks, 'But what does this "attitude of faith" or sensitive awareness accomplish that contributes either to the theological task or to the religious life?' the answer is likely to seem inconclusive, and the effort to justify its worth, somewhat groping. Early Protestantism overcame this ambiguity by attributing to it a personal assurance of God's goodness and grace which, when apprehended, released man, the sinner, from anxiety about his own destiny and thus enabled him to be mindful of his duty to others. Theological liberalism made a similar claim for its appeal to religious experience in so far as confrontation with the historical Jesus and his sense of vocation directed men to the community of good envisaged in the Kingdom of God. In each case the value rested back upon the capacity of each individual to have access to what is more than himself. The risk of subjectiveness here is obvious. Yet simply pointing out this risk is hardly sufficient to justify an individual in equating all such appeal to faith or to experience with subjectivity. This is a point which neither Barthian theology nor religious naturalism has adequately acknowledged. Both Barth and Wieman reacted vigorously against the subjectiveness of the liberal's method and sought to restore objectiveness to religious thinking by appealing either to revelation or to evidence. This, I think, is to detour attention from the nature of the existential situation with which both early Protestant and the theological liberal were basically concerned; and which, in the last analysis, is the point of mediation between whatever is objectively given and what is subjectively apprehended and received.

The folly of a sentimental dependence upon faith or the illusion of an uncritical appeal to religious experience are not profitably corrected by an arbitrary appeal to evidence except as something more than either of them follows. For if the sense of objective meaning is restored, the capacity for adequately apprehending this objective meaning remains uncalculated. In the one case, a skepticism with regard to man's nature and destiny is unrelieved. In the other case, something of the philosophic assumption that knowledge assures commitment blurs the fact that the problem of human salvation still remains unsolved, and, in a sense, unattacked, in this ardent concern to clarify the criterion.

Faith, then, we can say, is a precondition of thinking upon ultimate matters which gives some assurance of getting beyond the structural limitations of the thinking ego. By this one would mean that it provides a responsible relation with the ultimate concern on the part of the thinker, thereby increasing the probability of his response to such meanings or demands for meaning which may awaken religious discernment. This is tantamount to saying or assuming that a barrier stands between thinker and believer, between philosophic reflection and religious discernment — a barrier which is erected by the thinking ego itself and which can disappear only to the degree that the egoism of attentive thought is tempered by finding recourse to an attitude of faith.

Furthermore, in attempting to give a partial answer to the question, What does appreciative awareness, implied in the appeal to faith, contribute to the theological task and to religious living? I should say that it provides a condition of human response in which something creative can happen to man's total nature such that his habits of response can be transformed. Under these circumstances, even the very criteria which he envisages as being designative of the good may undergo radical change. Faith viewed as this openness to good beyond any definitive criterion of good, can thus be creative of new insight as well as of new vision compelling the reconstruction of criteria. It may do more than that. It may, by its very enlargement of vision and by the imaginative response which is quickened, elicit an affective response in thought, which is to prepare thought for commitment. Whether or not thinking issues in commitment, or in what Kierkegaard called *knowledge with concern,* determines its religious effectiveness; that is, determines whether or not the known result assumes a saving force or remains merely data of the intellect.

Protestantism from Martin Luther down to Jonathan Edwards has always implied that salvation is a problem of human affections and not simply a matter of works or of intellection. We can, in fact, characterize the whole Protestant effort, including evangelical Protestantism and theological liberalism, as a movement to awaken in men and women a religious affection that would transfer their lives from the orbit of themselves to the orbit of God. In this effort, religion has been known to wallow hopelessly in sentimental acts and expressions. It is a commentary upon our Protestant plight, however, that our only corrective to this emotional debauchery seems to have been rational reaction in which one extreme has followed up another. Modernism can be said to be both a direct attack upon the premises of orthodox evangelical thought and an indirect restraint upon romanticism in liberalism. Religious naturalism has continued the modernistic advance, but with more philosophical depth, having abandoned the sophisticated method of conceptualism which Kantian idealism had initiated. Religious naturalism has sought to escape from subjectivity and sentimentalism through the formulation of a criterion and the method of verification. The criterion has been made clear; the evidence has seemed unmistakable. Yet the capacity to embrace either of them as a guide to religious living or to the processes of culture is not assured by the attainment of this secure knowledge. The difficulty, as I have come to sense it, lies at this point with which theology has been continually concerned and with which Protestant theology, in particular, has been preoccupied: namely, the religious affections. Religious naturalism has clarified our sense of value; it has not been able to excite the mind toward that capacity for commitment whereby the philosophic quest might pass into religious devotion.

What, then, is the alternative to an exclusive concern for criteria? Must it be the relinquishment of all such concern? Must it be a retreat to contemplation and to mysticism? Obviously, neither of these is a solution. The solution lies in some kind of procedure in thought and action in which awareness and critical inquiry are continually kept in alternation. Critical thought should be able to sharpen the structure of meaning in which the sovereign good is visible and operative, but not to the point of being fully definitive. And the reach for absolute definitiveness may lead to an over-reaching of the mind wherein the act of awareness is progressively minimized and eventually routed. This is the route to abstractionism and to an intellectualizing of religion in which the affective processes can play no significant part. The act of awareness, on the other hand, should progressively advance beyond the stage of sheer awareness to some degree of affection for the good that is discerned. This will be achieved in proportion to the ability to recognize the redemptive good which is discerned as being genuinely operative in human life — an actuality of experience to which our emotions and active responses have relevance. The sense of a good not our own, yet imperative to our good as a never-failing source of grace and judgment, is precisely the feeling-tone that will awaken the affective regions of consciousness.

The solution, then, is in part a recovery of the orientation which Reformation Protestantism found in the appeal to faith. This orientation begins with acknowledging the grace of God in human experience as sovereign and saving, noting that this redemptive work of the Holy Spirit, offering forgiveness, has historical and symbolical meaning in Jesus Christ. Thus the Protestant appeal to faith rests back upon *the knowledge of Christ,* not as philosophic reflection derives knowledge but as the total nature of man, his appreciative and affective powers together with thought, *discerns* the redemptive good of experience disclosed in sacrificial love.

Now the validity of this discernment of faith, that the tender working of sacrificial love is a sovereign and redemptive good, can be rationally established. I think it has been so established at various times. Both Plato and Spinoza have given metaphysical formulation to such a notion. Various forms of Idealism, including Personalism, have done so. I am persuaded that the metaphysics of Whitehead offers a contemporary structure of thought of great relevance and significance for Christianity, providing, in fact, the source of a new theology capable of giving cognitive structure to the sentiments of the Christian faith. A philosophical theology availing itself of this cognitive clarification and support can be a resource of immeasurable importance to Protestant thinking in a time like this. Only it must be made clear that the appeal to 'the tendernesses of life' discerned in the redemptive act of Christ has force in its own right as a persuasive and re-creative element, capable of redeeming 'a world founded upon the clashing of senseless compulsions.'

The insistence upon this fact has been the chief force of the Protestant witness. Its reluctance to embody this discernment of faith in cognitive structures has followed from a sound sense of its authenticity as an operational fact apart from any attempt at conceptual clarity. The grace and judgment of God perceived in existential moments of beneficence or tragedy have been all too real to require elaboration. Thus the meaning of this gospel, it has insisted, does not wait upon intellectual defense or clarification.

What the Protestant thinker has often overlooked, however, is that the import of this gospel may be enlarged and made culturally more effective when given an adequate cognitive structure. Here, in fact, lies the chief weakness of the Protestant evangel. Its fear of all structures, pre-eminently of intellectual structures, as being potentially idolatrous, has led it to minimize the rhythm of man's doing and to stress the work of the Holy Spirit as if it were an operation without structure. The dynamics of faith have thus been represented as a superstructural activity in which man has been wholly passive and receptive. Faith as an act of awareness, albeit with penitence and humility, has been incapable of passing into a perception of goodness which, in turn, might be further defined and disciplined through critical inquiry. Thus the only Protestant alternative to idolatry has been a judgment upon structures, a protestation against all cultural formulations whether in the realm of thought or of creative effort. And the only safe course for positive action, apart from this act of judgment and reform, has been the profession of faith as an acquiescent response.

Granted that the redemptive good in experience, bringing grace and judgment to existence, affirms its own authenticity, and that its meaning does not wait upon intellectual defense or clarification, it must nevertheless be acknowledged that a fuller meaning of its gospel does wait upon the nurture of sensibilities and affections such that this concrete good which is in Christ as tenderness and love can affect the hungers of men's hearts. If the Protestant appeal to faith as a primary response can be directed to this nurture of the human spirit, it may hold the key to resources within our human reach which can serve the redemptive act in our lives beyond any limits we are able to define.

In lifting up the promise of the Protestant appeal to faith I have not meant to urge it as an alternative to rational effort in theology. That is a familiar emphasis in our day; but I am not echoing the voice of theological reaction. Rather, I am urging clearer recognition of the force of the Protestant appeal to faith in so far as it awakens our affective response to the redemptive good which is in experience. Whatever we do to reinforce this hungering and thirsting after goodness through intellectual means will broaden the application and increase its relevance; for it will thereby integrate the religious appeal with the communicable discourse of culture. But our acknowledgment of this redemptive good, our appreciation of its qualitative meaning and force in a world that is ruthlessly indifferent to it, as well as our dedication to it as our ultimate concern, these are expressive of sensibilities in our nature which precede and follow the rational analysis.

In the working out of our theological task we shall have to go beyond the historical, Protestant understanding of the interrelation of faith and reason, treating this concern, not simply as a problem of religious knowledge, but as a problem of relating religious affection to religious knowledge, such that awareness of the source of human value may issue in faith and commitment to the sovereign God, and thus offer a saving knowledge.

PART III

FAITH AND ITS ULTIMATE ISSUES

VIII

The Depth of Man's Nature

OUR UNDERSTANDING of the life-process as a structure of experience in which formative elements of great depth and antiquity continue to cradle and nurture the human spirit leads us to grasp more readily the way in which faith as a cultural energy operates to fulfill human life and culture. In part we are subconsciously molded as persons and as a society in the way that a mythos invariably imposes a distinctive character upon any people. In part, however, we are shaped by whatever decisions we may make to self-consciously appropriate the valuations that are thus transmitted. In the one case, we acquiesce to the passage of events within our cultural mediums and passively exemplify the coloring of the culture through the sensibilities which we acquire and the perspective which forms our mental framework. In the other instance, we may respond more heartily and with clearer insight to the formative power of faith through which God works to create events of human goodness, or to initiate in some form, occasions for actualizing his creative intent in human structures.

This is but a way of saying that a culture exemplifies varying degrees of conscious participation in the creative passage; though in no sense is it ever exempt from or independent of its formative power. Secularism is to be understood as an attitude and a procedure within society which ignores these primal depths, taking events on face value as simply human events within a social or geographical environment, with no reference beyond this meager measure or concern. The religious outlook upon life embraces some concern for the deeper view of events, though the specific character of this deeper view may not be indicated. A Christian conception of the cultural process specifically envisages this depth in the passage of events and in the nature of man within the imagery of the Christian mythos and seeks to understand man's meaning and the direction of his destiny in the light of the drama of redemption which may be viewed as the cultural extension or elaboration of the creative act of God.

We begin our inquiry into this topic of faith and the human psyche, then, by considering the implications of our perspective for understanding the depths of human nature within the context of the Christian faith. Our analysis of the structure of experience and of the work of God through its concrete structures has afforded us some grasp of the existential depth of the present culture in which contemporary man's life is being formed. We may now turn to inquire into the depth of what is ordinarily conceived to be man's individual or solitary nature.

I

It is not enough to say that man has evolved from lower structures. The philosophy of emergence points to an active tendency or operation in the natural structures which initiates creative acts. This creative operation is known by various names in the literature of emergence, but in the mature forms of metaphysical interpretation which have issued from this movement of thought a forthright doctrine of theism emerges in which God is viewed as a Creative Event in history bent on qualitative attainment, a sensitive nature within nature winning the creative passage for qualitative emergence.

The minimum metaphysical characterization of man is that he is an event. This means that he is a concretion: an actualization of meaning. Out of the indefinite flow of creativity and innumerable possibilities, he has been individuated as a concrete organism by the gentle hand of a Creator who, in the creative act, has wrested from the chaos and brute force of creativity some measure of order and sensitivity; and from the indefinite range of possibilities, some limited range of possibilities.

Birth is the emergence of some concrete order of existence, having a degree of meaning and bearing the visible marks of limitations. To be actual is to possess meaning to some degree. It is also to be limited, determined, or individuated by the fixed sensory facilities which define the living organism. Now the meaning that each one bears; or the meaning that is initiated in the mystery of human birth, is to be defined in three ways which somehow can never be actually separated. There is, in the first place, the creative intent of God — an expectation, if you please, which is laid upon each person by reason of the creative hand which has shaped this emergent into a concrete event. The image of God in the form of a sensitive nature becomes, as it were, a carrier of the divine anguish, providing a career for God, giving actuality in a human structure to God's creative intent, though in meager measure. The image thus borne, bears witness to the good that is creative of all meaning and which thus impresses God's nature upon each concrete event. In the human consciousness, this is, as we say, the cry of the heart, a hungering and thirsting after goodness; an impulse toward love.

These sensitivities which awaken the human creature to imaginative and creative venturing beyond the level of sheer well-being or to acts of dedication or of long-suffering, however the course of life may run, are qualities of our emergent structure which give evidence in our natures of the image of God at the level of feeling. In this sense, we are made for God. Whether conscious or not of this creative intention which permeates our every moment of existence, we bear its imprint upon our natures, if only in the form of ambiguous feelings or impulsions which restrain or complicate our egoistic will to live unto ourselves.

But the mystery of human birth initiates another dimension of our being. To be born, we have said, is to emerge as an event in the world of concrete events. To emerge in the world of the concrete, however, is to take on instantaneously relations with every other event. The full implication of this doctrine of prehension is that community is a constituent of the individual. It is not that the community absorbs the individual but that the individual must instantaneously claim the community as being of his own nature, integral to himself, necessary to himself; and that his life is fulfilled within its concrete existence by and through his relations with other men. In this sense we are made for other men, and they for us.

Yet the mystery of human birth is not fathomed until we see the significance of the I, the subjective self in the context of this social reality. For there is a sense in which we are made for ourselves. We may not overlook this essential condition of selfhood without loss of character and concreteness. The subjective orientation of the self is a fact. We cannot escape the given, physiological determinants of our nature, and the psychical thrust which issues from our center as a self. The uniqueness of the person is thus an indispensable doctrine. To be actual is to be limited, individuated by the fixed, sensory facilities which define the living organism. On the negative side this means that man exists under creatural restrictions which characterize every event. Every event must have a structure. The venerable word for it is finitude, meaning embodiment within certain defined limitations of creaturehood.

This structural nature of man sets the stage for the spiritual drama which is re-enacted in every human life. For every man is the bearer of a tension between the three simultaneous demands upon his being: the creative intent of God, the impulse toward solidarity, and the demands of the subjective experience. These are not necessarily mutually exclusive demands; yet they tend to become so as the growth process of the individual progresses and as the individuation of the person matures. Now the valuations of the Christian myth, in so far as they point up the fracture or the impairment and the consequent proneness toward sin in man's nature, relate to this tension and to the complexity of man's nature resulting from this tension. In the idea of the Fall, the myth has metaphorically noted the unfailing breach which widens between the creative intent of God in each human creature and the human ego as the process of self-emergence occurs. The formal theologies give their particular reading of this happening from within a given perspective. Quite apart from the systems themselves, with their particular shades of interpretation and elaboration, there is the concrete datum of human nature to which these characterizations have some relevance. We may better understand the truth of the Christian perception which is implied in the imagery of the Fall by attending to the emerging human consciousness wherein the concrete datum is observed.

In the present analysis we shall give particular attention to the concrete processes of interaction which form the person as a participant within the communal pattern of events, revealing the social character of existence within every individual life. In later chapters we shall concern ourselves with the tensions that develop in the subjective experience of individuals, giving rise to the concrete processes of sin and of human evil.

II

Man is an event in a context of events, arising as a concretion out of God's creative act. This means that each individual man is creation in miniature, carrying the intent of God to fruition within the unique pattern of relations that make up this subjective span of life. Man is a temporal-spatial episode in the drama of creation. As such, he derives meaning for his existence from the interplay of himself as event with other events. This interplay is possible because of the psycho-physical attraction and retraction between organisms and the communicative level of meaning that may thus arise out of mutual interaction.

The minimum basis for this interplay of creatural relations is the capacity for empathy. This is a psychical capacity which assures feeling response between subjective existences. It means the capacity of an individual to feel into a situation, imaginatively to take situations external to himself into his private experience in such a way that a kind of transcendence of egoistic barriers is achieved. The individual does this in aesthetic appreciation. The appreciative consciousness, in fact, begins in empathy, and without this minimum, psychical response, capacity for appreciative awareness could scarcely develop.

Empathy is the basic, organic capacity of the individual out of which all socialized responses develop.[1] Most people have this

[1] Roy G. Hoskins, *The Biology of Schizophrenia,* Norton, 1946, pp. 53ff.

capacity as an initially given feature of their psycho-physical organism. Consequently, most individuals make the transition from the egocentric orientation of infancy to social maturation without noticeable conflict or visible personal loss. It does happen, however, in some instances, that this transition fails to occur. The subjective life remains self-contained. Empathic feelers, these subtle fibers of human relations that weave the connections of human intercourse, simply do not mesh. They remain as arrested fibers whose nerve ends are exposed to every shock of human association.

Why this transition does not occur is a problem that may never be wholly unraveled. Failures in dealing with other individuals during the early years when socialization should have been progressing as a natural consequence of family life or neighborhood play, may, in part, account for it. Yet every opportunity for socialization may have been provided without avail. The only explanation that can be given under these circumstances is that a basic deficiency in the organic structure has precluded the emergence of empathy. The outcome of this organic deficiency or of such failure in socialization may be schizophrenia. The schizophrenic is the subjective life turned in upon itself. The circuit by which the normal level of human meanings are achieved through communication, outward attention, and the feeling into situations beyond the self, is closed. Fantasy replaces reality. Creation in such lives has reached a dead end.

Where empathy exists, however, a normal interplay of individual events takes place, out of which emerges the various patterned existences which we recognize as companionship, the family, the gang, the club, the religious fellowship, the community; all of which widen into a well-defined culture, the bounds of which are usually geographically, economically, and politically determined.

When we stand off and look at this patterned existence, evident in the lowest levels of creature life as well as in the human community, we are made to realize how far-reaching this communal character of existence really is. It is literally true that human nature, like creature life at every level, is defined by this interdependence and mutuality of existence.

Now this has theological meaning in so far as the contextualist character of existence illumines the nature of man (a) in his relation to God; (b) in his awareness of himself; (c) in his understanding of his responsibilities to the communal life about him; and (d) in his understanding of the whole gamut of creatural experiences, ranging from birth to death.

I think this means that man, in so far as he develops a normal creature-consciousness, encounters all experience as interrelational. This bears upon the basic theological idea of relationship between man and God, and such consequent ideas as sin and salvation, which have generally been treated as problems of man's solitary experience.

Solitariness, even in the sense in which Schleiermacher conceived the situation, where individual man feels the sense of absolute dependence, becomes a special form of interrelational experience. It is in one aspect, at least, communal in character. We commonly hear the expression that every man must, in the last analysis, meet God in his solitariness. 'Religion,' in fact, to recall one of Whitehead's arresting remarks, 'is what you do with your solitariness.' This is a familiar Protestant doctrine — the individual access to God, as Calvin phrased it. And Luther said, 'Every man must do his own dying.' This position has been recently stated in striking fashion by Benjamin Miller in an article, 'Toward a Religious Philosophy of the Theatre,' in which he writes,

The individual seizes upon the presence of other men as an immediate response to his inescapable awareness that he — the deeply fortressed 'I,' the unique core of his distinctive self-consciousness — is alone . . . This sense of isolation is never finally overcome in any human experience . . . This is life's tragic genius.[2]

Much that is said in expression of the tragic sense of life rests upon this underlying conviction of man's essential loneliness or aloneness in the ultimate sense. The force of existential philosophy in the particular mood of our times derives from this insistence upon the individual character of each man's life which stands in

[2] Benjamin Miller, 'Toward A Religious Philosophy of the Theatre,' *Personalist,* Vol. xx, No. 4, 1939, pp. 363, 373.

isolation as a lone event. Dialectical theology, too, reasserts this doctrine in its characterization of the 'divine-human encounter.'

The premise which seems to me to arise from the basic concept of dynamic relations would appear to question this understanding of man's solitariness in existence, even at the moment of death. Rather, solitariness is seen as a peculiarly intense, sometimes poignant, gathering up of this context of experience that includes all creatures, into one self-conscious creatural event. The world does not fall away from us in our solitariness; our fellows do not fall out of mind. Instead, they become peculiarly vivid in the perspective which solitariness gives. For the awareness that we then have of them is of a sort that can communicate to us total persons; while in conversation, the very act of attending to them restricts our intercommunication.

Solitariness may be the moment when our creatural life as creation in miniature becomes peculiarly real to us, such that the significance of being concrete may bear in upon us with the force of a revelation of our meaningfulness.

Even death is not solitary in the sense of aloneness; for death, in its basic meaning, is the disruption of relationships. And if it has any meaning beyond this conscious span, it implies the emergence of new relationships. Attending only to the evident experiences that accompany the death of any individual, we should have to say that, in most instances, death is the event that brings a person vividly into focus to his fellows. 'No man is complete until he is dead!' an ancient seer once said. And this completion means the social envisagement of a life that now stands out starkly as a total system of meanings whose intent and character have become clarified. Death is clarification. To whom? To the social community that embraces this life, now ended, as an intention heretofore observed, but not pondered or fully perceived.

If this is true of the relationship with the wider community, it is even more true of the relationship that is intimate and companionable. Grief is a social response. It acknowledges the pain of an uprooted relationship. The cruelest thing about death is what it does to those who live on in full awareness of this person who is no longer communicable. Just the sight of maimed lives that linger on to lament the departed wife, husband, or lover, should impress us with the social nature of death. The imagery of going on into the great beyond *alone* is not an accurate imagery. We go attended by all the social witness that grief and public acknowledgment acclaim — and perhaps much more. A play such as Thornton Wilder's *Our Town* may help us to realize this fact.

Solitariness and death are discussed here chiefly because these are instances of extreme individual experience which seemingly point to the atomistic nature of life in its ultimate aspect. The implications of the metaphysical concept we have been considering leads to a theological revision of the understanding of these basic, creatural experiences, and therefore of all creature experiences. Life, except as it is mutilated or maimed by organic deficiencies, or by social tragedies that preclude the normal release of empathic response, is marked by an inevitable solidarity.

This insight has important consequences for the sheer act of living. For it means that relations are not merely external, formal, subject to dissolution; but they are internal, intimate, and indissoluble by reason of the texture of existence itself. It is through, or out of, these internal relationships that the real sustaining and redemptive forces of life issue. These are the avenues of grace and redemptive love which save the individual life from what would otherwise be the tragedy of aloneness.

This concept of dynamic relations, then, presents human nature as inescapably social, not in the superficial, environmental sense, but in the basic existential sense — in the extremities of death and solitariness as well as in the concourse of communicative experience.

III

The reverse side of this truth, however, is also important. Here the meaning of the subjective life is involved. Man is an event in a context of events. Man is also individuated. Individuation means being particularized, set apart with uniqueness. This is the mystery of creation, that individuation occurs simultaneously with socialization. We cannot understand existence in any profoundly religious sense except as we keep these two processes poised and in tension with one another. The problem of religion, we repeat with Whitehead, *is* the problem of individual in community.

Now what does it mean to be an individuated event? We have said it means to be creation in miniature: The sea water flows in our veins. The minerals of the earth lie embedded in our bodies. The rhythms of the tides move within us in the rise and fall of passion, in the alternation of moods, and in the varying secretions of the endocrine glands. All of these identify the individual event with all events in the sense that they represent existence in its constituent parts; but they distinguish the individual from the many other events in that the many are here gathered into a unique organization of structure, bearing limitations peculiar to the self as well as aptitudes and tendencies which are singular.

The uniqueness of organic structures is more than a physiological fact; for it is by reason of this distinctive organic structure that the spiritual life of the individual emerges in its peculiar way. Let us put it this way. Two sources determine the nature of the growth of the individual personality: the mechanisms of the organic structure, and the resources of the culture which are, in time, internalized by the individual through the facility of those mechanisms. The process by which the individual internalizes the meanings and resources of the culture is called symbolization. Symbolization is the procedure of creating meaning and of interrelating meanings through communicable symbols. This has become an elaborate procedure at the human level, though its range of complexity is extensive, being, on the one hand, the elemental conversations essential to basic problem-solving, or even the simplest form of musing or daydreaming; and, on the other, the abstruse discourse of higher mathematics and metaphysics. Animals engage in a minimum degree of symbolization, but there is relatively no range of complexity in their discourse.

Man's distinction as a person arises from his capacity to engage in symbolization ranging from the most concrete thought, imagination, and expression, to a highly abstract, compounded form of thought, imagination, and expression.[3] Each person, however, is able to participate in this humanizing, spiritualizing process of symbolization to the degree that his organic structure permits of sensible interaction with the cultural meanings.

Symbolization is not unlike the digestive process. It is this process extended to the realm of meanings. The perceptual and cognitive powers of the person draw into the individuated experience the stuff of culture in much the same way that the person eating imbibes food. Musing and reflection are like mastication. The stuff of cultural meaning is literally chewed over and absorbed by the reflective mind in ways peculiar to the particular mind and imagination at work. There is a highly complex organization of parts in each person determining how this mastication and digestion of meanings proceeds. Prominent among the determinants are the genes, which carry the basic unvarying physiological elements of creaturehood in the individual, the endocrine glands and the cortical mechanism which adjust the range and degree of sensitivity in human perception. With these clearly differentiated facilities for participating in the culture of meanings, it is obvious that there is no simple mass context of meanings. The articulated culture is the medley or symphony or chaotic dissonant interchange of these partially appropriated meanings.

Each of us lives in a maze of mystery which we shall never wholly comprehend by reason of the limitations of the very mechanisms with which we must engage in symbolization. No creature can escape this limitation. It is the price of individuation. Yet we are impelled to overcome this limitation to whatever degree is possible within whatever scope of relations may be possible, since the conditions necessary to existence and the pursuit of our significance depend upon that interchange and interrelation.

This analysis will reveal how difficult the matter of human association really is. Human association would not be possible

[3] Carl G. Stromee has undertaken to show that personality emerges as a structure of value from the accumulative valuations at this level of symbolization in *An Interpretation of the Self as a Structure of Value and Its Implications for the Christian Doctrine of Man,* Ph.D. Thesis, The University of Chicago, 1947.

if it were dependent solely upon the interchange of meanings at the communicable level. This is where empathy as a sublingual force in our natures enters in, weaving our internal relations together through feeling, and giving a depth to our human association which our communicable level could neither achieve nor understand. This is what we mean by *rapport* — a factor in human living which makes possible such profound degrees of human association as companionship, love, and devotion. This is what we mean by faith underlying our knowledge: depths in our natures, fortified by the accumulations of yet unanalyzed impressions and discernments, give assurance to our stride even though, on intellectual grounds, we waver.

The mystery of all living is in the realm of internal relations, for these constitute the stream of experience, the psychic flow, the creative flux in which and through which events have their primordial reality. This is the level of creaturehood, a level more profound than consciousness, though in rare moments of upheaval, of relaxed awareness, or of heightening, as on the Mount of Transfiguration, some hint of this profounder orientation may reach our consciousness. We should not confuse this primordial depth in our natures with the more superficial area of subconscious experience. The subconscious is a more mediate level of semi-communicable meanings. It is of a piece with our conscious life, though it bears the imprint of prior, conscious experience; in fact, it is prior conscious experience inverted, repressed, twisted perhaps; and as such it has a cumulative force in its control of conscious experience. This, however, is still the person's self, the individuated life-span operating in terms of its fixed, organic limitations under conditions imposed by the sequence of happenings that have composed its span of experience.

Deeper than the self is the creative passage, the creativity, the on-goingness, the space-time continuum, where the event seems indistinguishable from events. All living is contained in this medium and is sustained as a temporal-spatial event by reason of being continuous with it. To say that at this level of creaturehood the event seems indistinguishable from events is not to resolve the analysis in a complete monism. It is merely to acknowledge the limit of articulation and to say that there is this depth in our nature that brings our subjective life into creatural rapport with all creatures, and with the creative Source of our being. This is the most basic level of feeling which we can apprehend. I use the term feeling here in the metaphysical sense of Schleiermacher's *anschauung,* and of Whitehead's doctrine of prehension.

The nature of man, then, is seen to be defined by these aspects: (1) the initial interdependence of all created life; (2) the individuation of each event determined in character (a) by the organic structure that provides the facilities for symbolization and (b) the cultural matrix out of which meanings appropriable by the organism may be internalized and made integral in the self; (3) the bi-conscious life, or the two levels of self-consciousness, (a) one in which attentive perception and reflection operate — what is called conscious awareness, and (b) another in which the cumulative force of previously conscious events are operative — what is known as the subconscious; and (4) the primordial depth of existence which contains each event in the sense that space-time as creative process sustains all happenings. The complexity of man's life lays upon him his problem of existence. *He is made for God* in the sense that he, like every created event, bears the intent of creation, and has concourse in his deepest range with the creative passage. *He is made for his fellow creatures* in the sense that all events participate in an interdependence that is of the essence of concretion. *He is made for himself* in the sense that concretion occurs as an event of individuation, i.e. subjective lives are essential, sensory mechanisms to the actualization of spirit in concrete form. The creation of spirit through individuated lives depends upon these three interrelated intents happening simultaneously.

IV

God, as divine intent, the concern for significance in events, arising out of the infusion of feeling, reaches man, in part through what Schleiermacher called the *sense of absolute dependence,* or something comparable to this — that interior rapport with primordial existence which can occasionally reach man's consciousness through exceptional sensitization of his nature. But God may more readily reach man's consciousness through the very process of symbolization wherein man takes into his experience the articulated meanings of the culture. The articulated meanings of the culture, bearing this message of sensitivity and persuasion, as the basic reality of existence, rise out of the events that describe the Christ. The meaning of Christ in the culture that provides us with resources for symbolization is that 'the tenderness of life' give intimation of its depth and core. Feeling, as a sensitizing of force, is the basic category.

Christ, then, is the concrete alternative to mysticism, if by mysticism we mean this singular, internal awareness of Feeling.

To say Christ reveals that God is love states the matter too conventionally to convey this insight sharply; though this traditional statement has metaphysical as well as historical justification. A more precise statement of it within the metaphysics which we have sought to interpret, would be to say that Christ bears witness to the tenderness of life as the primary attribute of God and as the most ultimate, creative force, qualifying all force wherever concrete events exist. The theology that avails itself of this constructive insight must do more, however, than reiterate the words, God is love, or that Christ disclosed God as having a tender regard for his creatures, important as this disclosure is. It must make clear how this insight becomes communicated as a revelation in the culture of Western man, such that it reaches the human consciousness in the very act of symbolization. A proper treatment of this phenomenon would go far toward giving a cultural-anthropological interpretation of revelation, and relate what is vividly known to us in a pictorial way through the song and poetry of our Christian tradition to what the psychologist and anthropologist are now saying about the formation of personality. An adequate Christian doctrine of man, as well as a contextualist understanding of revelation, waits on this formulation.

The psychologist leads us to a clue to a reinterpretation in saying that we emerge as persons by the process of symbolization, which means taking into ourselves such an integration of cultural meanings as our facilities permit. But the range and depth of cultural meanings is not inquired into. Just as there are hidden depths in the solitary experience, reaching to the level of creaturehood, so in the communal experiences that form this network of relations that we describe as our culture, there is the undertone of inherited meaning, stemming from the Christ-event that carries the same sense of creaturehood. Hidden and obscure as this Christian revelation of our meaning is in the contemporary culture, it is nevertheless there as a constituent of its life, awaiting recognition and response to become operative and creative.

The concept of dynamic relations thus seems to provide a new orientation for such basic theological doctrines as: (a) the nature of God and his intent for his creatures; (b) the nature of man, both in his superficial aspect as a conscious structure, and in his creatural depths, relating to his solitariness and to his cultural connections; (c) the relevance of Christ as a source of revelatory and redemptive love in the culture, reaching man through the symbolization that creates man's personality; and (d) the meaning of the Church as the community within the cultural community, bearing and nurturing the revelation of these historic events in which tenderness was disclosed as a creative force.

The importance of the Christian community within the culture, then, consists in this, that it bears witness to the message of persuasive love that was released into culture by the events of Christ's life. This Christian community within the cultural community serves to keep the social stream of meaning impregnated with the redemptive force of those events which persists from age to age. This points to a doctrine of the church which we cannot develop here. It is enough to say that such a view would represent the church, not simply as an institutional witness to an inherited faith or as the custodian of a tradition; but as the actual bearer of the seminal meanings which can reawaken people again and again to what is deepest in their natures and in their history by reason of these revelatory events that characterize the Christ. To the degree that the church can render these seminal meanings vivid, significant, compelling, through the sensitively spoken word, through dramatic art, through the great musical epics such as Bach's *B-Minor Mass,* Mozart's *Requiem,* Brahms's *Requiem,* Handel's *Messiah,* the numerous chorales, significant hymns, through whatever medium that is consonant with the message of these events; to that degree the church provides resources within the culture upon which symbolization can feed, as it were; or, to change the figure, such that symbolization in the culture can, by reason of these resources, reach the depth of creaturehood.

The church in any given community may not be the sole mediator of these meanings. It may not, in fact, be the most effective mediator. It happens in some instances that the church formalizes these meanings to such a degree that they are not communicated beyond the cultus. It also happens that the church through lack of sensibility, reverence, or perspective, degrades these meanings through excessive informality and sentimentality so that their redemptive power is dissipated.

The church, as the initial bearer of this continuing revelation, has the responsibility of striving toward effective communication of this to which it bears witness; and when it fails in this, such secondary media as literature, art, education, and so on, may seek to replace the church in this role. But these apart from the church can never be as effective in this role as these in collaboration with the church.

IX

The Source of Human Evil

INQUIRY into the depths of man's nature leads to a familiar, though baffling, problem: the problem of human evil. Human evil is the dissolute and destructive turn of events which arises from human nature itself and from the accumulative results of human behavior. What man is and does creates conditions in existence which are not only destructive of good and of the creative intent, but productive of rival forces that turn power and structure into aggressive agents of evil doing. Theologically, these operations of human evil have been characterized by the word 'sin.' In this discussion we shall undertake to designate the source of human evil in the concrete processes of human behavior as it appears at various stages of human growth.

Discussions of sin constantly move between a formal discourse which attends to abstract relations between man and God, and a realistic discourse which seeks to illumine concrete facts of existence. All mythology is a way of dramatizing internal processes so that man can look upon himself as if he were *out there* — projected. Theology, to a considerable extent, in so far as it has remained within a formal discourse, has followed this mythological procedure, projecting each man into universal Man and then setting him in a universal drama in which the concrete processes of existence have been made vivid by enlargement and intensification. Man's life has been given cosmic scope; his good and evil have been portrayed in the sharpest tones — sins that are scarlet, evil that is of the blackest hue; goodness that is as white as snow.

Theology has always implied a dramatization of the human predicament. Now unless dramatization is taken to mean falsification, this characterization will not be disturbing. Actually, dramatization implies heightening, bringing hidden facts and motives vividly to the fore in such representative form that each man may find himself in the portrayal. Theology that is good dramatization can be as faithful to the concrete facts as art can be. Theology that overlooks the fact that it is dramatization will become a literalizing universalization of the human situation which obscures or formalizes all concrete facts.

Now this is pertinent to the concept of 'sin.' Sin is one of those generalizations upon the human situation which can communicate only formal meanings — i.e. meanings that derive from some particular theological pattern without reference to concrete equivalents; or it can convey a comprehensive understanding of actual processes in human existence which, in turn, are available to concrete observation. The former was the more common procedure before Liberalism, and gave rise to a theological discourse paralleling scientific inquiry, without being continuous with it at any point. The latter was intended in Liberalism, but it tended to become identified with scientific analysis so completely as to be its equivalent. In this, the value of a theological perspective was lost.

The real danger in the theological thinking of Barth and Brunner, and to a modified degree, in that of Reinhold Niebuhr, is their inclination to return theological thinking to a formal discourse — a picture-thinking that derives its imagery from a formal pattern. Theology in this form, we have said, is no longer continuous with concrete facts of existence, but supervenes them in a way that mythology has always done. Kierkegaard is the safer guide in these matters for the very reason that he holds the concrete and formal meanings in their proper relations. This may be because Kierkegaard is the better artist. His sense for concrete meanings is very vivid. Niebuhr is much the better artist than either Barth or Brunner and is therefore more sensible of the concrete than they. Barth and Brunner are almost without perspective in these matters. They slide back and forth between formal and concrete meanings as if no distinctions were to be observed. Thus their theology has the scope of mythical constructions but the definitiveness of literal truths.

Kierkegaard's analysis of the concept of dread as being a presupposition of original sin is an illustration of his deftness in handling theological insight. It is to this analysis that we now turn by way of beginning our inquiry into the source of human evil, for Kierkegaard's analysis of *The Concept of Dread* [1] is one of the most discerning studies in the nature of sin at the initial stage of human growth that is to be found anywhere.

I

Dread, says Kierkegaard, is a normal, psychical accompaniment of the innocent mind. The innocent mind is the child-like mind, one that is as yet without those capacities for distinction, discrimination, judgment, or choice that give rise to responsible action. The innocent mind is as yet without a clear knowledge of good and evil; nevertheless, in so far as spirit rises in its nature, there is apprehensiveness which forecasts the possibility of such knowledge. It is as if the child anticipated freedom in its creatural sense before he actually arrived at a self-conscious awareness of human freedom.

Dread is the feeling of insecurity that attends possibility. It is therefore a creative fear, the kind of fear that enables the human being to rise above animality to pursue spirituality. In the child where innocence prevails, says Kierkegaard, spirit is present in a state of immediacy, a dreaming state. In this state, spirit is an ambiguous power in the child's life. It fills him with strange expectancies and, at the same time, with fearful misgivings. There is no escaping this state of mind during innocency: The human mind cannot 'sink down into the vegetative life' since it is determined by spirit. Neither can it flee from dread. The child wants to, yet he doesn't want to; for he loves this state of apprehension, wonder, and mystery. Yet he does not really love it.

Innocency is this dreaming state of spirit wherein the child is

[1] Søren Kierkegaard, *The Concept of Dread,* trans. by Walter Lowrie, Princeton University Press, 1944.

filled with a sense of knowing, but is constantly enveloped in a cloud of unknowing.

Kierkegaard, without the aid of modern psychology, saw that this self-awakening of the child, in which dread was a pervasive mood, intermingles with prohibitions, on the one hand, and with emerging sexuality, on the other. And it is in this complex of happenings, wherein the child emerges a knowing person, conscious of guilt and self-consciously sexual (that is, aware of sexual distinctions and accordingly responsive to them), that the idea of original sin takes on meaning for Kierkegaard.

Original sin is seen to be a condition of existence that is bequeathed to each new individual in the sense that the processes that shape every creature at the human level at a certain stage of conscious awareness re-enact the miracle of self-emergence in every individual. Original sin is like birth and death; it is part of the time-span of every creature.

In psychological language, we should say that Original Sin is the theological equivalent of puberty; or, more accurately, that the happenings within the self of spiritual import with which the theologian is concerned when he speaks of original sin, is this complex of events which the psychologist loosely designates puberty. There are psychological meanings here, and there are meanings that carry the picture beyond the psychologists' interest. Now just as the concept of dread carries a double meaning, implying misgiving and possibility, so original sin, in this context, takes on a complex character. It is not something simply to be decried in the human creature; for it is the mark of spiritual potency. Apart from original sin there can be only innocence and a state of childhood dreaming; or animality. The concept 'original sin' initiates the drama of the spiritual life. The nature of the drama is tragedy. Original sin announces the tragic sense in man's creation at the same time that it affirms the good in this event. This double meaning gives to the Christian interpretation of the child and of man its dramatic and unpredictable character. The dread never really leaves the human situation — i.e. the dread of expectancy and of apprehension.

To be able to sin, therefore, is a mark of spirituality. Sin itself may give rise to grievous evil; yet sinfulness, like sexuality and sensuousness, bespeaks a qualitative level in the human consciousness that cannot be dismissed as sheer evil. Studies of saints and sinners, as in Gamaliel Bradford's *Naturalist of Souls* and *Damaged Souls,* have vivified this fact.

Original sin, understood as the event of spiritual awakening in the human psyche such that the stage of innocence gives way to the stage of responsible thought and action, defines life as tragedy, pointing it, nevertheless, toward blessedness. Life is made poignant by this insight. Birth is seen to be a sobering event. Growth is hazardous. Existence is unpredictable. Dark shadows, along with shafts of light, deepen and intensify the contours of every human venture. And death looms as inevitable mystery, at once culmination and a haunting intimation of further emergence.

In this happening, therefore, wherein the innocent girl passes into womanhood and the boy becomes a man, we have one of the crucial events of the creative act. The early religions had a sound sense of its importance, as evidenced in their initiatory rites. Modern psychology and education have come to focus upon it as the strategic dividing line in human beings.

In this context of man's spiritual emergence, the Christian thesis regarding the *Fall* is especially illumined. Christian theology, both in its Roman Catholic and Protestant form, has been concerned to designate a deficiency in human nature which is so deep-seated and universal as to characterize the human being as such. The drama of the Fall provided a formal exposition of how this deficiency came about. In Roman Catholic theology, following Thomistic influence, the Fall was interpreted to mean the loss of a supernatural nature. Natural man thus stands constantly in need of the supernatural grace that is mediated by the Church if he is to complete his spiritual destiny. In Protestant theology, under Calvinistic influence, the Fall has implied an impairment of will in the individual human being such that the use of human freedom led to rebellion against God. Thus, of himself, through his reason or his volitional life, man is unable to attain to his intended end as creature.

A person accepts or rejects these formal characterizations of man according as he accepts or rejects the pattern of thinking which the total theological system, in each case, provides. Yet underlying these formulations themselves there is the concrete datum of human nature to which these characterizations have some relevance. We may better apprehend the truth of the Christian perception that human nature carries a deep-seated deficiency by attending to the emerging human consciousness wherein this concrete datum is observed.

There is a stage of human growth, we have said, wherein the child passes from innocence, with its accompanying condition of dread [2] to a state of spiritual emergence. In this transition the ambiguous, dreaming state of spirit takes on the clear individuation of a person. Here the capacity for sinfulness, as well as for spirituality, becomes an active, self-conscious capacity. The sharpened individuality accentuates both the degree of good and the degree of evil that is attainable through this human consciousness. Greater intellectual force, heightened sensitivity, add to the range of spirituality that is possible to a person. They add, also, to the possible range and intensity of sinfulness in the life-span.

Individuality is not in itself sinful or evil because it is the creatural condition by which persons are possible and through which both good and evil emerge in the human being. But the inevitableness of sin arising from the individuated consciousness, to which the concept of original sin has reference, associates sin and individuality, since individuated existence implies, not only being oneself, but being committed to self in ways which our subjectivity requires.

Sin may not be equated with subjectivity, however. Sin arises from subjectivity, but it is not the subjectivity as such that constitutes the condition of sin. Why does subjectivity require commitment to self? Because there is no other way by which internalization of meanings, essential to conscious existence in any sensory organism, can take place. This is our predicament as persons; and the more individuated we become as persons, the more acute becomes this self-attentiveness. Freedom is the increase of possibility in human response that follows upon our individuation as

[2] Ibid.

persons. Thus, the emergence of freedom in any single life-span opens the way for more and more self-assertiveness and self-expression.

To this burden of subjective process, which defines each individual life, is added whatever survives from childhood in the way of infantilism. Infantilism is a peculiar, circumstantial exaggeration of the ego acquired during cradle days by every infant. How much of it he outgrows, and how fast, depends on many things. That all human beings do not outgrow infantilism, but carry it through their adult years, is one of the depressing facts about human nature; though this is to be distinguished from the more universal feature of subjectivity to which the theological term 'sin' refers.

The emergence of selfhood, when not only the self as an individuated person, but the world in its more mature meaning, breaks in upon this tender consciousness, is a time when infantilism as well as innocence may be cast out. The parents look hopefully toward this period for signs of sanity, by which they mean maturity, action that makes sense in a responsible context. It is a time also, unfortunately, when loss of sanity may break without warning upon the growing child in the form of schizophrenia. Understood in its simplest terms, schizophrenia is the retreat into innocence.

Self-emergence is one of the great mysteries of existence — fully as impressive as birth itself; in fact, it is birth fulfilling itself in the spiritual sense. We can say that the body is born at birth; the spirit, fourteen years later when the person in the body awakens to himself and to the world. At no point is the complexity of the human person more vividly dramatized. What he would do, he does not; what he would not do, that he seems to do. The child's way of expressing it is, 'My mind's all mixed up.' Or, there appears a flood of new aspiration when the world seems to be opening up wide; then follow moments of depression when menacing walls seem to be closing in on him with suffocating effects.

This condition of being 'mixed up' is something more than inadequate orientation; although this contributes to the problem. It is basically the contradiction of impulses that comes to consciousness in the human being who has emerged beyond innocence and who confronts the demands and lures of his own nature and, at the same time, the pressures and possibilities of the more than himself which is mystery, yet actuality.

The *dread* of the innocent years may now give rise to more explicit anxieties and insecurities, issuing in new forms of rebelliousness — a rebelliousness that often seeks false security in becoming assertive, and secretive. Not infrequently, the youngster, not yet in college, achieves a parade of sophistication that serves to insulate himself from his fears. The battle of the ego may thus be driven underground and become almost cankerous in effects. It may, however, precipitate a deeper reckoning, forcing the spiritual issue to the fore. It has long been known that during these 'impressionable years' the child is peculiarly susceptible to the appeal of religion.[3]

We sense in these freshly awakened youth, also, a marked concern for solidarity, a will to be just like the others, not to obtrude. This becomes a kind of oblivion that reassures the ego. Often this concern to conform within the group has been taken to be a premature conventionality. 'There is no conventionality like the conventionalism of youth' goes the remark. At this stage of the person's growth, there is no practical alternative to such acquiescence. The dangers of isolation, of withdrawal, and consequent psychosis, lurk in the path of the young life that does not find such reassurance.

Psychiatrically, being absorbed into the group in this way is the road to health. Religiously, it is a necessary concession to the ego. We should not mistake this social acquiescence for socialization. Socialization awakens the self to the goods of community and ultimately orients the individual in the community. This is a higher level of integration and requires not only insight into the nature of existence but real discipline over the demands of the ego. This salvaging of the self through accommodation to the group is an early manifestation of the self-protective practices to which human beings resort in lieu of a religious relationship with

[3] This observation was made as early as E. D. Starbuck's *Psychology of Religion* (1899) and James's *Varieties of Religious Experience* (1902).

reality. In adult life it becomes a network of face-saving devices, conventions, and proprieties by which a static, conventional society is achieved, insulated, so it is assumed, against the insecurities that are most clearly envisaged and feared.

In this adolescent protection of the ego, the concrete operation of sin can be seen. Theologically, this procedure is to be described as an idolatry of the ego. The self becomes the organizing center of existence. What it fears and what it demands become the chief motivating forces in the individual life.

Now it is not enough to say, having observed this fact, that we must suppress such egoistic action, or rout it. For the sanity of the human being is involved here. Obstruct this egoism, and a condition more baffling than the ordinary person can understand will result. This is the predicament we encounter. It is this condition that often brings the psychiatrist and the moralist face to face in open hostility.

Sin arising out of subjectivity, then, is a complex problem of the emerging self. There is no easy escape from it, if, in fact, there is any escape from it whatsoever. It is not a condition which psychiatry can cure, or education easily redirect; for the psychiatric process, concerned only with the sanity of the mind, may simply lead the individual deeper into its subjective orientation; and education, attentive only to a conventional level of socialization, may not even be aware of the spiritual problem that is involved in the growing child.

The sin is this persistent response of the ego in seeking to alleviate its insecurity through protective practices which lead to organizing existence around the self, thereby obscuring, even shutting off from the individual altogether, the real center of human dedication which is God, the source of all creative good.

II

I have been discussing this process at the level of adolescence where individuation is most critical. Sin arising from subjectivity proceeds at an even greater degree and with more tragic consequences in adult human beings. It is in this area of the problem that Reinhold Niebuhr has contributed such suggestive insights.

The story is not different from that of youth; it is only more accumulative, more deeply entrenched.

This persisting, creatural insecurity, appearing as dread and wonder in the child, passing into a forthright protective concern in youth, assumes a more subtle form in adults. It is doubtful whether the real ingredients of human evil in this mature situation can be isolated. Psychoanalysis undertakes to do so in critical instances; but this is perhaps, at best, only a working analysis of the complex. Something of the unanalyzable complex remains.

There is some value, however, in singling out the most evident elements of the human situation which give rise to evil, as Reinhold Niebuhr has done; for, apart from giving us a realistic grasp of our situation, they actually illumine the concrete datum of sin in so far as this deep-going trait of human nature can be isolated.

Chief among the manifestations of our nature which point to this concrete datum, says Niebuhr, is anxiety. Anxiety attends the human situation almost as a constant mood. Anxiety, Niebuhr sees as the 'inevitable concomitant of the paradox of freedom and finiteness in which man is involved.' [4] Man is anxious, not only because of his limitation which stands as a threat to his autonomous ego, but he is anxious also because his possibilities are seemingly without limit. To be both bound and free in these contradictory ways is to find his situation ambiguous — an ambiguity that cannot easily be relieved. Anxiety, in this form, adds Niebuhr, is at once the source of man's evil and of his creativity.

This theological generalization of man's situation may be further itemized. Man's freedom, understood as the index of his possibilities, confronts him with the same kind of apprehensiveness that attends the child; only the possibilities in the adult take on more definitive character as hopes, expectations, ambitions, strivings, plans, and enterprises, to mention only the tangible evidences of his outreach. Over and above these are the less easily articulated concerns of his being which gather into the reach for fulfillment. All that points him beyond present achievement,

[4] Reinhold Niebuhr, *The Nature and Destiny of Man,* Scribners, 1941, p. 182.

that gives him a sense of becoming and of overcoming experience or the existent reality, belongs to this dimension of freedom. Niebuhr would add to this, no doubt, further overtones suggested by the word transcendence; but these are certainly a piece with whatever we mean to define as transcendence. Man is forever in a state of being fulfilled; and this incompleteness in his nature affects him with an uneasy hopefulness that is both a promise and a threat of defeat.

The freedom that opens up possibilities in man's nature is readily transmuted into some form of enslavement: it may be vocational or avocational. In any case, it takes the form of pressing man's efforts and energies toward some yet-unrealized-end. Vincent van Gogh, driving himself to madness in the ceaseless effort to capture the yellow of the fields in the medium of his art; Gandhi, fasting himself to near-death in pursuit of an objective that accords with a principle; Schweitzer, relinquishing all else in dedication to the one purpose of relieving pain because of a reverence for life; these are exaggerations, possibly caricatures, of the concern that is common to all men, namely: to realize with one's life the measure of significance that is above all else meaningful and compelling to one. The ends vary enormously in their significance, some being of the commonest kind of careerism or the pursuit of well-being; some being dedication that is well-nigh selfless in motive. Enslavement and the threat of anxiety increase in proportion as the end is self-seeking. The magnitude of man's sin mounts as he uses his freedom for self-seeking; for he not only becomes enslaved to purposes and processes that define himself, which is self-idolatry; but he becomes increasingly protective of these purposes and processes, thus becoming incapable of perceiving any good, save as it is *his* good. Yet, no man, however noble his end, actually escapes the condition of anxiety which the use of freedom and this transmutation of freedom lays upon our human destiny. Even the saint can never completely rise above sin, because saintliness, however pure, is never without human motivation. The dedication rests to some extent, if only as its sublimation, upon an initial condition of anxiety that impelled the individual toward the higher goal.

The limitation that is imposed by what is sometimes called our finiteness, on the other hand, is more than a stubborn impasse, a frustration of our freedom. It is a positive source of apprehension that takes many forms. Its basic form is a fear of death. Now people do not consciously fear death. Yet, deep in the human consciousness is the realization that life is precarious, *their life* is precarious. All that they cherish rests upon this slim margin of consciousness that is sustained by a soundly working organism, or by the assurance of an organized society capable of providing for basic needs.

Death is a constant intruder. It consults no one. This fact, generally known and acknowledged, places the whole matter of living on a tentative basis. We pursue life's interests as if they were of permanent significance to us; that is, we give ourselves wholeheartedly to them. Yet the fact of death points to their culmination and to our dissolution. Anxiety is deeply rooted in this subconscious clinging to life in the face of its acknowledged tentativeness.

But the fear of death becomes pyramided into numerous other attending fears: the fear of ill-health, the fear of physical or mental inadequacy, the fear of economic disaster, the fear of losing friends and loved ones, the fear of loneliness, the fear of incompetence, of ultimate failure. All of these fears rest back upon the basic realization that the life-span of man is limited, both from the point of time and of circumstances. Life may be unfulfilled! This fear accelerates self-attentiveness.

This underlying state of anxiety, which in the last analysis is a creatural condition, gives rise to further complications in thought and behavior that serve to insulate us from the creative source of our good. This insulation, in turn, serves to develop incrustations of the self which accentuates the condition of autonomy because interchange and communication become increasingly feared. Security is sought by narrowing the range of interest and by developing fixations which make the personality rigid, inflexible, incommunicable. The self becomes a fortress, protective against outer invasions.

The total effect of this autonomous self is a pretentiousness in manner which conceals its essential insecurity. Yet the insulated life does not dwell upon its insecurities; in fact, the success of its compensatory responses depends upon its keeping the shell intact so that intimations of this insecurity do not penetrate the protective surface. Thus the protective device becomes assertive. The best defense is an offense. Arrogance, domination, tyranny, or just smug complacency, these may be the normal accompaniments of the assertive and proud man.

Such a person, tucked away in a citadel of his own building, towers precariously over his fellows, removed, not only from the warmth of companionship but from the community of being that is in God as well.

Pride is paramount and full blown in some individuals; it is incipient in others. For the compensations that follow upon insecurity are not all in this direction. Insecurity may move toward insulation from tragedy, suffering, defeat, or dissolution by cultivating absorption in whatever offers itself as an immediate escape from the peril of the person's predicament. These escapes are numerous. Sex, as Niebuhr has pointed out, is an obvious one — not only actual sexual excess but the whole traffic of sensual participation that may assume the form of entertainment, literature, art, even becoming in some instances a cult of the body.

Insulation from the issues of life may be achieved by higher forms of preoccupation. It cannot be denied that for some people, art or music have become an alternative to religion. I say this not with contempt but with considerable understanding. For others, business has assumed this role. Activity, whatever the form, or regardless of the goal, may take on the intensity of a faith. No one of these is easily evaluated. None can be dismissed as sheer idolatry, although they involve just that; for they are also adjustments within the particular individual experience by which life is given focus and a sense of direction.

If happiness is taken to be the chief human goal, I think we should have to acknowledge that these vocational alternatives to the religious solution are, in many instances, reasonably successful — except when the major crises of the life process intrude themselves. They insulate the person against monotony and meaninglessness, and against the fear of crises; against the crises themselves, they may not hold.

A more important objection to these alternatives to the religious solution, however, is that they integrate life around an egoistic affection, however refined this affection or appreciation may be. Somehow, in instances of this kind the self remains unredeemed, despite the increasing depth of appreciation or dedication. The problem of individual in community, which is the religious problem, simply does not touch the consciousness or the human psyche under these circumstances.

III

Our analysis so far of conditions giving rise to sin, makes for a formulation of the doctrine of sin for which the Reformation doctrine of forgiveness and assurance of grace provide the redemptive solution. But sin is a more virulent condition in our natures than this Reformation doctrine implies. Or, to put it more accurately, the implication of sin arising from fear of death and its accompaniments, is but a partial exposition of the circumstance in our creaturehood which makes for inescapable evil — evil which we of ourselves are helpless to overcome, or even mitigate because the overcoming requires that transformation of our natures which, in part, is our undoing; not our doing.

The virulent character of sin is due to its positive character; its tendency toward sovereignty in man's nature rivaling that of God's. The figure of the rebelling, fallen angel in the ancient myth is not too strong to express this truth.

This tendency in man is aided by two factors which become interfused and difficult to distinguish. One is the assertiveness of force, the lifting to dominance of that which in the very nature of concreteness, is required to be subservient if order and meaning or value are to result; the other is the assertiveness of the subjective life, which is a particular channeling of force and creativity such that a false sense of independence emerges in the creature, doing violence to the interrelations that sustain him.

The assertiveness of force over sensitivity is a commonplace in individual lives and in social institutions. By this I do not mean to suggest that all expression of power is sinful; but that power unattended by such discrimination, restraint, and concern that looks to the creation of meaning, is, to recall our figure, the wild, spirited steed on the loose from the redeeming, restraining, quality-giving grace of God's tender working. On its negative side, or as a negative expression, it is unresponsiveness to, indifference toward, disregard of the persuasive good revealing the lure of God's working.

Sin is grounded in insensitivity as truly as it is grounded in fear. And when this insensitiveness becomes assertive, it can become an even more heinous source of evil whose destruction of good may have magnitude far in excess of the human impairment we often ascribe to sin. In fact, sin in its social consequences cannot be adequately envisaged or appraised until it is seen to have this impersonal, even demonic, character and power — a fruition of the human consciousness just as surely as is spirit.

This insight reveals the enormity of the vitality that is in the human structure, or that may rise from it. Its extensive facilities for symbolization, accompanied by its organizing and administrative gifts, enables it to compound its effective energy through institutional or other corporate means so that the net result of the human psyche is a huge potency, whatever its ends may be.

Mankind under this aspect is a terrible creature among the inhabitants of the earth. His emergence has released a potentiality of terror and destructiveness upon the earth which no other creature can so far emulate. This was true before the atomic bomb appeared. It has released similarly a potentiality of creative meaning, actualizing good, which no other organic structure can provide. All this means that through man, creation-in-reverse can reach a magnitude of evil which is unique by reason of his capacities for organizing energies; just as creation, through him, can attain a level of emergence exceeding that of all prior levels of structured existence.

This dual character of our natures is not as paradoxical as may seem, once we have seen the source of the duality. We are no different in this respect from every existent thing since actuality, the coming into being, implies the fusion of feeling and force. We are born of this miracle that turns the flood and chaos of brute force into a creative event. The good that is implicit in our natures waits for its fruition upon the continuation and completion of this creative act which human birth initiates. Actually, the reverse of this process gets under way at the same time that a deepening of sensitivity may be occurring. Every person is shaped simultaneously by contrary and contradictory impulses that may awaken him, on the one hand, to the possibilities of good in his nature; and, on the other, to the possibilities of evil in his nature. No human being is free from this warfare of rival impulses. In fact, no human being is ever free from the possibility of his entire nature being overwhelmed by one or the other organization of impulses. The predominantly evil person may undergo, in fact has undergone, a complete reversal. We are fairly familiar with this phenomenon in religious conversion. But the opposite is always imminent too. The good man, the person with love in his heart, may be brought to a crisis in which love is inverted. These facts compel us to recognize the dynamic character of human nature; which suggests the instability of both our good and our evil and hence the ambiguity of human goodness.

This assertion brings us to confront the astounding words ascribed to Jesus in the New Testament, 'There is none good but one, that is God' (Matt. 19:17). These words imply that all else is an intermingling of good and evil. The gospel writings voice frequent judgment upon those who have presumed to be good people. Thus judgment has usually been explained on the grounds that many of Jesus' words were addressed to legalists who defined goodness in meticulous terms of the law. Generally the legal good was externally conceived, leaving the inner problem of motive or intention uncalculated. Jesus, it is said, preached a gospel of love transcending the law; and by this higher standard the so-called good people were obviously deficient. I do not mean to ignore the issue between legalism and love; but I am impressed by a deeper vein of meaning in the insistence that our human goodness is ambiguous. It is a judgment that penetrates even beyond the level of motive and intention to the operational level where intimate events of joy and sorrow are being wrought out in actual lives. It is the living tissue of experience in which the decisions and acts of men and women persist far beyond their memories. Here in the characters that they bear and that their children bear, the judgment upon these decisions and acts is more stark and real. In the institutions that give visible form to the structure of experience, human decision, long since forgotten, stands forth as a present reality to be judged. At this level of actuality the ambiguities of human goodness become apparent.

Consider a certain man who was devoted to his wife and family. In any analysis rating he would qualify as a good husband. He provided for the family's needs. More than that, he was actually enterprising in anticipating their needs, not only in the routine matters of the home but in their recreation beyond the home. He arranged well in advance for the family holidays. He saw to it that each member of his family was provided with whatever he or she might need on vacation. He thought of everything: he even thought of what his wife might wear and ordered it. She liked it, yes. She had learned that it was better that way. And the children, too, knew that what Dad decided was, in the long run, better. Year in and year out this man was busy being a good husband and a good father until — in desperation his wife left him, and his children, out of sheer rebelliousness, which even they did not understand, became delinquent.

Where is the justice in such a situation we ask? Is there no gratitude left in people these days? The fact is, the stark, operational fact is that this man, with all his good intent, imprisoned his wife and children with the world of his appreciations. The good he presumed to do was hopelessly entangled with self-interest and self-assertiveness, leaving him utterly unaware of *their* good as it actually existed. This was his good, imposed with all the magnanimity of the self-assured. Consider a more poignant parable: the way of good parents with their child. These parents were not assertive. Their intentions were of the best. Their knowledge of child psychology was above the average. The wife was technically informed on child care. The husband had pondered the intricacies of human psychology. But the intimate associations of people are subtle. Under some circumstances they do not know each other. They may know many important facts of theoretical significance concerning human relations; yet some crucial facts affecting the living situation may escape them. How these young eyes, looking out upon this or that act, gave hint of the way the child responded to the situation, they may ignore completely. How this word uttered or this gesture unwittingly annoyed or offended the other person, they may overlook. And so the unseen signs and intimations of disaffection accumulate: the understandable ignorance of the parents, the reticence of the offended one, the years and years of seeming rapport that were only half interpreted, the tensions that became explosive and then resolved, but only partially so, the stored resentments, the fantasies arising in the child's troubled mind, the efforts at escape, and then the tragedy! How many youth walk in darkness or on the edge of the abyss despite the memories of a good home and good parents!

The evil that arises out of a clearly recognizable hell is no problem to the understanding. It is the evil that intermingles with the good which confounds us and causes us to cry out in desperation, 'Our good is not enough! Our good is not good at all.'

I am impressed, too, that our human good, however genuine, however intense and wholehearted, is an unstable good. I have seen love between two young people twisted into hate. Their love had been genuine affection, based upon mutual interests and the appeal that each one made to the other. As college companions they were simply two people who had attained a common zest in discovering the reaches of the mind in Plato, Bach, and Goethe. Their intellectual and aesthetic affinities, together with their mutual respect, seemed to bind them inevitably to each other. Then the cold, hard reality of family and class intruded. The young lady had come of professional people, distinguished, proud, and enterprising. The young man was a gifted, sensitive member of an immigrant worker's family. And on the issue of family their love struck an unyielding rock.

It was then I realized what depth of evil opens up out of the inversion of good. We know these things through our acquaintance with tragedy in the great arts; but here it could be witnessed in its stark actuality. Hate is all the more deadly when it has once been love. And the alchemy of human emotions which transforms the one into the other is so little known to us that human nature appears dark with mysterious terror once this strange new depth is opened up to us. Hate, when it has once been love, becomes demonic; for love inverted carries a memory too poignant to be rational. It is too full of pride to be understanding, too fully over-come with resentment to be forgiving. When it has once been love, hate releases the full weight of virtue in a desperate act of destruction.

This same dynamic quality in human nature which makes for instabilities of good and evil in individual people appears in groups as well. The group, under some kinds of provocation, can rise to a degree of goodness and magnanimity which no single individual can emulate. Under other kinds of provocation it may reach a depth of hate and frenzy which would seem beyond the imagination of the individual: Witch hunters, ancient and modern, Ku Klux Klan, race rioting, war fever, and the like. These uncal-culable depths of passion in human nature, often righteously moti-vated, at times pent-up, held in check by a slight margin of pro-priety, authority, or coercion; but more often not pent-up at all, become emergent evil strangely arising from its opposite. Such inversions of good sober us with the realization that we do not really understand what good and evil in men mean until we view them as phases of a dynamic process in which the two interpene-trate and shape each other. And we do not grasp the import of this fact until we understand human nature as a dynamic event.

IV

That there is good in man, I am not denying. Let no one take this analysis of the source of human evil to imply a complete dis-paragement of man. There is a glory that rises out of the human structure which emulates the flowering of the fields. The glory that is there in human beings to be appreciated is a kind of fruition that follows upon long years of human growing. Sometimes it flares forth in an insight heretofore hidden from the human mind. At times it is a dedicatory act of great suffering and sacrifice, or of unselfish help to another. At other times it is steady courage or patience or companionship. The glory of the human spirit often manifests itself in creative art. The enormity of human creation in thought, in music, poetry, and architecture, in science and skilled labor would be beyond designation. What we celebrate as tradition is chiefly this heritage of creative hands. What we live by, in large measure, is the dependability of other human beings.

I am meaning only to point out in this discussion of human evil that the good we *will* is a good intermingled with evil; and that because of the dynamic character of human nature, it is a precarious good: a good often bordering upon depths of terrifying evil.

I am not willing to isolate these instances of self-assertion, insensitivity, or inversion to which we have pointed as special and peculiar occurrences. Human nature is remarkably similar, though the conditions under which people pursue their labors may differ considerably. Our conditions often insulate us from the peril of ourselves. The inertia of our existence may blind us to the instability that is actually concealed behind this façade of moral well-being. Under provocation, how shall we stand?

If it is true that the dynamic character of human natures makes for instability in our goodness, which is the core of the frequent assertion that men are sinners, then we must see the folly of the recurrent, simple injunctions that are designed to make us good. This opens an enormous problem: the problem of the religious life. How shall a person pursue the good life? Shall he seek out specifications of the good life and develop the disciplines that will assure him of a good character and a good way of living? We may not dismiss the inquiry lightly. People of stature have searched out this problem and have labored for a lifetime exploring its possibilities. But there is vanity in this effortfulness; and few who pursue this course escape its vanity. They become self-conscious in their achievement of goodness and become possessed of a strange air of holiness that is deficient in humility and kindliness. The thesis I have been insinuating throughout these remarks argues roundly against this kind of self-culture. All the discipline and nurture we can provide should be secured; and it is fair to say that we have hardly begun to explore the possibilities of nurturing the sensibilities or of luring the affections to more sensitive ends. But all this must be done with a realism regarding the dynamic character of human nature which gives no assurance of a permanent solution to human evil; no sure road to perfecting human goodness or human righteousness.

It is when we confront this stubborn conclusion staring out from the ambiguity of our good and the continual threat of human evil, that we begin to feel the force of the Christian doctrine of forgiveness and redemption. At some levels of human failure there is no more constructive step to take than the penitent cry, 'God! help me a sinner.' How can a man reconstruct the years that have shattered his home? How can penitent parents reclaim the lost opportunity to give security and sanity to their child? How can the lover whose love has become hate renew his affection?

It is in these desperate failures of human goodness that we take adequate measure of ourselves and cry out, God, help me a sinner! There is no hope save in the good that is of thy redeeming love.

The Christian doctrine of redemption holds this view of man in focus: that all have come short of the glory of God. In this sense, the judgment upon man remains. But forgiveness implies a realistic understanding of this human predicament, not in the sense that all evil is tolerated, but that man, in his failure to attain the good, man in his shortcomings, will be accepted where there is a contrite will to be received. It implies that, in some sense, if an individual is to retain his sanity, he must accept himself. Redemption is a social doctrine which removes the sense of guilt, the sense of failure and remorse in the penitent heart, without relaxing responsibility, the hunger for righteousness, and the love of goodness.

There is a goodness beyond our own efforts that works silently on in experience and in history to redeem us from the consequences that would otherwise follow, were it not to intercede. The most intimate experiences of our lives give intimation of this goodness. We do not earn the love of our parents. It is given. It is a gift of the relation that somehow transcends the law of cause and effect. We do not earn the love of our children. It is given. And when it is given, it often wrings our hearts, and wrings from us the confession, 'God help me a sinner who could have done more; who could have done so much less of injury had I known.' We do not earn the goodness of companionship. However it comes, we recognize it as a beneficence that is given. So it is with the tendernesses of God that re-create our hopes and reclaim us from our own dissolution. This is a goodness not our own, given where there is capacity to receive such goodness.

To be sure, in each of these instances we do invest ourselves, and in some measure we reap what we sow; but neither the good nor the evil is visited upon us in direct proportion to our works.

X

The Problem of Human Goodness

THE AMBIGUITY of human goodness need not lead us into a radical cynicism that denies all good in existence; nor may it justify rash doctrines of depravity which dissociate man from every natural capacity to enjoy and to exemplify goodness in living. The clear fact is that goodness in many forms does grace the human scene.

A man who has seen goodness in men and women, or beauty of spirit, or who has felt its surge in his own heart, warming and heightening his bodily feelings will forever afterward confront an empirical datum which will not let him go. What is this grace of goodness and beauty? Whence does it come?

The destruction of tyranny and tragedy, violence and hate do not counter the importance of this persisting good; nor do they demonstrate its impotence or its irrelevance. For the most demonstrative events of destruction, of violence or hate will themselves prove ultimately impotent, except as this healing good, what the modern psychologist is now beginning to call 'the dynamics of love' intrudes in redemptive acts. Existence, I have been moved to affirm again and again, is sustained in most instances by a perilously slight margin of sensitivity. I invite anyone to brood over that observation. He cannot, I feel sure, escape its truth or fail to sense its significance. Sometimes in family relationships, what holds the group together, where relations are strained, is the capacity of one person in the group to keep the members in communication or on a negotiable basis. This applies to larger groups and communities as well. In the individual organism, too, it applies. At times the sanity of the individual rests upon such a margin of sensitivity as may occur in the relationship between himself and one other person.

The depths of tragedy or of ruthless force reveal in poignant and shocking ways how indispensable is this margin of grace and goodness. The creative moments, the times of transfiguration, of dedication or joy, exemplify its abundance and its fulfilling power.

The fact that there is goodness in existence presents no less a problem than the fact of evil. Professor Wieman, in preparing to describe, in *American Philosophies of Religion,* the philosophy of F. S. C. Northrop, calls attention to a basic observation which underlies the work and inquiry of such men as Whitehead, Einstein, Jeans, Eddington, Bavink, and Northrop. Says Wieman, 'The fact that all these men seem to see the same basic fact and the same cosmic problem would indicate that the fact and the problem are genuine no matter how diverse the outcome of their several efforts to find a solution.' This common fact, Wieman goes on to summarize, is that the universe is made of highly active units whose activities are highly independent of one another. There is nothing in the nature of these units to keep them from frustrating and destroying one another and producing a hopeless confusion. Yet as a matter of fact, they do not fall into such confusion. How, they ask, can we account for this creative condition of order? Whence does it come? In each instance, in answer to this basic problem, there developed a thesis or theory of God.[1]

My attempt in this work and in others has not been unrelated to this approach; though I have been concerned more and more with this creative happening as it appears in the operations of the human psyche and within human cultures. In this context the datum appears to be a dynamic relation of sensitivity which works creatively and redemptively both to form meaning of a quality which under some circumstances assumes a response of love, or of beauty; and to restore relations conducive to these responses

[1] H. N. Wieman, and B. E. Meland, *American Philosophies of Religion,* Harper, 1936, p. 241.

when such relations have been broken. These configurations of qualitative meaning which yield a resource of grace in living confront us with some questions too. This is the problem of goodness.

Empirically speaking, the fact of evil is no surprise. When all the pretensions and rationalizations that provide a concealing façade are removed, the evil of life is stark. It is no more so in times of war and social chaos than during quiescent periods; except that during times of upheaval the pretensions and social rationalizations are difficult to sustain. Life takes on more naked meaning. And there is much of it that overwhelms us with its terror and deception, both as calculated and wholehearted evil, and as ambiguous evil in which some mixture of good intent survives.

In the wake of tragic and evil circumstances, the problem, empirically speaking, is in the appearance of goodness and beauty and in the thirst after righteousness which break upon the world in season and out like a branch of blossoming peach against a menacing sky.

These operations of uncalculated goodness which intermittently and spontaneously come into human relations and into the human character under varying conditions have been rightly designated *spirit*. By this term is generally meant a transcendent quality or movement of grace which has its source in God, or in a realm beyond man's world. The implication here is sound in so far as it insists upon the objective character of such happenings. For it is not enough to speak of these occurrences simply as *our* goodness, or our ideal ends. It is rather a goodness in existence itself, which discloses to us a spontaneous, transformative working within the human psyche and within history at various times and places.

The notion of spirit has a way of slipping out of hand the moment we try to grasp its meaning. Are we talking about something alien to man's structure, of a different order, or do we mean to identify it with the human psyche? The reluctance to identify Spirit and human spirit has generally grown out of a conviction that this dimension is supernatural in origin. Humanism, concerned to reject the overtones of supernaturalism, has insisted upon a thoroughgoing truncated view of man in which the human spirit is interpreted to convey solely ethical and aesthetic values. It is my concern to break through this impasse and if possible to grasp the meaning of man in his most sensitive dimensions without severing either man or spirit from its empirical source. This task is a difficult one, for it requires a more subtle handling of the human response than is generally evident when man is viewed either within a scientific perspective or within a framework of formal theology. The problem narrows down to a concern to grasp the objective meaning of spirit while at the same time understanding its subjective associations. This amounts to designating the sense in which man, in his behavior, attitude, or character, actually transcends himself as a structure, actually becomes the bearer of meaning which can be called a good not his own.

The sense of wonder is undoubtedly the most elemental expression of spirit in the human creature. I wonder what this is? I wonder what is beyond us way out there? I wonder what will happen next? I wonder what would happen if I did this instead of that? Wonder is the stimulus to thought and to creative effort, and in this sense underlies the whole of the human enterprise. If analyzed at its level of emergence, wonder would be designated as the spontaneous play of thought not focused by any functional purpose. It is but a level above reverie in that it is usually directed toward some expectation; but like reverie, it is thought playing over the surfaces of fixed realities. It is like the primordial moment at creation; in fact, it is the primordial moment of every creative act. And it is fair to say that creativeness is always attended by wonder, implicitly or explicitly. Without wonder creativeness lags.

The sense of wonder, expressive of the spiritual dimension, can best be envisaged as (1) open awareness, (2) appreciative awareness, and (3) creative awareness. These may be stages of a single, continuous response, but they indicate degrees of integrating receptiveness and the conscious response which add discipline and directive effort.

Open awareness in its simplest terms is receptiveness to the full datum of experience. Life tends to become channeled and fixed in routines of behavior. There is almost an inescapable tendency among living things to seek assurance of survival through dependable and repeatable procedures. The risk of novelty is thus discouraged in well-ordered societies.

This adherence to the tried and true serves to insulate the individuals who conform to this ordered existence from stimulus beyond these routines. Thus society becomes closed to spontaneous appeals, to new emergents, or to any form of reality that stands apart from the social routine.

The moral consciousness arises out of this concern for fixed values and for the procedures that assure the conservation of fixed values. Primitive societies afford the clearest examples; but all organized society tends toward this pattern. And social groups within the larger society become similarly fixed about special conventions and thus intensify the effect of this insulation. Social clubs, political parties, and in many instances, churches, erect these invisible barriers insulating their members from the flux of experience.

There is a sense in which open awareness is denied to any living creature, individual or organized; for every living thing must live in terms of a structure. And the structure is in itself delimiting, operating as it must through the sensory facilities that are available to it. The world is offered to every man only in terms of 'these five windows clear.' Thus open awareness is never quite an actuality in human response, but a condition sought. And the very concern to achieve it tempers the tendency toward insulation. This means that the more elemental levels of man's existence, where stimulus and response are almost automatic (visceral) in nature, tend to dominate man's behavior. In Bergson's language, 'men lapse into matter.' Matter here suggests the most elemental level of existence. In this sense, all life tends to lapse into matter. And man is no exception. Societies of men are no exceptions. Economic and political processes, instead of serving the spiritual life of man, become dominant as ends in themselves because of their evident power to control or to coerce other phases of man's existence. And this is to invert man's structural organization.

The difference between the human consciousness pitched toward wonder and the one closed within its structural barriers is so marked as to introduce a new dimension of human response. Thus we can speak literally of the person being *saved by wonder* as over against the person who is lost to fixations.

Appreciative awareness connotes a more positive expression of the sense of wonder than sheer open awareness. While it implies also a relaxing of the egoistic barriers, in personality or in institutional practice, it implies further an open awareness toward the end of *knowing* the reality *out there* in its own right. Beyond being receptive, an individual thus reaches toward rapport with what is given in the object beyond himself. He seeks understanding and discernment of what is cherished in the situation which is seemingly external to himself. And by this readiness to establish an interchange of meaning that may well require a reorientation of his own outlook or situation, he renders his own system of meanings, to some degree at least, less insulating. To the extent that interchange of meaning is possible, a real reconstruction of meanings may actually occur. What we often describe as teachableness in the child or in the growing person is a by-product of such awareness. We say the mind is flexible or that the nature is pliable. These are figurative ways of saying that the system of meanings which comprises the valuation pattern of the person is, as yet, not wholly formed into a rigid structure such that concourse with new meanings or meanings alien to the mind-set may be received and retained.

Now it is generally assumed that the mind of the person in maturing takes on such rigidity in the very process of attaining character. This assumption overlooks the fact that the capacity for appreciative awareness can itself become part of the habitual pattern of response in which case, instead of closing the personality structure to new and wider ranges of meanings, maturation actually heightens the degree and discipline of appreciative awareness when awareness is retained.

Creative awareness means simply wonder becoming a creative force. The line between this stage and the one just discussed is slight indeed. Whenever and however attitude passes over into habitual action, the appreciative capacity becomes a form of energy affecting, not only the structure of personality that embraces it, but also the structure of relations that defines the whole context of living in which this individual participates as a person. Several people living together with a readiness to establish such rapport and with intercommunication, establish a situation in which the spiritual dimension of man is given abundant release and nurture. The degree of *felt* understanding, or discernment of intention and expectation at the level of feeling is greatly increased; thus anticipatory action — the kind of prehension that a mother can exemplify in relation to a child, or a lover toward the beloved, becomes a feature of the social group on a much more generalized level. To the degree that the measure of such anticipatory action increases at the level of common action we can say that love becomes a social energy. Wherever this occurs, spirit in man becomes a transformative power of social magnitude, and can thus be translated into civic and political energies.

The community is always possessed of such potential spiritual energy, but the release of its working waits upon the increase of appreciative awareness that can pass into anticipatory action, looking to the emergence of a wider range of meaning which can contain, not only a person's own system of good, but the good of others in relation to which his life is cast.

One reason why the sense of wonder, in one or in all three of these facets, is a primary expression of spirit is that it defines the pitch of the organism, as we might say, by which the human being reaches toward its new level of emergence. It is man moving toward his fruition at the level of spirit.

Spirit as a structure of response is more vividly indicated by the word freedom, understanding this word to mean such release from the coercion of limiting conditions imposed by the parts as to enable the self to act as a *total* self. Freedom is awareness of possibilities and a capacity to respond to them selectively. The human structure of consciousness is made for choice. The exercise of choice is, in itself, a humanizing activity. Potentially it is a spiritualizing influence. I say potentially, because the exercise of choice per se, though humanizing, that is, capable of extending the distinctively human dimension in man, may issue either in good or in evil. Man choosing evil is still man acting at the human level. Humanizing influences as such may not assure the emergence of this transcendent quality of goodness; they assure it only in proportion as choice turns men selectively toward the realization of good. The word good in this context will be seen to imply qualitative meaning arising from the fulfillment of relationships in response to full recognition of the authenticity of the self. Choice issuing in egoism is the denial of such relationships and precludes the emergence of qualitative meaning implicit in community. But choice issuing in communalism that enables relationships to cancel out the sense of the authentic self reduces the quality of community to a condition in which freedom is made inoperative. Choice in awareness of relationships and in recognition of the qualitative differences that emerge out of the legitimate nurture of authentic selves, contributes to the growth of qualitative meaning in its most inclusive dimensions, relating the self and society, the world and the individual, God and man. In this sense choice becomes a spiritual act.

Now obviously, whatever aids the possibility of choice, of selectiveness, or discrimination, extends the human capacity or dimension of our consciousness which is creative of spirit. Whatever crushes it, obstructs it, or dissipates it, lowers the level of conscious activity and of consciousness. What is it that crushes capacity for choice? The obvious answer is tyranny, oppression, slavery; mechanization of social processes such that the coercion of lesser goods precludes the rise of higher goods. What is it that obstructs capacity for choice? This may be ignorance of alternatives, due not always to a lack of intelligence, but to an impoverished imagination or an inactive imagination. It may be indecision, due either to double-mindedness in Kierkegaard's sense, or to the lack of a criterion by which degrees of better and worse may be discerned and sharpened. It may be lethargy, or the absence of inclination to will one thing rather than another, or indifference to processes that might actualize what is envisaged or desired. What is it that dissipates the capacity for choice? The readiness to rest back upon impulse, routine, or the coercion of the moment; the readiness to acquiesce unreflectively to the decisions of others more assertive than oneself; the bovine beatitude that the body is more blessed than spirit.

What, then, can aid the capacity for freedom and thus extend the human expression of spirit? The answer can be in one word: Decision! There is something peculiarly impressive about the act of decision. Decision is the 'I' defining itself. Decision, says the child psychologist, is the act by which character emerges. Decision has all the implications of creation or of the creative act. It is the way by which existence as passive being assumes the form of responsible act. In this it not only defines its own character, but it defines the nature of its vitality in relation to other personal centers of vitality as well as to what is ultimate in the nature of God. In this sense, Brunner is justified in speaking of decision as the moment of the divine-human encounter.[2]

Decision is the elimination of possibilities and the assertion of one direction of actuality. In an individual's decisions the quality and purpose of the self is exposed, and the force of his being — what Gandhi spoke of as the soul-force — is impressed upon the world of fact and relations.

Whatever enriches the act of decision through appreciative awareness, through sympathy, and the critical understanding of possibilities, aids man's capacity for freedom; and to that extent provides conditions for the emergence of spirit. Contrariwise, whatever precludes the act of decision, confounds it, or frustrates the clear articulation of the self in relation to other selves, impairs the capacity for freedom; and to that extent destroys conditions essential to the emergence of spirit.

The man in whom some form of invalidism has blocked the development of his powers is not free; but the man in whom these limitations are functionally overcome *is* free. The man for whom slavery, oppression, or imprisonment has crushed the human psyche such that he acquiesces in sheer animality to his condition, is not free; but he whose spirit continues to sing amid prison walls, who fashions out of the impoverishing circum-

[2] Emil Brunner, *The Divine-Human Encounter*, Westminster Press, 1943.

stances some creative expression, this man is free. He who is bound by sensuality or by any other sensory response, is not free; but the individual for whom the sensory life is a resource of vital energy and of creative expression *is* free. He who becomes bound by the circumscribing conventions of an institution through which he labors is not free; but he who clarifies his sense of responsibility, both to himself and to the enterprise with which he works, such that each is enhanced by the empowerment of the other, this man is free. He who is bound to the sovereign God through fear of punishment or concern for his own reward is not free; but he who loves God with his whole heart, and in utter adoration serves God with a pure heart, this one is free. The man who is bound to his friends by fear for his reputation or by ambition for social success is not free; but he who is appreciatively aware of their companionship and who enjoys them for their sake as people, *is* free.

Freedom is always release from the limiting circumstances that would otherwise empower what is less than good, or what is a lesser good to coerce what is of higher value. The lack of freedom results in mechanism. The presence of freedom creates holism in which spirit is sovereign.

Besides being the release from the coercion of what is lower than value, freedom is also the capacity and incentive for choice, or for the capacity to recognize and to choose value. The man for whom better and worse do not exist is not free, for he is bound by the mediocrity that possesses him. The man in whom indecision prevails for lack of understanding, or because of commitment to conflicting goods, is not free; for he is tyrannized by his own inadequate sense of values. The individual for whom alternatives do not exist and for whom no capacity for discrimination is available is not free; for he must then be dependent upon the choice of another.

Freedom is a clear perception of the good and the full commitment to it. To be thus bound is to be free — i.e. free from the coercive control of what is less than the sovereign good. Where freedom exists, either in release from what is less than the greater good, or in affirmation of and commitment to the good, spirit rises like a flame in the wind.

While the conditions creative of spirit provide this sense of freedom, spirit is always discerned in relationships. Thus the topic of religion, as Whitehead has said, is *the individual in community* where fragmentation is overcome through whatever recourse we may have to wholeness.

Wholeness as the ultimate condition of the spiritual life is generally associated with a monistic metaphysics. In Absolute Idealism, for example, religion and wholeness came to have identical meaning. Wholeness in this sense is always in danger of obscuring the individual, as Josiah Royce well knew,[3] and as William Hocking has clearly indicated in stating his principle of alternation.[4]

The insight that is implied in the notion of wholeness can be stated in other ways so as to bring out the importance of structure without minimizing the sense of the self. Modern psychology speaks of the structure of personality, meaning to gather the many facets of the person, including its relationships, into a valuational unity. Whitehead has conveyed this insight in his explanation of the present moment under presentational immediacy and causal efficacy. These different ways of presenting the *whole* nature of the individual or of the individual event lift up one basic term as defining conditions that are creative of spirit. It is the word *relatedness*. Spirit, or the realm of spirit, understood as the stratum of sensitive meanings, heightening the sense of the person, is actualized and sustained by a growth toward community.

We come more nearly grasping the meaning of spirit as a fruition of man's encounter with such relations by examining the capacity for joy and sorrow; for these are especially expressive of this dimension.

Joy and sorrow would seem to be at opposite poles, the one antithetical to the other. This, however, is not really so. Joy and

[3] Cf. his *The World and the Individual.*
[4] Cf. his *The Meaning of God in Human Experience.*

sorrow have a common basis in feeling and in the capacity to respond feelingly toward life's events. They are the light and shade; but light is not the opposite of shade; nor is shade the absence of light. They appear simultaneously, the one emphasizing the presence of the other.

The opposite of joy is cynicism; and the opposite of sorrow is callousness. Cynicism implies capitulation to despair, with no other recourse than wit and invective, or perhaps sensuality and the idolatry of beauty. Cynicism is oriented to the search for happiness. Its mood becomes acrid because of frustration in the search for happiness. Now happiness can be of doubtful virtue, and is certainly a questionable end for human life.[5] It often culminates in the sheer satisfaction of desire or in irresponsible egoism. If it does not lead to cynicism, the search for happiness may lead to the cocktail lounge with its maudlin sentimentality, or to a bovine absorption in the concern for well-being, which results in mediocrity.

The capacity for joy is of a different order than the concern for happiness. For one thing, it is grounded in appreciative awareness. It is not concerned with egoistic satisfaction, but with participation in the actual goods of life, a giving of oneself to the appreciable meanings within experience.

Theologically, joy has its basis in the oft-repeated refrain of the creation story, 'And God saw that it was good.' This is to acknowledge that created goods, for all their potential evil, are actually good, praiseworthy, enjoyable. And to enter into the joy of their existence, is to share the Creator's satisfaction in the fruits of creation. For a parent to enjoy a child is a spiritual act when it takes the form of envisagement which attends to the child for its own sake. Such envisagement involves appreciative awareness of the child as a human being, pondering the child in one's heart, recalling the miracle of growth as it has occurred in these young years, participating in the discoveries that now lure

[5] The writings of John Cowper Powys, *The Meaning of Culture, The Art of Happiness; In Defense of Sensuality,* and *The Philosophy of Solitude;* and of his brother, Llewellyn Powys, *Love and Death,* which provide a candid expression of the hedonist faith, seem to me to illustrate both the virtue and the folly of the spiritual path founded upon happiness.

the child into new growth, contemplating this life, imaginatively, in maturity. This is to enter into the concrete fullness of the young life now emerging, for which a person may have some responsibility. It need not be his own child. It may simply be *a* child.

Enjoyment of people in the sense of finding joy in their being themselves, is of this spiritual level. Receiving the world's goods appreciatively, as when enjoying a field of grain, a broad meadow, or a woodland, the desert peace, or the over-arching field of stars of a night sky — these are elemental experiences that have found their way into the lives of all of the earth's peoples, as the testimony of their sacred writings will acknowledge. Simple as these experiences are, they are genuinely spiritual responses in the human creature; for they render us attentive to existent good and identify us appreciatively with it so that we can say, in the Creator's phrase, 'This is good!'

Being capable of joy is being receptive to the common graces that abound in the midst of evil and tragedy. They who have joy, who can find joy in living, bear the enterprise of good in their natures and thus make it concrete, actual and communicative, where otherwise it might be but a hope, a faint hint of deliverance from strain and frustration and failure.

The capacity to praise life, like the capacity to lament, reveals both deliverance from the tyranny of self and a mature adjustment to the exigencies of life itself. Where the demands of the self are upon a man, evil is exaggerated in the mind, the scope of evil is exaggerated. Good is made unreal except as it serves the desires at hand.

The praise of life can be uttered by the mature spirit in the very act of acknowledging a tragic loss; it can be made parallel with lines of lament. One of the distinguishing features of the Hebrew psalms is this parallelism of praise and lament, attesting to a highly disciplined condition of spirit. Where there is genuine acceptance of tragedy and loss, the clinging to existence, which intensifies greed and self-love, is relaxed. A man no longer sees circumstances through the desperate focus of his private concerns, but sees them as they are in relation to all relevant facts of existence. Thus the good that is present, operative, and real is not obscured by self-attentiveness; but is properly appraised and received. No life has fully emerged as a spiritual creature until this kind of discrimination is possible; until the good appears as discernible as the evil.

The affinity of joy and sorrow must be insisted upon. The capacity for joy without the capacity for sorrow gives evidence of a distortion in perspective. This is to praise life in excess and to blur the fact of evil. Often this happens because we mistake sorrow to be the opposite of joy. And the command to be joyful thus takes on the compunction to resist being sorrowful. Joy, unattended by the capacity to become sorrowful, becomes artificial and forced, and lacks the quality of tenderness that can enter understandingly into suffering and loss.

The pose of joy, in disdain of sorrow, can even be ruthless, pressing upon people or situations, for whom grief and consolation are the only natural graces, an unyielding injunction to be joyful. This pose of joy becomes also sentimental and degrading; for if a person is not persuaded by theory or fact that the joy is unmixed, he must depend simply upon repetition of the sentiment. He must don the spectacles with rose-colored lens.

Sorrow is an appreciative response in the same sense that joy is appreciative. It is also a feeling response, one that identifies the sorrower with the situation of loss. That 'He was a man of sorrow and acquainted with grief' was to recommend the Suffering Servant as Savior. 'Blessed are they that mourn,' was said to commend grief as a spiritual expression. Sorrow is bearing one another's burden, in so far as understanding relieves the weight of misfortune. It is acknowledging the interdependence of life and its internal relations.

To be capable of grief is to have a tender regard for the frail events of existence which attest to value, despite their frailty. It is one of the mistaken notions in theological thought, which reasserts itself from time to time, that value is of spiritual import only if it is stable and endures. This at once dismisses a vast amount of simple enjoyment of the concrete good, for clearly its beauty is but momentary. 'I cried over beautiful things, knowing no beautiful thing lasts,' wrote Carl Sandburg. Tschaikowsky's

Pathetique, often maligned as a morbid utterance of pessimism, anticipating his end, was, in fact, as a letter to his nephew suggests, a voicing of this anguish that all sensitive persons know who have contemplated the transiency of beauty and of all concrete goods. To be dependent upon beauty that does not last, so the counsel runs, is to court folly. Only God endures! All else is chaff!

True as this statement may be, it issues in a ruthlessness which quickly dissociates God from the existent goods that are frail and passing. It enables us to come to a swift solution of the problem of value by isolating the Supreme Value as solely sovereign, thus leaving the lesser goods actually uncalculated. For if they are potentially evil, in what sense are they good? And how is their good to be appropriated and enjoyed?

The capacity for sorrow is not evident where this ready disregard of the passing good is possible. And religion, when it becomes unqualified devotion to the Sovereign Value without actual sense of loss in relinquishing these frail goods, becomes deficient in sensibilities. The problem of idolatry may not be so easily dismissed.

Sorrow may become a preoccupation, just as joy may become excessive. So pursued, it, too, becomes either sentimentality or a distortion in perspective that sets joy and sorrow in opposition thus making them mutually exclusive.

This apprehension of good in existence, or the spiritual sense, becomes a working function of the human consciousness in proportion as man participates in the enjoyment of good. It is precisely the same process by which people become competent in perceiving other values. The mind is lured toward the object of its vision. The psyche of the person is shaped by its controlling affection. The qualitative structure of the personality is developed through its sensibilities. Thus the nature and extent of one's sense of beauty, one's sense of justice, one's discriminations of right and wrong, better and worse, the nature of his enjoyment, as well as what comes to him in the nature of a demand, indicate the level of one's psychical orientation.

Noticing these instances of spirit in the human situation is always a matter of pointing, of appreciating, of enjoying, or of sorrowing. We can say that spirit may not be directly sought or self-consciously pursued. It is never attained. When it comes it is given to a person in existence out of relationships that have oriented him to its good.

It has come to me with the force of conviction that we encounter instances of this transcendent good in the human structure whenever we experience acts of repentance and forgiveness.[6] Such responses indicate a working of spirit in the human structure which moves upon a different plane of motivation and causality than is ordinarily experienced in the give and take of human relations, even when these assume an orderly form within the calculated or measured responses of moral or legal behavior. It is as if a change of wind had occurred, to modify the climate of thought and feeling, once such an intrusion of spirit occurs. What seemed impossible of achievement suddenly happens in the situation where people have become repentant, or where they are actively forgiving. The release of tension which heretofore had frustrated effort and had bound the individuals to a fixed point of resistance suddenly floods the relationship with new resources of grace, transforming the situation completely. Similarly, when love as an appreciative response to another human being, quite independently of self-interest, arises as an organizing emotion within the personality, it alters human relations dramatically. What had seemed an impasse between persons suddenly presents openings offering new opportunities for negotiation in a number of directions.

The intermittent and spontaneous character of these instances argues, I think, that, like creative visitations, they are not subject to calculation or regulation in the way that moral and rational behavior is. In this sense they are not characteristic features of the human consciousness, but are graces of the spirit at work in the human structure, giving intimation of a tendency there and of an implicit order of qualitative meaning, pointing man to his intended destiny.

[6] I have argued this point at greater length in an essay 'The Perception of Goodness,' in *The Journal of Religion,* Vol. xxxii, January 1952.

Spirit, thus evidenced by fugitive instances within human behavior of acts of repentance, forgiveness, or love rising spontaneously and intermittently from the human consciousness, though not uncommon, is clearly not a sustained feature in the human creature. And when it appears, it is intermingled with a complex of counter tendencies making of spirit an occasional burst of beauty so rare that it seems to be a gift to man's nature, a beneficence unearned, under heightened circumstances.

Now these qualities of the human response which appear in acts of repentance and forgiveness, and, at a more elemental level, in wonder, freedom, community, joy and sorrow, are clearly psychical activities in the human organism, made possible in part by the facilities of its structure. Yet they may not be readily subsumed under the human dimension as if they were wholly typical or representative behavior of its structure. There is a degree of spontaneity and of incalculable meaning which seems to point beyond the more visibly structured responses of the moral and rational consciousness. A more marked degree of sensitivity and concern appear in these responses suggesting the play of affections and sensibilities that belong more properly to what I should call the appreciative consciousness.[7]

The goodness that appears in the structure of the human psyche in these more sensitive forms, however, is not to be thought of as a tendency wholly countering moral and rational good; nor as being irresponsibly set apart from them. It can no more be related to them in a one-to-one ratio, however, than inert matter or the level of mechanism can be related in a simple sequence to psychical life. Spirit in this form of sensitive goodness subsumes the good of the moral and rational consciousness in the way that all higher levels have subsumed the facilities of lower structures. Yet, in the emergence of these sensitive responses something creative has occurred to provide a new center of meaning, a new motivation, a new organization of concern, issuing in something qualitatively new.

Perhaps the most fruitful area for exploring the operation of

[7] See Chapter v, 'The Appreciative Consciousness' in my *Higher Education and the Human Spirit,* University of Chicago Press, 1953.

spirit in the human consciousness would be those heightened and poignant moments of a man's history when the sense of extremity is upon him through experiences of remorse, or defeat, or through occasions of unbounded joy when his cup runs over. The study of them, however, might be quite disappointing; for their very nature precludes such direct and analytical inquiry. In part this is so because the human mind would be attending to a datum that defies ready description or categorizing. To be sure some psychological interpretation could be given; for the processes within the human psyche are in part observable; but only partially so. The inaccessible aspect, that which seems to point beyond the human structure to a good not its own, has the quality of an emergent which may not be readily assimilated by the discourse of description or analysis.

Rather than pressing for a method of understanding this emergent good, we might do better to sharpen our perceptions to notice its occurrence and to quicken a zest to attend to its dynamic and creative happening. I am persuaded that in becoming sensitively aware of this emergent quality of response and occurrence in human events, we may be brought to a level of perception where the Biblical witness itself may become more vivid and compelling; and in becoming so, add profoundly to the resources we now possess. It is not altogether adequate to say simply that the gospel stories are poetic or mythical or even indirect forms of discourse. They are so precisely because they deal with instances in which this emergent good stands forth again and again. The impulse to mythologize these meanings derives, not so much from an elemental consciousness as from a sensitive, yet frustrated, one that recognizes the depth and import of the mystery to which it is attending. It thus strains to report what is so vividly and profoundly encountered, but which exceeds the bounds of the human mind.

The stretch of time which separates our world from this ancient experience does not really dissociate us from these events. Our creatural extremity is no less actual. The dimension of the human consciousness is no greater with us than in the ages of Biblical faith. It is true that, at certain levels of our society, we have passed through a greater measure of disciplined inquiry which certain critical facilities of thought have made possible. The full import of these intellectual disciplines is not easy to assess, so much of it is negative in its results, and much is irrelevant to the deeper issues. Some have claimed that our capacity to deal sensitively with profound issues of our existence is in inverse proportion to our increased capacity to become analytical and descriptive. There is some truth to this assertion, if for no other reason than that the focus of thought and concern has progressively shifted from ultimate to immediate issues as our instruments and methods of thought and inquiry have become sharpened. Yet the assertion is misleading also; for it overlooks the small margin of persistent inquiry which has never relaxed its concern to see the empirical meaning of this datum of goodness, and to sharpen men's sensibilities as well as their minds for attending to its claims. Despite the dissipation of faith which has accompanied the search, and which, in some respects, was a consequence of it, decisive gains have been made in reorienting man's inquiry into psychical meanings that relate to problems of spirit; and into the nature of structures in which the human mind and spirit have been cradled. The mystery of the human equation is not better known by us; for we, too, are limited structures of consciousness. We, too, see through a glass darkly. But it has become a dimension of our being which can be approached with some discernment as well as faith since we are able to attend more sensitively to processes within our structure which give intimation of its creative working.

Although it would be misleading to suggest that we can grasp the meaning of this horizon of spontaneity which awakens us to the mystery of our existence, it is proper to suggest qualities of the human response, or capacities in our structure which render us more sensible of their emergent operations. The human consciousness should be viewed as a highly dynamic and creative context in which habitual and emergent tendencies contrive to form a persistent duality in human nature. This duality is not the distinction between animal and human characteristics; or between man and nature, to which Idealism pointed. It is a duality in the human structure itself, precipitated by the creative activity which constantly presses the human organism to perform simultaneously, acts directed both to functional and imaginative ends. Bergson saw this duality of intention when he described the *closed* as over against the *open* society.[8] Yet he obscured the importance of this insight, in my judgment, when he ascribed these emergent tendencies toward openness to rare individuals who rise above the mores and structured life of the community, as in the mystics. This is to individualize the occurrence to the point of dismissing the really precious operations of grace which are at work in all men, however rigid or habituated their modes of life may become. To be sure, these rare and decisive emergents appear in the culture — not only as mystics but as perceptive and dedicated men in different vocations. But they exhibit more decisively and continuously what is incipient and intermittent in the great mass of human folk. A closer look at these nameless people, many of whom live as members of one another rather than as individuals, would reveal a far more sensitive and perceptive response among them than Bergson's theory has suggested. The cultural anthropologist, for example, who makes a specialty of exploring the communal life of some one people in great detail,[9] never fails to notice the creative and responsive qualities of their life as a group. The sensitivity that has become individuated in the mystic or the creative artist is here corporately expressed in their crafts and in various rituals which they create to deal sensitively with one another and with the great powers that are thought to be inhabiting the environs. In a way they are a closed society; but only in regard to certain fixed mores. In their arts and in the play of the human spirit as it appears in celebrative or sober events and in their more casual, festive encounters, something spontaneous seems to appear to suggest that even here there is openness to a freedom that transcends the mechanisms of living.

Similarly among people of more differentiated societies, these qualities of spirit appear. Here it may be in the family group, or

---

[8] *Two Sources of Morality and Religion,* Holt, 1935.

[9] Cf. the works of Margaret Mead, Ruth Benedict, R. R. Marett, Robert Redfield, Robert H. Lowie, et al.

in groups formed by special interests or by common dedications. What Durkheim noted as a heightening of the group consciousness in ceremonials and in other forms of group participation, and attributed to the suggestibility of the mind under group stimulus,[10] can be interpreted quite differently. Under some circumstances this heightening follows as a release from the mechanisms of ordinary routines as the individuals are enabled to respond to that level of their consciousness which is appreciatively motivated. The occasion, together with the temper of the group, serves as a transcendent point of focus. What is incipient, though habitually cramped and inhibited in the personality, may then find release and become refocused around this higher center of consciousness. It is not mere suggestibility, or the illusion of experiencing something greater than oneself. It is an actual reorientation of the psyche. It is a genuine encounter with a good not one's own. Something in oneself enables the psyche to be responsive. It is, as I have said, the incipient play of spirit in the human consciousness pressing toward emergence. But the communal event has, in such instances, served as an objective center to bring what was incipient into dominance. The fact that it is occasional and intermittent makes it no less real, no less genuine as a transcendent act.

[10] Emile Durkheim, *Elementary Forms of the Religious Life,* Macmillan, 1915.

XI

The Redemptive Good

REDEMPTION is the renewal of the creative act in human life by which the sensitive nature which is God is made formative and fulfilling in our purposes. We are saved from our own acts of dissolution to the degree that this sensitive nature can reach us. Whatever happens in our lives to open up our natures to the tendernesses of life which are of God is redemptive. These happenings can be discussed under the topics of grace and forgiveness.

I

Grace and forgiveness, while familiar Christian concepts, have particular force of meaning in relation to the Reformation analysis of the human situation. Here all confidence in the devices of men to transform themselves — good works, ethical progress, education or Christian nurture — has been abandoned. The ills of human nature, the Reformers held, are too far-reaching, too deep-seated in the human ego, to be affected by these step-by-step alterations. Furthermore, they insisted, it is not in the human ego to initiate or to effect the change which the human situation of despair requires. Thus for them the self confronted a cosmic dread which was paralyzing as long as the person had only the merits of his own situation with which to bargain for his destiny. Except as some power or good other than human resources could give assurance of relief from the perils of human destiny, Reformation thought insisted, man's life is engulfed in utter despair. Grace and forgiveness, therefore, made meaningful by the love that was disclosed in Christ, were seen to be all that stands between the man driven to despair and the man who is able to take hope.

Whether or not this Reformation analysis over-dramatizes man's predicament, we need not be concerned here to decide. All theology, all philosophy, in fact, and, we may add, all dramatic art, falsifies concrete existence in this sense. It lifts up the life of man in a generalized, sometimes formalized, pattern. No generalized version of the concrete event portrays concrete existence in its true, empirical form. It bears resemblances to it as the play characterizes life's experiences.

The Protestant analysis of the human situation, which magnifies man's dependence upon grace and forgiveness, nevertheless calls attention to an empirical datum which may be analyzed as follows: Every human life pursues a subjective course by reason of its sensory orientation. This is a *given* of existence, itself. It is the way human consciousness has actuality. But this subjective life bears hidden relations to the vast context of all life and to the creative force of life which fact lays upon each individual, demands that can be fulfilled only by concessions which the socialized existence, the community, make to the individual. The individual spiritedly declaring, 'I'll pay my own way! No one need look out for me!' is either blind to his social dependence, or is simply chafing under an acute awareness of it. Strong-minded men of wealth, unaware of the social basis of their holdings and much impressed by their own initiative, illustrate the former. Elderly people, compelled by circumstances to fall back upon the support of their children, illustrate the latter.

Grace takes on meaning in our vocabulary in proportion as we come to understand the accumulative evil of subjective existence in this communal context of living; and to the degree that we appreciate this social dependence — our need of our fellows and of God, the Creator. It is literally true that no one pays his own way in the sense that he gets on by his own resources and efforts alone. This is not to deny responsible concern for our obligations; but to insist that the best of our efforts fall short of sustaining our existence, of meeting the demands of our creatural needs, to say nothing of demands for spiritual and moral health.

It can be said that we live upon the grace of one another. No one can estimate the extent of this dependence; only we know the scope is vast. The relations between two people in love accentuate this dependence, so that the grace of companionship, for example, becomes a vivid fact. The relations between people intimately bound into a small community again vivify this interdependence in which the limitations of each subjective existence are made clear. Not only are these limitations physically felt, but they are spiritually discerned. People cannot rise to their full stature as people except as they respond to one another in meaningful ways. A Mexican, describing this feature of village life as he had known it in Mexico, put it quite quaintly, saying, 'In the Mexican village we make music out of our common life together. We play upon one another as if each person were an instrument.' This is the true imagery of the relationships out of which grace arises. Individuated existence bears the limitations of segregated instruments. The qualitative meaning of human living is as communal as the symphony.

Grace is empirically discerned in companionship, in human understanding among people where no explanation is needed; in the affections of people that affirm and appreciate the good discerned in human life. In the even run of affairs, this sustaining goodness is a slumbering, community sentiment; in evidence, but unassertive, except in quiet, reassuring ways. In times of crisis, in grief, personal failure or loss, and in common crises such as war, flood, or famine, this slumbering sentiment becomes the most evident sustaining power, without which the suffering and grief might become unbearable.

Grace is always a gift of the goodness that waits to be apprehended in any situation to soften the sting of evil or loss, and to reassure the broken or defeated spirit of man. Whether or not grace has actuality in an individual's existence will depend upon how ready he is to receive the good that awaits him in each such situation. Every moment is a creative situation in which lethargy, evil, and the good that is of God's working, contrive to be sovereign. The quality of existence as well as the quality of our expectations is determined by the capacity to penetrate the concrete situation, and to be aware of these constituent elements.

Now this analysis places the operation of grace in the commonplace human relationships wherein the sociality of existence is illuminated. Obviously, from the point of view of the metaphysics which we have been lifting up, this does not exhaust the nature of the concrete event in which grace is observed. The ultimate source of grace is God, through whom the infusion of feeling in concrete existence is made possible.

'Grace' has been defined as 'the abundance of good in any concrete situation which our own efforts did not create.' The fullness of the sensitive working of God is never adequately known by any one of us. We cannot know the fullness of good that hovers over every situation, for we are able to experience good only up to the limits of our capacity to receive it. Another way of saying this is that there is always more good in any situation than any of us is able to acknowledge or appropriate. Just as our minds are limited in observing the facts at hand, so our perceptual powers grasp but a meager proportion of the concrete goodness that meets us in any situation. We are equally inattentive to the magnitude of evil that confronts us; but this is another problem.

This goodness which is beyond our ken, but which nevertheless affects our existence, is the source of a beneficence that we do not seek, do not plan for, and often are not ready to receive. In our estimates of life, this abundance of the concrete good is left uncalculated because it is unperceived. The perception of ill and of evil is more acutely developed in the human response. This tends to give rise to a common depreciation of life's worth and to a ready response of fear and distrust, with its compensatory reactions of egoistic assertiveness.

The doctrine of grace is the affirmation of this good in existence which can 'do exceedingly abundantly above all that we ask or think, according to the power that worketh in us,' and the insistence that a redemptive power works in our lives by reason of this abundance of concrete good.

We may say this in various ways to bring out the point more

sharply: No life depends wholly upon its own merit and achievement for the sustenance of life. We are not rewarded according to our due, but according to our capacity to receive the good that is in existence.

Now this view of grace illumines the problem of subjective existence, which, as we said earlier, preconditions every sensory life for a sinful existence: i.e. a life absorbed in the demands of the ego, compelling the orientation of energies around the self. The assurance of grace — this abundance of concrete goodness in existence which awaits our capacity to receive it — is the objective datum that can release the ego from its preoccupation with protective procedures. This is always relative, to be sure. Subjectivity is never completely overcome; but the intensity of the focus may be tempered, and ultimately, the egocentric focus may give way to a genuine dedication to the concrete good that is of God's working.

To be redeemed, then, from the point of view of this aspect of the analysis, is to be rescued from the strictures of our own individuation and from the insensitivity to our good, which gathers in force as we pursue the demands of the subjective life.

But the capacity to receive this grace of spirit that redeems the subjective life waits upon our sense of forgiveness. This has been presented in formal theological patterns as a dramatic act of the deity in relieving sinful man of the anguish and fear that arises from his sinful state. In concrete terms, it involves an awakening of the individual consciousness to the goodness of God that is in himself as a concretion, and in every concrete event, and to the communal context in which all life is gathered into community with God and men.

There is a sense in which the *giveness* of man, his subjectiveness, is accepted by the community of God in recognition of the further fact that his individual life exists in community. The evils of subjectiveness are not canceled out; nor is the good of subjective existence discounted. Forgiveness is a kind of divine understanding of man's plight, as it were, opening the way to a fuller freedom from that plight through greater recognition, both of the communal demands that can reorient the focus of the individual life, and of the vast resource of good that envelops every man by reason of this communal context of existence.

Our concern in this discussion of Grace and Forgiveness has been to establish the empirical datum that gives objective meaning to the redemptive experience that is indicated by the terms grace and forgiveness. That empirical datum, we found to be the abundance of concrete good that is in each situation which is beyond each individual's perception or even apprehension. This abundance of concrete good arises from the mutuality of existence which inheres in the fact of God's relevance to each existent thing and in the relevance which each existent thing bears to every other event. Abstractly speaking, the rich fullness of events is contained in every individuated life; yet concretely speaking, no individuated life can fully apprehend the qualitative richness of events which meet him in each situation. This is true as regards his relations with his fellows. It is more true as regards his relations that go beyond his fellows, namely, the fullness of meaning that is in God. Everything depends here upon a person's ability to enter into the radically dynamic character of relations that characterize events in every situation. There is no static you or static me, no static community, no static history, no static God. The core of our durable qualities moves in a shifting matrix of varying depths and gradations. As persons we bear a uniqueness that is our peculiar individuality; but we bear also the image of God and the image of our fellows. The range of our conscious awareness of this divine and human image which we bear beyond our unique individuality determines the depth and breadth of our valuations of experience and thus of our capacity to perceive, acknowledge, and receive the good that is in each situation.

Redemption is a renewal of creative good in our natures, accentuating the lure of the divine and human image in our subjective life by reason of our access to this abundance of concrete goodness. It is the goodness of God at work in these concrete events that renews the impetus toward goodness in our natures and thus saves us from the sinfulness implicit in our subjective orientation. It is this abundance of concrete good in the tenuous relationships between people, in the depths of men's dedications where they have envisaged good beyond themselves, in the beauty that unsuspectedly crowds our path, in memories of one life or of one people that gathers 'the greatness incarnate' of a culture into an acknowledged and cherished tradition — it is this abundance of goodness that saves man from his frustrations, his failures, and from tragic loss which every life, in some measure, encounters. These abstract goods which we call relationships, dedications, beauty, memory, always meet us in vividly concrete form: in our love for some person, or in our oneness with friends; in our feelings for the Christ, or in some clear glimpse of ultimate truth; in the curve of a hill or a certain path that has become as a shrine in our thoughts; in particular events in history or some moment in our lifetime when life's meaning was illumined — experiences such as these are for every man the means of access to this redemptive good that hovers about him daily. In grief, in times of desolation, these are the structures through which the grace of God is mediated as a healing force. In such times, these meanings which have furnished our minds or given quality to our experiences become the staff of life, the bread upon which our spirits feed to live. The grace of God is terribly real in these desperate hours, and no theological analysis can amplify this fact.

Now the force of Christian faith seems to me to mount in proportion as this sustaining, concrete good in existence becomes real to us. We may struggle to make the doctrines of faith intelligible and convincing; we may analyze Christologies and theories of God, but these are as chaff until the concrete fullness of this pervasive good in existence reaches us as an empirical reality with which we can live, upon which we can rely, and to which we can have recourse, not only in days of disaster but in every day that we live.

Each life touches the vast complex of existent things at a tiny point of existence. Our focus of existence within our individual lives is meager, indeed; yet this is the living source of such authenticity as may come to our thoughts. We may find criteria, we may achieve a rational exposition of our insights and thus provide for objective verification of our beliefs (I have no concern to minimize their importance); but the assurance that roots us unfailingly and unquestionably in the love of God is deeper than thought. It is the witness of our own tiny point of existence as it touches this vast exterior. It is the aperture in our own natures, receiving with concrete awareness, some datum of the sensitive nature within nature, communicating this primal truth that life is good, and that goodness is the creative force in all existence upon which all actuality ultimately depends. To the degree that this pivotal perception of good infuses our thinking and our living, the meaning of Christian faith, I feel sure, will gain in clarity and persuasiveness.

The Christian faith brings this perception of good into sharper focus, designating Jesus Christ as the source of faith. In moderate theological versions of the faith, Christ is the luminous point in our culture, attesting to the good that may be more widely discerned. In radically non-empirical theological expressions such as those of Barth and Brunner, Christ alone is designated the Mediator of this grace that is of God. Obviously this makes for a fierce dependence upon Christology and for the complete depreciation of all structures of value that are in any sense continuous with experience. What dictates such a theological stand is itself an empirical persuasion; namely, the complete sense of despair with regard to creatural experience. Grace is seen as wholly other than these structures of experience because experience itself has become so devoid of grace. This, in itself, is an empirical datum.

How low can this tide of sustaining grace within the structures of experience get before we relinquish our trust in it as bearer of our good? Obviously, the European experience has, at certain historic moments, actually reached a spiritual desuetude such that the zest for life has been dissipated. The intent of creation, which is life and meaning and beauty, and, in their total aspect, goodness, has been lost from view. This magnifies the sense of evil in existence so that no glimpse of the good is psychologically possible. There are no eyes to see!

Shortly before the last war there came out of Germany a very poignant novel by a German writer under the title, *Das Lobe des Lebens* (The Praise of Life). The author, discerning the signs of the times, saw that Germany was moving swiftly toward war and toward inevitable catastrophe. He wanted to record the sheer joy and beauty of living itself as one came to know it in a quiet, German village before the senses were too numb to perceive it. Donald Culross Peattie wrote *Immortal Village* shortly afterward, lifting up this same spiritual essence as he had found it in a French village years earlier.

Faith as a structure of experience is supported by fragile fibers, numerous, tenuous tendrils that rise out of social intercourse like tender shoots. From one point of view, this is an exceedingly delicate structure — a web of relations about as tenuous as the spider's finely spun strands. Under normal circumstances, these subtle connections with existence, channeling the assurance of spirit to our consciousness, are perishable enough. At times the upsurge of faith is robust and compelling; but often it gives but a faint intimation of hope and zest. In times of great destruction, when the physical supports of life themselves fail, there is similarly a great shattering of these subtle connections with existence which provide and nurture faith. Out of the despair that rises from this shattering, come violent reactions against all spiritual dependence upon humanly discerned resources. With these subtle connections shattered, God is seen to be completely other than these resources of our lives. Man stands at the edge of an abyss that has been created by the collapse of these sustaining relations. This is the real meaning of discontinuity. Man is placed in a psychical condition where he is without access to God, to the resources of Grace, through the concrete channelings of his own existence. Only an emergency structure, it is claimed, a mediating bridge thrown across by God Himself, can span this aching void that separates man from God.

But this desperate recourse to the *Word* which is in Christ is not abandonment of the concrete channeling of spirit after all. It is a falling back upon the deepest reserves of the culture. Christ is a datum of the concrete experience. He is not mere idea, imagination, theological concept; He is fact, event, actuality! He is, as Whitehead has intimated, an eruption in history in which the good that is in God and the tendernesses of mere life itself came visibly

to view; [1] yet, not as miracle, disavowing the reality of all existence, but as life abundantly lived and as death tragically, yet
expectantly, embraced. This was real man, real human existence
reaching its magnitude in achieving access to the concrete abundance of good.

The appeal to Christ is not the abandonment of the concrete
events of history; it is the fullest envisagement of its concrete
depths which our culture affords. Revelation? Yes, in two dimensions; not one: revealing God and revealing man — bringing to
the fore in one concrete span of life the intent of creation wherein
the tender working of God was actualized in a human structure of
consciousness and made creative of a community of love.

The appeal to Christ as the source of faith in this Grace that
works toward our redemption is a return, then, to the concrete
depths of our own existence, to this aperture within our natures
through which the good is made vivid and actual to ourselves. By
his love we are redeemed in the sense that this aperture, this tiny
point of existential witness to God's tender working in ourselves
is given fullness of meaning and we, as subjective selves, are overcome with goodness in the same way that brute force, in the act
of creation, yields to God's working, thus issuing in creative
events.

II

The redemptive process can be looked upon as a form-giving
process in the same way that creation is a changing of the formless
void into structures of meaning. Or, to hold to the imagery of
emerging structures, we may say that redemption is a level of
emergence in the human structure of consciousness following
precisely the sequence of emergence in lower, physical structures
in which a new organization of impulses arises. At the level where
physical and chemical compounds are in dominance and where
psychical life is only incipient, inorganic structures are observed.
The emergence of psychical life to a sufficient dominance transforms sheer physical structures into, say, vegetation; at which

[1] A. N. Whitehead, *Adventures of Ideas,* Macmillan, 1933, p. 214.

level we say life appears. The emergence of animal existence follows upon a certain sequence of events which gives rise to consciousness and to sensory feeling. Human consciousness as a sheer structure results from the refining of physical mechanisms which advance into organisms with a central nervous system; but the miracle of personality is the result of this new emergent: that is, conscious awareness interacting creatively with symbols and signs that designate this concrete abundance of good awaiting human recognition and enjoyment.

In each of these stages of emergence, constituent parts are responding to the lure of an organizing factor; and the creative result of this process by which the many become one is a unity. The vitalities have become functionally related through form. Growth in the physical organism is the continuation of this form-giving process by which the organizing features of the psychophysical organism shape the individual life. Simultaneous with physical growth occurs the formation of the self, which is more than a bodily event since it depends upon symbolization. Now the formation of the self is the crucial, complex happening of human emergence.

It is apparent that the range of human emergence is vast, indeed; for emergence depends upon the facilities for symbolization and the nature and depth of symbolization itself. And these vary enormously. The subjective growth of one person may include but a meager process of symbolization in which the barest human meanings are brought to conscious awareness. In some, the rich content of an earlier humanistic civilization may be explicit, with only a meager embodiment of the modern, technical insights and values. In others, the full dimension of our modern era may be embodied, but with meager, almost negligible, consciousness of the inheritance of values upon which the modern era rests. In some persons the most sensitive meanings implicit in music, religion, and poetry are incarnated; in others these meanings are as non-existent. In their place appear the rough sentiments of an essentially muscular mentality. So the differentiations go, on and on — almost endless in their variations. Human emergence manifests a vast variety of individuated consciousness.

Now redemption opens up a still greater range of difference in human emergence. Redemption is emergence at that level of human consciousness where symbolization reaches beyond sheer egoistic satisfaction to embrace the qualitative meaning of this unity that is higher than the individual organism — first in community, then the community of God. These are concentric circles of relations that designate the gradations of creatural emergence.

Redemption differs from growth in that it is a transcending of the organism and of the self. From one point of view it may be regarded as the reverse of growth, especially where redemption is spoken of as the *breaking of the self*. Self-denial, self-relinquishment, these are often associated with redemption. I should like to offer an alternative figure which seems to me to be truer to the process of redemption: Not the breaking of the self, not even the losing of the self (though the import of this New Testament expression is preserved), but the lure of the self into a higher unity; the attraction of the self toward a higher emergence of form by reason of a qualitative advance in the organizing features of self-activity. 'For me to live is Christ!' is not just the loss of self-awareness, but a refocusing of self-consciousness about a higher center of conscious value. 'The old self is cast away,' yet not altogether; for something of the old self endures in this reorientation in which new form is attained.

Redemption, then, is still symbolization — the same process by which the human organism achieved social growth — only it is symbolization that reaches a new depth of cultural meaning. It is the human consciousness feeding at the level of spirit. It is the human consciousness finding access to the concrete abundance of good as cultural meaning, which becomes organizing and sovereign in experience. It is human consciousness opening itself to the creative working of God's sensitive nature through affection for the good that is in Christ. This is to acquire a new pattern of organization in life: one in which the range of human meanings becomes inclusive of the most ultimate meanings with which the human mind, at its level, can be concerned.

Redemption as form, giving structure to experience in relation to the deepest meaning, which is God, expresses one aspect of the process; perhaps the external aspect. On its internal side, re-demption is infusion of feeling. This figure is not too happy, for it suggests an artificial injection of something into the human creature. Actually, we mean to suggest the subtle emergence of sensibilities in the human being, arising from his religious affec-tions.

Both Schleiermacher and Whitehead have had a preference for feeling as the ultimate concept, depicting both the elemental nature of the religious relation and the nature of the religious reality. This involves a significant alteration in world-view as over against those theologies and philosophies that designate mind as primary (Hegel and the movement of Modern Idealism), or moral good as primary (Kant and the strand of ethical idealism in Liberalism; or the theology of ethical decision in dialectical theology; and even the neo-naturalist concern with criterion of value). Concern with feeling implies a subjective ordering of im-pulses without external compulsion, except the lure of objective good arousing the affections.

The stress upon the reorientation of feeling has significance for all expressions of redemption. For one thing, it implies a total transformation of a person's character or of his situation. It is remarkable, when we think of it, how completely interpretations of man have ignored the body in dealing with the person. Con-sciousness, to be sure, is a dominant element in human personal-ity; but it is in association with visceral, sensory, affective proc-esses which either deeply enhance conscious commitment or work at odds with it, even obstructing and frustrating its intent. Intel-lectual analysis of the problem of evil or of sin, clarification of the criterion of value, conscious understanding of what is right and wrong — these are steps in the right direction; but, alas, knowledge of good and evil simply does not redeem man from his situation. Redemption advances only as we feel into the situation with our bodies such that our feeling-self cries out in affection toward the right or the good; in any case, so that the feeling tone of our bodies accords with our conscious awareness in relation to ideas, facts, or situations. Redemption is never assured by mental assent; it waits upon the co-ordination of feeling with intellectual assent. This argues for the nurture of sensibilities along with conscious dedication and critical knowledge.

Good will or love in the form of a generalized sentiment is not the same as sensibilities that restrain or refine action in the interest of a cherished good. Good will is often an ambiguous feeling that is unrelated to the processes that define human action. It may be but an attitude at the conscious level — only a surface play of the mind, as it were, with no visceral connections. Moralisms can be like that: consciously affirmed ideals that supervene upon action, remaining unimplemented.

Sensibilities are quite otherwise. They may rarely enter the conscious level or be rehearsed as intellectual sentiments. They simply form the deeply laid restraints and appreciations in a person or a culture which give rise to a certain character or quality of action. Sensibilities are related to a clearly conceived good; in fact, constitute the reflection of that cherished good in practical decision and action. Sensibilities are acquired, not through sudden decision, nor through coercion; nor are they achieved through self-conscious effort; they are like spirit — qualities of response that arise slowly in human personality or in culture as a result of persistent affections or appreciations.

Redemption, in its inward working, is the nurture of sensibilities which carry the transformation of life, implied in dedication, to the inward parts. It can be said, in fact, that redemption as an act of conversion is never actualized until it has passed from conscious affirmation or dedication to unconscious sensibility; until, in other words, it becomes feeling in the visceral sense. This matter becomes more vivid when we transfer the concern for redemption to the problem of suffering and tragedy.

III

The transcending of suffering and tragedy is not just a mental adjustment; it is a deeply creative transformation that reaches every cell of the body, else transcendence does not come.

The person struck down by grief, by the loss of a loved one in death, is himself a casualty. Death envelops him as it has the one who has actually met physical death. In the one instance, death has dissolved the body as well as the living person; in the other, it has brought death to a vital portion of the living person. Death in life is the cruelest burden that we must bear.

Is it a lingering death? Or does it move from death to life? Does the cross remain, or does it issue in a day of resurrection?

> O Friend, we never choose the better part
> Until we set the cross up in the heart.
> I know I cannot live until I die —
> Till I am nailed upon it wild and high,
> And sleep in the tomb for a full three days dead.[2]

The death of a loved one must be taken into oneself; absorbed into one's feelings; not consciously suspended, held off as if it were not true. Grief itself is a creative process through which the death of another passes through our bodies, our deepest, emotional selves. Some will grieve silently; others more demonstrably; but however it is done, it will take the grieving individual down into the valley of the shadow of death. And when the body can weep no more; when it is emptied of its grief, a quiet healing, as miraculous as birth itself, will begin to mend the connections that had been fragmented by death. The miracle of the resurrection occurs time after time within any one human life-span where body and spirit of the grieving one has lain in *the tomb three days dead*.

As friends of the man who grieves, we should not be insensible to this creative process that redeems broken lives from recurrent tragedy. Our task is not to rescue them from sorrow; certainly not to provide them with redemption, but to help them where we can to avail themselves of this redemptive process that follows upon full relinquishment of their selves to the cross. More theological talk may not suffice. A life torn by grief is hardly receptive to intellectual analysis; though in some instances, this in itself may be reassuring. Certainly indulging in talk about the benefits of tragedy or about good that can come out of it, is misplaced. This crisis is like illness; and must be dealt with as a physician

[2] From 'Follow Me' by Edwin Markham. Reprinted by permission.

deals with illness — i.e. provide conditions by which the illness can run its course toward healing.

Perhaps all we can provide is friendship. This is exceedingly important, for it is here that loss has been sustained. Furthermore, this connection enables us to offer what depths of resources are in our own nature to sustain the grieving one, or to open the mind to resources of faith we may hold in common.

The advantage of the minister long in residence and intimately related to his people is that in times of crisis, he becomes the point of entry into this abundance of good which initiates the redemptive process. The same may be true of a professor whose relations with his students are of this personal sort. Here a person is not required to argue the pros and cons of death and immortality; or the purpose of suffering; but simply to open doors that will free the vision from the cramped foregrounds that now have become suffocating. The intent of such effort is to enable the person in grief to receive the grace that is in this situation, offering healing and renewal of heart.

Redemption from tragedy as infusion of feeling, then, is a creative process that transforms the very depths of our natures to accord with the facts given in the tragic situation. We do not escape the cross; for it may not be a part of our destiny that the cup shall pass from us; but in commending our spirit to the Source of our good, the cross that we are made to bear is transmuted into a cross we are able to bear. And it is literally true, at least within the life process, that they who yield themselves up to the cross when it intrudes upon life rise again. They who insist that the cup pass from them, who resist the transmutation, prolong the tragedy and forego the redemptive experience.

IV

This fact of death in juxtaposition to life is a mystery. And the transfiguration which transmutes the tragedy and evil of death into a triumphant good is an even greater mystery. No one of us who stands on this side of the ultimate mystery of death can speak with knowledge of the ultimate mystery of life. Yet, we know that a renascent process has been encountered in experience. It has restored hope among people who have seen their world crumble. It has renewed the will to go on in men and women when the things they cherished most were wrenched from them. It has brought orderliness of mind and a confident spirit to a child, lost in the living death of his own confusion, when maturity broke through the debris of his shattered dreams. The healing of the heart and the renewal of zest, where the will to live has atrophied out of a loss of hope or incentive, is the most visible assurance we have of the redemptive love that works on in the world. This love, issuing in a redemptive grace, is real energy, a good not our own, which re-creates our ambiguous good, restoring the wastelands and making the crooked paths straight. The Christian faith affirms this resource as a never-failing source of life and hope.

To extend the evidence of these experiences into an assertion of knowledge would be too facile; and it would be to speak beyond the limits of our frail minds. Yet, to ignore this evidence, to be unaffected by the wonder and expectancy which it creates, is to fall needlessly and insensitively into a premature finalism.

How the mystery of death unfolds beyond the life-process is not given to us to understand. The Christian faith affirms the resurrective principle as ultimate and thus envisages tragedy overcome in a final sense in a way that corresponds to the lifting of grief in this present existence. According to this Christian affirmation the very character of our cultural *élan,* the distinguishing aspirational drive which points to the meaning of existence for our culture, is given in the doctrine of the resurrected life. This should be understood as a valuation of the life-process — the Christian man's conception of himself as participant in it, together with his claims concerning the ultimate nature of whatever shapes his destiny. It answers the human cry for meaning. The problem of human destiny, which defines the meaning of existence, can be said to be resolved only when we can truthfully say, 'Life is good; so also is death good.' Except as attachment to life and relinquishment of life can be carried simultaneously in the human spirit, it cannot really be said that the religious issue has been resolved. Where attachment to life is sought as an alternative to the life of relinquishment, something of a short-range exaltation of mere existence ensues. Where relinquishment of life is made the alternative, however, the essence of existence is made an unreality. Man then clings to a shade that refuses to become fully embodied. Attachment and release are two dimensions of living which provide for a fullness of being in the human creature. Attachment is to be understood as a sensuous embracing of the goods of existence as they are conveyed or communicatd through the perceptual powers of the creature. It involves the exercise of the appreciative powers in man toward many different kinds of goods in experience. It implies a generous degree of expansiveness in one's nature toward evident values, wherever discerned, eliciting a response of joy or praise over their existence; and, at their death or dissolution, evoking in one genuine grief. This tender attachment is in no way contradictory to the capacity to release from existence what must be taken away, or be given up in the creative passage of events. It is the source of a pathos that gathers like a gossamer web about the whole fabric of existence, giving to it the tenuous quality of spirit which only regret and the shattering of great joy can bestow. Where it is accompanied by capacity for release this tragic attendance of a sense of loss and grief infuses into the spiritual life of relinquishment a softened ardor which rescues the religious man from his own ruthlessness.

Devotion to creative value without such tender regard for created goods can make of religion a cruel enterprise, and of the religious person an impoverished man. The attachment to life which can be taken to mean a subjective enjoyment of the concrete events of life is the source of that persisting yearning of the human spirit for more of life — more than can be granted to any individual existence. It is what rises in protest against the mortal limitations of the life-span; and what presses the human consciousness to define its ultimate meaning when this specter of dissolution appears before it.

Heaven and immortality are not spiritual concepts in the sense that they voice the summit of human devotion and dedication;

they are the transmutations of the will to live. They are in fact desperate creations of the religious mind to justify in an ultimate sense this subjective enjoyment of concrete events. Nevertheless these concepts that carry the human venture to an imagined fulfillment designate a spiritual concern which cannot be set aside without doing violence to the human spirit. Crude as they often are, they bespeak the necessity of carrying this two-dimensional thinking of attachment and release beyond the embodied life.

The Christian faith may be taken to affirm the inseparableness of these two dimensions, adding as a third dimension the concern to hold this principle of life and the principle of death in tension. The cross is the symbol of the one, the resurrection is the symbol of the other. The cross without the resurrection is the search for value without awareness of the concrete good.

These seed affirmations define the spiritual outreach of our human psyche in the West. As we have said, this response of faith can be stated in terms of two levels of valuing life. At the elemental level it joins with the spiritual response of other religious cultures in acknowledging the sacredness of life. In its disciplined and mature expression, it transmutes the simple will to live into a will to live significantly, which is to join attachment to life and relinquishment in a simultaneous acknowledgment of vital human joy along with the tragic sense.

On its deeper side, the story of the Christ may be said to be a transfiguration of this elemental hope of the human race. It is the tragic sense of life transmuted through love and sacrifice, which gives assurance to the Christian that he who loseth his life shall find it. The elemental truth carries the age-old yearning for more of life. The transmuted truth lifts this yearning to a noble faith of relinquishment in which the sense of attachment is not disowned, but transfigured.

XII

God as Hidden and God Discerned

THAT THERE IS a dimension of mystery which continually attends our experiences, giving them depth of meaning and re-creative occasions, is a conviction that steadily takes hold of the inquiring person who confronts instances of sensitivity and spontaneity such as occur in acts of forgiveness, repentance, and love. This is a minimum conclusion to which emergent thinking comes as it analyzes the movement of faith in the life of the culture and in the human psyche. This redemptive life, though a mystery still, is a sensitive working which has been a resource of renewal and a source of judgment to human effort throughout the long years of cultural history among diverse people and places.

Any attempt to inquire directly into the nature of this redemptive good that reaches our human structures in transformative ways is doomed to disappointment. To this extent theologians who have insisted that God must come to man, and that man cannot first come to God, have been right. For it is not in the capacity of any given structure to define or to observe as a datum, the movement of spontaneous and creative meaning which intrudes with greater sensitivity and import upon its structural order. Some awareness of its emergent quality, of its judgment and transcendent good, may be possible; though even this will require discernment and humility in the organism to enable it to be receptive to what is other than its habitual path of response and beyond its full comprehension.

The difficulties theologians have confronted in dealing with this problem of God's coming to man are well known. When the matter is stated in its usual Protestant form, namely, that God, through the work of the Holy Spirit, prepares the heart and mind of those whom He chooses to have respond to His divine initiative, there is, to say the least, an uneasiness about what this can mean. It can be settled, as it has often been settled, by simply insisting that we must accept *on faith* what happens here, that to inquire further into the matter is to trespass upon holy ground.[1] In so saying, however, the Protestant theologian takes a decisive step toward dismissing the relevance of structured meaning, inferring by this dismissal that God's work is without structure and thus fortuitous. The absence of a Protestant philosophy of faith and culture stems from this decisive act and its implications.

Now to be sure, the structures that define and limit man's acts may not be generalized into a divine or absolute order, even when these structures can be defended as being 'the highest we know,' or as the ideal extension of man's best efforts. The fallacy of the Hegelian dialectic and of Absolute Idealism in general becomes clearer the more this matter is pondered. Similarly, the inclination of most liberal thinking to project its delineations of the ethical good into an affirmation of God's character must be regarded as an over-reaching of the human structure. By contrast, the restraint of Kant in his reticence to cross the boundary of the thing-in-itself appears humble if not actually perceptive. The readiness of the dialectical theologians of our day to stand with Kant on this point, however much they may press his formulation of faith back to its Reformation ground, and to counter all subsequent Idealism with their strictures upon its idolatrous logic, can be understood and defended as a proper sensibility. The Scriptural warning that God's ways are not man's ways may not go unheeded by the theologian who would be concerned to give evidence both of discrimination and proportion in his thinking. This is not simply a matter of religious concern: it is a matter of logic in its most subtle and sensitive form; knowing the limits

[1] Cf. John Calvin, *The Institutes of the Christian Religion*, 6th Amer. ed. rev., trans. by John Allen, Phila., Presbyterian Board of Christian Education, Bk. III, ii, sect. vii, p. 496; also Chap. xv, ii, p. 197.

of one's own logical structure, on the one hand, and, on the other, recognizing how the discernment of faith may enable one to peer through the glass darkly when these boundaries of the human structure are reached in thought.

Yet it becomes obvious, I think, that dialectic theologians, however discerning, cannot do more than repeatedly sound this warning. Theirs becomes a theology of negation for lack of its concern with structures; or because of their readiness to dismiss all structured meaning as being man-made and thus irrelevant to the Word of God.

The mystery of depth or transcendence to which Christian theologians have persistently pointed can be spoken of in emergent terms without doing violence to Christian sensibilities. The effort to do so can accomplish two results: first, it can move our thinking suggestively beyond the impasse to which the Kantian *Critiques* brought theological thinking without issuing in an idealism that blurs the distinction between man and God; and second, it can permit us to engage constructively in understanding the movement of grace and judgment to which the Christian gospel has borne witness. The conviction that this course of inquiry could open up to us the meaning of the Christian witness and suggestively point up its directives for our time has led me to press constructive theology in this direction. In pursuing this course I have come to certain conclusions which I now set down as summary statements somewhat in the nature of a credo:

(1) I believe God to be a reality of grace and judgment which both interpenetrates and transcends the life of man in the way that the hopes and judgments of a father transcend and intermesh with the life of his son. The imagery of parental care which the Hebraic-Christian faith has employed to convey the personal relationship between God and his creatures is sound so long as the imagery is not used to reduce God to human stature and thus to mythologize a meaning which really transcends man's mind even as it cradles and nurtures the whole of man's existence.

God stands to man as one structure of meaning stands to another. This is the import of the father-son imagery. The actuality here is, I believe, a matrix of sensitivity and meaning of subtle and vast dimensions, transcending our own, in fact all human structures, which serves as the ultimate ground of our meaning and the source and center of all that we are and of whatever else we might become in the mystery of creation and re-creation.

God is a structure of infinite goodness and incalculable power. The empirical evidence of this fact is in the working of grace as a redemptive power which carries implications and consequences of judgment in situations of grief, remorse, suffering, dissolution, tragedy, and defeat; and in the creative experiences wherever a foretaste of fulfillment is attained. The historical witness to this fact of God's goodness and power within the Christian community is the Biblical account of the redemptive work of God in history and the continuing witness of the Church to the good discerned in Christ. The confirmation of this empirical observation and of the historical witness appears when we seek to understand the primordial act of creativity metaphysically wherein sensitivity and what seems to be an ordered concern transmutes brute force into meaningful events. The metaphysical analysis of the creative act of God, implicit in every event of actuality, thus renders intelligible what is given more concretely in the historical witness and in present experience.

(2) I believe God to be both hidden and discernible. What is hidden is the range and depth of the transcendent structure of meaning which is beyond our comprehension. This dimension of God's meaning, our human consciousness and sensibilities with their limited structure can only dimly apprehend. What is discernible is that measure of the concrete nature and working of God which reaches our sensibilities, awareness, and attentive minds. Specifically, it is the concrete working out of creative and redemptive occurrences as these touch our lives in events of joy and sorrow, in experiences of guilt, remorse, judgment and forgiveness, in the lifting of grief, and in the summit vision of peace, in so far as the human spirit can rise to such fulfillment of meaning.

In my understanding of revelation within the context of emergence, the hiddenness of God refers to the fullness of sensitivity as a transcendent structure of meaning which nevertheless interpenetrates and subsumes every other structure. It is the 'not yet' and 'beyond' of all that is. It is not wholly remote since it is immediate, ever present, and efficacious in every event or occasion. Yet it is a depth of mystery to which our structure of consciousness simply cannot attend except in a mood of awe as in a holy presence.

What we say or do here will, in the nature of the case, tend to be an over-reaching. So long as it is simply a straining appropriate to the reach of our structure, it need not be an over-reaching. On the contrary, it may serve to deepen the sense of dedication and to heighten the mood, if not the meaning, of these events in experience in which the concrete work of God is discernible.

Whether we may presume to reach further into the hidden dimension of sensitivity and meaning in God is, to my mind, a serious and disturbing question. Thus I am led, on emergent grounds, to recoil from mysticism, if not to distrust it. At this point I would seem to converge toward dialectical and existential theologies, though my reasons would be stated differently. It would seem that I should be intrigued by the efforts of Gerald Heard who sees possibilities of impelling the human structure to evolve toward a higher capacity for sensitivity through a more disciplined differentiation of consciousness.[2] To some extent I have been impressed by Heard, but I resist his magic on the same grounds that I distrust the mystic. To bring the human structure to its full capacity of sensitivity and dedication is, I think, our obligation and spiritual aim. But how far can we properly pursue this course without seeming to manipulate the creative process? At this point I find the proportion and the humbling response to God's otherness in Reformation teaching a welcome corrective.

(3) I believe Jesus Christ to be the revealer of God and the mediator of God's redemptive work to men. By revelation I mean a decisive instance of a structure of meaning, more complex and sensitive in its relations, breaking with the force of disclosure and re-creative power upon a more simple structure, thereby impelling

[2] Cf. Gerald Heard, *The Eternal Gospel,* Harper, 1946. See also *The Ascent of Man,* Harper, 1929; *The Source of Civilization,* Harper, 1937; *The Third Morality,* Harper, 1937; and *Time, Sex, and Pain,* Harper, 1939.

it to a new level of awareness and sensitivity. Such an instance would be an encounter between the limited, human consciousness together with its bodily feelings, and any intimation of a transcendent structure. The gospel story bears witness to such an encounter in the person of the Christ who, in turn, became the mediator of this transcendent structure of meaning within the human community wherever the witness was borne. This means to me that Jesus Christ, though human, embodied in his structure of consciousness the dimension of this transcendent structure and thus actually effected the work of God, not only in human events through the impress of his person upon them, but within the human personality in so far as this matrix of sensitivity which is God's structure could be transmitted and made expressive through human thought and feeling. To the degree that this interpenetration of sensitivity in thought and feeling occurred in the consciousness of Christ, a coalescence of structures occurred in which a novel advance of spirit was made manifest.

The antecedents of this emergent event lay in the developing moral consciousness of the Hebrew people with its intermittent witness to the redemptive power of God in history; and, to a more limited, yet real, degree in the developing rational consciousness of the Greek culture with its persistent search for the sovereign, ethical good.

The sensitivity of spirit conveyed through the parables and narratives of the New Testament expresses a new dimension of goodness to which such terms as grace and judgment, repentance, forgiveness and love point. This transcendent good was not wholly unknown to the Hebraic and Greek cultures. Occasional and tenuous strands of its sensitive meaning rise like a mist from the recorded events and reflections of these two historic peoples, as in the more tender and decisive utterances of the prophets; or in the more profound and sensitive reaches of Plato's anticipations. But in the Gospels this sensitive meaning breaks upon the ear with a release and redemptive power that suggests its full creation as actualized event. The structures of moral and rational good are not denied or disowned; but they are re-created by this novel power of grace and forgiveness. The old structures are as

stalks to these flowers that are in bloom, whose beauty and promise break upon this company of troubled and disheartened men
and women as a new horizon of hope, yet with demands and a
counsel of judgment that is inescapable.

The revelation of God in Christ, then, became concrete, dynamic, formative, and impelling within the human structure and
in a living community. This was a world event as truly as the
atomic bomb, even though, like the release of atomic power, the
facilities for its emergence first appeared in but one time and
place.

As a novel advance within the human structure, this emergent
life of grace and redemptive power has effected *a permanent
revolution,* to use a familiar phrase.[3] The culture of the West has
never been the same since its innovation. And it continues to
release men from their restrictive egoism as well as from the
mechanisms of their own humanly contrived orders of logic and
justice, enabling them to participate, in part, in this more sensitive
order of meaning, despite the dominating frustration of their
characteristically human structures. Thus the cruelty and folly of
this human structure, tempered at times to be sure by a sense of
virtue and idealized good, which at best is ambiguous and in-
stable, is continually under judgment of this perennial innovation
of spirit and within reach of its redemptive good as well. To have
Christian faith is to affirm the reality of this redemptive power
as a continuing and ever-present energy of judgment and grace.

This grace and judgment, issuing from the transcendent structure of sensitivity and meaning which is God, reaches the structures of cultures through both mediated and immediate ways.
As I see the matter, the revelation in Christ became a cultural
energy in the West which assumed structure and dynamic power
through the symbolisms and organizational witness of repentant
and dedicated men and women, the emerging community of witness. Christ is therefore more than a memory in the minds of

[3] Reinhold Niebuhr ascribes the phrase originally to Trotsky. Cf. H. R.
Niebuhr's use of it in *The Kingdom of God in America,* Harper, 1937, and
The Meaning of Revelation, Scribners, 1941. See also Bernard M. Loomer,
'Neo-Naturalism and Neo-Orthodoxy,' *Journal of Religion,* XXVIII, April
1948.

living Christians. He is the persisting structure of sensitive meaning which works at the level of cultural institutions and creative effort, pointing men to the real energy of grace in their midst. By whatever metaphysics we may designate this persistent force of the living Christ, we must acknowledge it to be formatively present within the mythos of our culture to which we bear witness in innumerable ways.

(4) I believe the Holy Spirit to be real God. As Christian language has employed this term, the Holy Spirit is the immediate working of the concrete nature of God. It is the discernible and apprehendable working of God in human nature and events in so far as there is a direct and immediate encounter between God and man's present, structured experience. In saying that the Holy Spirit is real God, I mean to acknowledge that it is the actual working of God in human life; but in being discerned or apprehended its working partakes of the ambiguities of the human structure: i.e. its actual effects contend with the limitations, in part to transform them, but under conditions imposed by the sensibilities, consciousness, and will of the human structure.

There are two reasons for this limitation upon the working of the Holy Spirit. One is that the 'Comforter' is inevitably the power of God conceived in relation to explicit human needs and demands. This means that God, as Holy Spirit, stands to the human consciousness as the parent stands to the child. In the child's experience of the parent there is a focusing upon realities that are explicitly relevant to his needs and demands. The child is often oblivious to the nature of the parent in his fullness of meaning as a person. What this person he calls father or mother was before the child himself appeared; or what each of them is in roles which are assumed beyond the family circle, may be of little moment or as nothing to the child's world as it intersects that of the parent. At best it may be but an ambiguous fact of the past or of the remote present of which the child can make little sense. To be sure, much of the meaning of the parent, his hopes, his compulsions, his anxieties, all of which affect the child's present experience, are of a piece with the complex of mystery which supervenes upon what the child views as the actual parent. Yet the parent is known to the child and responded to by him through a role and within capacities which have been called into play by the demands of the parent-child situation. The analogy has its difficulties, but I mean to suggest that similarly, God as Holy Spirit, God in his concrete nature, tends to be known and experienced within the human structure in terms that are defined and restricted by the purview imposed by men's practical purposes.

But the ambiguities of this encounter arise also from the structural limitations of the human consciousness by which God is apprehended. Thus the visible working of God as known and experienced tends to be distorted or fragmented by the way that the human situation bends God to men's purposes and perspectives. To a considerable degree, then, the work of God in human life is subject to the limitations and obstructions of the human structure. God as Holy Spirit, a sensitive structure interpenetrating other structures, must work through such structures. Operationally, then, the work of God or the actualization of his purposes in human life can be no more than the yield of this interpenetration.

Shailer Mathews used to speak of Calvin's doctrine of the inner working of the Holy Spirit as an anticipation of the liberal concept of religious experience. This, I think, is what we should have to say within any one of the philosophic frameworks of liberal theology. The advance of process or emergent thinking over liberalism in its earlier philosophical orientations is indicated by the ability of the emergent formulation to recapture the objective working of God in this notion of Holy Spirit, while at the same time giving full account of its identity within the human consciousness and experience.

(5) I believe that the work of Christ as mediator of redemption and the work of the Holy Spirit may be distinguished; yet they stand related. By reason of the work of Christ, the work of the Holy Spirit (as the concrete nature of God) actually reaches men and transforms them, if not by reconstructing their conscious lives, at least by quickening their sense of sin, their awareness of a good not their own, and, possibly, by impelling them to an affection for this good that is of God. Christ thus becomes

the re-creative or redemptive energy within culture, in part because of the symbolism that arises about his life and work; in part because of the sentiment awakened within the Christian community centering around the revelation in Christ; but also because of the persistent witness to him at all levels of human discourse. If an individual is to carry forward the emergent interpretation of the gospel, he must take this redemptive activity seriously. In doing so, he would be on the way to developing a cultural conception of revelation to which cultural anthropology could speak significantly.

We cannot speak of this cultural mediation of redemptive energy as the work of the Holy Spirit; for it is not the concrete work of God in its immediacy. It is, rather, the revelatory event of Christ continuing as a redemptive activity within culture and within the structures of human personality through the medium of witness, thereby providing conditions within the human structures for the working of the Holy Spirit as a direct and immediate interpenetration of the transcendent structure of sensitivity. Culturally speaking, this continuing redemptive energy preparing men to respond to the work of grace as a direct impartation of the Holy Spirit, is the living Christ within the social organism.

This observation points us back to the resurrection as an inescapable facet of the Christian faith. The overcoming of death in the resurrection remains a mystery in so far as its ultimate import is concerned. The recognition that Christ as redemptive energy survived the cross is simply the discernible event within the human structure of consciousness. There is a hiddenness here, just as there is a hiddenness in God as transcendent. This is not to imply a 'non-material presence of some kind' or a non-material order supervening upon what is discernible structure. It implies, rather, that just as the structure of meaning, which is available as explicit meaning to the human consciousness, moves continually upon a frontier of sensitivity that points to a more subtle and complex order of meaning; so every occurrence within nature and in human history carries adumbrations of meaning beyond their discernible dimensions. This is why we can speak of the height and depth of existence in intelligible terms, intimations of which do come to us in vivid encounters with God's concrete nature or with the witness to Christ's revelatory event. So long as this is true, we cannot properly truncate any event, least of all one so charged with intimations of emergent or transcendent meaning as the resurrection of Jesus Christ.

The import of this observation is to affirm the revelation of God in Christ as discernible and available redemptive energy within the culture in the form of a ministry of both grace and judgment; and to live in Christian hope in the face of dissolution, death, and tragedy by way of affirming the openness of events in so far as they participate in the structure of sensitive meaning transcending the human frame of conscious existence.

(6) I believe that the church is the self-conscious and continuing witness to the revelation of God in Christ. As such it is a cultural organism. It is the body of Christ through which the sensibilities of faith are mediated. The church is a distinctive and exceedingly precious instrument of grace, being the organic, cultural carrier of the revelatory event in all the ways that are suggested by a concern with doctrine, worship, pageantry, creative art, and the ministry of prophetic action as these persist through the care and dedicated labors of the believing community. In this sense, the church is the responsible bearer of the formative myth as it articulates the import of the revelatory event. To the degree that it is faithful to this obligation it remains the luminous center of its witness within the culture.

Yet, being a corporate expression of the human structure, however selective and dedicated it may be, the church is a fallible instrument of grace. Its failings have been enormous to the point of being an offense to the Christian faith. The evidence of this betrayal is clearly documented in the record of the church's climb to power and its struggle to cope with the issues of faith and culture in every generation since the inception of its role as a witnessing community.

The sources of these persistent failings can be traced, in part, to the ambiguity of human goodness, however expressed: whether in the solitary efforts of individual men or in the corporate strategies of institutional enterprises. They can be traced, in part, also to the problem implicit in the relation of power and goodness and to the complexity of relating the demands of religion and culture respectively. Yet the crux of the matter seems to lie basically in the indecisive character of the witness itself. The church, in one expression of its institutional role, has been prone to arm itself with the power of God and to assert its authority as an ambiguous voice of the divine, forgetting its frailty as a human structure, and by this very act of self-deception, becoming less and less perceptive of the quality of infinite goodness to which, presumably, it has borne witness. In this self-assumed status of a divine monarch, the church has wielded the power of its prestige over culture with little concern for, or recognition of, the sensitive working which is the essence of grace. And conversely, where it has relaxed its authoritarian temper in seeking to serve as a community of believers, the church has dissipated both the power and the goodness implicit in its witness through an easy-going identification of piety and faith, or of gregarious sentiment with the dedicated work of the kingdom.

The good that is discerned in Christ, that is disclosed in the revelatory event of Christ, exhibits a peculiar and even paradoxical interrelation of power and goodness. The power is a 'gentle might' of infinite consequences, as the parables of the kingdom insistently portray. The goodness is a working of grace with inescapable intimations of judgment. To be equal, in some measure at least, to the task of witnessing to this good not our own within the culture, the church must recover this sense of 'the mystery of the kingdom' with its interplay of gentleness and incalculable power, and its unrelenting message of judgment and grace.

That God was in Christ, reconciling the world to Himself, thus becomes a formidable fact of history — a fact of overwhelming importance to each living man. It is the decisive event that sets all events and human structures in a radically altered perspective. For the structures of moral and rational good, the virtues of law and the logic of cause and effect, though not wholly canceled, are subsumed and transcended, and thereupon transmuted by the spontaneity, the freedom, and grace of forgiving love. As the act of forgiveness may transcend the impasse that has formed under the demands of causal connections, and bring healing to the broken relationships, so the structure of consciousness in which grace and love are regulative, transmutes and redeems the brokenness of men.

In the midst of the evil that well-nigh overwhelms us; in the face of our human failings and the tragic consequences that tear at our hearts, there is a working of grace and of suffering love that confounds the measure of our days.

The implications of these conclusions may be obvious, but they are worth noting: They point to a conception of the Christian witness which at once intensifies its responsibility within Western culture and justifies its hearty and spirited venture into cultures beyond the West. Its responsibility here lies in the recurrent need for bearing forth the Christian *élan* as a re-creative or redemptive life within every life and within every generation of living persons. Something decisive has been released into the structure of experience of Western life by which every life, nurtured within its social matrix, participates in and benefits by the concrete operations of the goodness of God. For every life to live within this matrix *is,* to a degree, Christ; though the clarity of this maxim must vary with the degree of self-conscious identification and dedication with which the individual affirms and receives this witness to the living Christ.

By way of this Christian motif, which is given operational meaning in the fact of the living Christ and through the Christian witness which rises from its seminal intent, the fullness of time, as it may be known and experienced in the concrete circumstances of culture, reaches into every momentary, conscious event. This is why the revelation of God in Christ is to be conceived as a perennial experience of the culture. It is a dynamic in the flux of life itself. It is a resurrected life for every age. For the incursion of the redemptive consciousness of Christ is an integral part of the creative act of God in every moment of history. There is no other way by which this depth of our cultural life can become concrete and manifest save by the recurrent witness to the living Christ.

The second observation is equally valid and relevant: namely, that the Christian witness beyond the culture of the West is appropriate and necessary. It does not follow, because the notion of the living Christ is a Western heritage which can have compelling meaning only for the human psyche which has known this inner orientation and nurture of the historic faith, that the witness to Christ is localized within these cultural bounds. This would mean that people of different cultural heritages could never communicate with each other at the profound level of experience where the issues of destiny emerge. But there is a right way and a wrong way to pursue this communication. The wrong way, according to the analysis of faith and culture which we have pursued in this book, would be to intrude the Christian evangel upon non-Christian peoples with an arrogance that brushes aside every other revelatory event within that culture. Again, the wrong way would be to minimize or denature the Christian witness in an effort to tread softly and inconspicuously with Christian wares upon alien soil. Both intolerance and an indulgent show of tolerance are misplaced in this respect. For the witness of faith must be candid, forthright, and hearty or it is no witness at all. What, then, is the alternative? The alternative to intolerance and to a sentimental tolerance is a full-bodied confession of the Christian commitment which declares 'Here I stand' by virtue of the light that has been given me. This is the existential witness to the goodness and judgment of God which has reached the individual within his cultural bounds. With explicit candor and with an earnest disclosure of the dedicated spirit, the Christian can convey to another culture the religious situation of the Christian West at the stark, creaturely level where basic human sentiments, in relation to ultimate resources and demands, can be acknowledged. Whether or not the comparative note intrudes may be of little moment. If it does intrude, the person of commitment can do no other than to avow the superior claim of his existential witness; but even this can be done without arrogance or without absolute denial of counter claims which may issue from equally dedicated spirits of another faith. For the witnessing of man must bear the limiting marks of his individuated, cultural perspective. And this is to acknowledge, in the very act of our hearty affirmation, that the work of God in its creative and redemptive events, is no respecter of persons or of cultures. With the objectivity of rain and sun, His judgment and grace fall upon the just and the unjust, the cultured and the uncultured, the men of East and West. Within and through these various mediums, the witness to God's work is more fully borne.

The intensity of the Christian witness thus invites an equally intense and candid communication of non-Christian people. Thus at the level of their creaturely encounter, where the witness to God's work can be vivid and compelling, more vivid, in fact, than man's reflections upon it, and thus less given to the bitter encounter in the confusion of tongues, something deeper than evangelization or universalization can occur. It is the deep speaking to the deep through the medium of creaturely rapport which alone can transcend or circumvent cultural barriers. From within another perspective, which we can only imaginatively assume, it is the creative event carrying revelations in experience to their ultimate cultural fulfillment through the interpenetration of these unyielding acts of witnessing among dedicated men.

Index

Alexander, S., 8

Allen, John, 210

Ames, Edward Scribner, 52

Anthropology, cultural, 4–6, 80–81

Anxiety, sin rooted in, 156–8

Appreciative awareness, faith as, 119–22; nature of, 174–5

Appreciative consciousness, Christ and, 86

Aquinas, Thomas, 71, 151

Aristotle, 24

Bach, Johann Sebastian, 58, 146, 164

Bacon, Francis, 18, 21–2, 25–6, 46, 56

Baptists, 77

Barth, Karl, 123, 148, 197

Bavink, B., 170

Benedict, Ruth, 5, 188

Bergson, Henri, 4, 8, 34, 40, 48, 89, 173, 188

Biblical events, 42, 47; emergence as seen in, 214–15

Bradford, Gamaliel, 151

Brahms, Johannes, 58, 146

Brunner, Emil, 28, 83–4, 86, 89, 92, 148, 177, 197

Buck, Peter H., 5

Calvin, John, 74–6, 137, 151, 210

Carlyle, Thomas, 117

Cassirer, Ernst, 5, 83

Causal efficacy, 37

Christ, *see* Jesus Christ

Christian faith, culture and, 99–102, 145–6, 213–23; dynamic of the, 10–13, 32, 64–79, 86–7; meaning of the, 113; *see also* Faith, Witness

Christian Witness, *see* Witness

Christology, 197, 213–19; *see also* Jesus Christ

Church, nature of the, 219–20; predicament of the liberal, 32ff., 56–9; role of the, 145–6

Creativity, 108–9

Cross, the, 208

Dante, 71

Darwin, Charles, 3, 4

Dawson, Christopher, 18

Death, fear of, 158; meaning of, 138–9; mystery of, 207ff.; transcending grief in, 203–5

Deism, 23

Depth, dimension of, 34–40, 92

Descartes, René, 9, 18, 21–2, 24

Dewey, John, 19, 26, 107–8

Disciples of Christ, 77

Divine Comedy, 71

Durkheim, Emile, 189

Eddington, Sir Arthur S., 170

Edwards, Jonathan, 124

Eliot, T. S., 110

Emergence, 39–40, 43–5; man within the perspective of, 132ff.;

Emergence (*Continued*)
myth within the perspective of, 86–7, 97; redemption within the perspective of, 199–203; revelation in the context of, 212–14; spirit understood within the perspective of, 184–7; symbolization in, human, 200–201; transcendence in relation to, 211

Emerson, Ralph Waldo, 107

Emmet, Dorothy, 93–4

Empathy, 50, 135–6

Enlightenment, the, 10, 18, 20–29

Ethics, and ritual, 29

Ethos, 20

Evil, demonic, 165; prevalence of, 171; radical, 28; source of human, 147–68

Evolution, conceptions of, 3–4; emergent, 8–9, 39–40; *see also* Emergence

Existentialism, 34

Faith, appreciative dimension in, 119–22; collapse of, 11–13, 18–31; as a cultural force, 114–16; elemental forms of, 63–4; in relation to despair, 74–5; as individual attitude, 70ff., 101; institutional forms of, 65f.; nature of, 14–18; lack of a Protestant philosophy of, 210; and Reason, 22–8, 117–28, 122–6, 128; Reformation conception of, 70–77, 119ff.; as psychical energy, 63ff.; tradition distinguished from, 100

Fall, imagery of the, 135; meaning of the, 151

Feuerbach, L. A., 22

Ford, Henry, 107

Forgiveness, Christian doctrine of, 167; Grace and, 190–95; Reformation doctrine of, 160; Spirit evidenced in acts of repentance and, 184–6

Form, redemptive significance of, 199ff.; vitality and, 160–62

Franck, César, 58

Freedom, 92, 152–3; paradox of, 156–7; Spirit and, 175–9

Freud, Sigmund, 34

Frazer, James G., 80

Gandhi, 157, 177

God, the creative act of, 108–11, 113; culture and the work of, 102; grace and judgment of, 126, 192–5, 199, 215; hidden and discernible aspects of, 209–23; image of, 133; Jesus Christ as revealer of, 213ff.; philosophical conceptions of, 170; redemptive activities of, 97, 190–208; structure of, 211–12

Goethe, Johann Wolfgang, 164

Goodness, ambiguity of, 162–5; empirical evidences of transcendent, 184–6, 192–5; operations of uncalculable, 171; problem of, 169–89; qualities of human, 165–6

Grace, empirical evidences of, 191–5, 214ff.

Greek Orthodox Church, 51

Grief, the redemptive process in, 203–5

Händel, G. F., 58, 146

Harnack, Adolf von, 56

Hartshorne, Charles, 45

Heard, Gerald, 213

Hegel, G. W. F., 3, 4, 9, 34, 84, 202

Herrmann, Wilhelm, 52, 56

History, function of inquiry into, 105–6; meaning of, 104

Hocking, William E., 179

Höffding, Harald, 110

Holy Spirit, 51, 77, 126, 127, 210; Jesus Christ and the, 218; meaning and nature of the, 216–18
Hoskins, Roy G., 135
Human nature, complexity of, 132–43; source of evil in, 145–68; goodness in, 169–89; instability of, 164–6
Hume, David, 21–3

Idealism, 33, 56, 126, 210
Imago Dei, 133
Immanence, 32–4, 57–8
Immortality, 207–8
Intuition, 40

James, William, 4, 8, 44–6, 48, 69, 89, 154
Jeans, Sir James H., 170
Jesus Christ, 8, 9, 25, 28, 29, 42, 49, 51, 52, 54, 57–9, 86–7, 99, 101, 113, 122, 126–7, 144–5, 162, 196–9, 208, 212–22
Joy and sorrow, Spirit as seen in a capacity for, 179–84
Jung, C. G., 69

Kant, Immanuel, 3, 4, 9, 17, 18, 21–6, 56, 125, 202, 210, 211
Kierkegaard, Søren, 34, 124, 148–50, 176
Ku Klux Klan, 165

Langer, Susanne K., 5, 83, 89–92, 95
Language, and religion, 82ff.; of theology, 95f.
Lawrence, D. H., 33
Liberalism, the Christian myth in theological, 51–4; reconstruction in theological, 32–60; loss of faith in, 14–31; new resources for theological, 3ff.
Linton, Ralph, 5

Locke, John, 21–6
Loomer, Bernard M., 215
Love, rule of, 48–9
Lowie, Robert, 5, 188
Lowrie, Walter, 149
Luther, Martin, 69, 74–6, 124, 137
Lutheran Church, 51

Malinowski, B., 5
Man, Christian estimate of, 10f., 27–9, 134ff.; emergent perspective on, 132ff.; 'loneliness' of, 137–8; contributions of the new metaphysics to an understanding of, 98–116, 131–43; summary of the nature of, 143
Marett, R. R., 5, 188
Markham, Edwin, 204
Marxism, 29
Mass, Bach B-Minor, 58, 146; Roman, 71, 112
Mathews, Shailer, 52, 217
Mead, Margaret, 5, 188
Messiah, Händel's, 58, 146
Metaphysics, the new, 9–10; Christian conception of man informed by the new, 98–116, 131–43
Millay, Edna St. Vincent, 109
Miller, Benjamin, 137
Milton, John, 58
Modernism, faulty perspective upon man in, 107
Moral Consciousness, Christ and the, 86; concern for fixed values in the, 173; impoverishment of the, 27; Spirit and the, 185, 207, 214–15
Morgan, C. Lloyd, 4, 8
Mozart, Wolfgang A., 58, 146
Mysticism, 144, 213
Myth, and the Biblical writings, 47–9, 59; Christian, 19–20; content of Christian, 42; and culture, 80–97, 98ff.; empirical implications

Myth (*Continued*)
of Christian, 211ff.; meaning of, 40–43, 58; metaphysics and, 84, 90–91; nature of, 87; numinous experience in, 88–9; religious education and, 55; and sensibility, 47–9; and structure of experience, 98; revelation and, 86; theological interpretation of, 95–7; truth and, 92ff., 117–19; valuations of Christian, 134–5; and worship, 51f.

Myth-consciousness, 6, 87ff., 93–4

Mythos, Christian, 18, 20–21, 26, 47, 78, 132; meaning of, 20

New Testament, the, 48, 162, 214ff.

Newton, Sir Isaac, 4, 47, 48

Newtonian world-view, 47ff.

Niebuhr, H. Richard, 215

Niebuhr, Reinhold, 92–3, 148, 155–6, 159, 215

Non-conformity, psychical effects of, 68–70

Northrop, F. S. C., 170

Otto, Rudolf, 25, 89

Pan-psychism, 44–5

Paradise Lost, Milton's, 58

Peattie, Donald Culross, 198

Personalism, 3, 56, 126

Pietism, 77

Plato, 34, 126, 164, 214

Positivism, 4

Powys, John Cowper, 180

Powys, Llewellyn, 180

Pragmatism, 56

Protestantism, conception of faith in, 70ff., 119ff.; dissociation from structure of experience in, 71f., 100–101; prophetic force of, 101–2; conception of man in,

151; reconstruction in liberal, 3ff., 17, 20, 32–60

Psychology, depth, 29, 34; and religion, 6–7

Quakers, 77

Rationality, Critique of, 32ff., 117–28

Rauschenbusch, Walter, 29

Reason, faith and, 22–8, 117–28

Redemption, Christian doctrine of, 167; Christian drama of, 46, 52, 72, 87, 113; empirical meaning of, 190–95; sensibility and, 203; symbolization and, 200–201

Redfield, Robert, 5, 188

Relations, dynamic, 131–46; mystery of internal, 142

Renaissance, 27

Requiem, Brahms', 58, 146; Mozart's, 58, 146

Resurrection, 206–8, 218–19

Revelation, cultural anthropological interpretation of, 144–6; emergent understanding of, 212–14; myth and, 86

Ritschl, Albrecht, 3, 17, 29, 52

Ritual, Greek Orthodox, 51; Lutheran, 51; Roman Catholic, 51

Robinson, H. Wheeler, 47

Roman Catholic faith, 51, 65, 70, 151; discontinuities between Protestant and, 73

Romanticism, 25, 27, 78

Royce, Josiah, 179

Sandburg, Carl, 182

Schleiermacher, F. E. D., 18, 21–6, 51, 137, 143, 202

Schweitzer, Albert, 157

Selfhood, emergence of, 133–6, 139–42, 152–4

Sensibility, good will differentiated from, 203; law and, 48–50

Sensitivity, 188, 209; assertiveness of force over, 160–62; creative ground of, 111–13; frontier of, 218; in the Gospels, 214; image of God as, 133ff.; matrix of, 211; Spirit as, 184–6; transcendent character of acts of, 43–5

Sin, 147; concrete datum of, 156–60; egoism and, 154f.; insensitivity and, 160–61; Original, 150–55

Smith, G. B., 19

Smuts, Jan, 4, 8

Sorrow, joy and, 179–84

Spencer, Herbert, 3, 4

Spinoza, Benedict, 126

Spirit, emergence of, 86; emergent quality of, 209ff.; nature of, 171–89

Starbuck, E. D., 154

Stromee, Carl G., 141

Structure of experience, 54–5, 72, 96–116; faith as a, 198; history and the, 104–7

Suffering, transcending, 203–5

Symbolization, 140–2, 200–201

Symbols, use of religious, 95

Theology, two modes of discourse in, 95–6; faith and reason in, 28–9, 117–28; language of, 96–7, 147–8; Christian interpretation of man in liberal, 32–60; modern

task in liberal, 32f.; new resources for, 3–13

Thoreau, Henry David, 107

Tillotson, John, 21–2

Tindal, Matthew, 21–2

Transcendence, 41, 101, 184–9

Truth, faith and, 117–28; and myth, 117–19

Tschaikowsky, Peter, 182

Tylor, E. B., 80

Urban, W. M., 84

van Gogh, Vincent, 157

Webster, Noah, 20

Western culture, Christian faith and, 10, 14–31, 49, 53, 78; expressions of faith in, 70; revelation in Christ as a revolution in, 215; Christian witness within and beyond, 221–3

Whitehead, Alfred North, 14, 34, 36, 37, 45, 48, 50, 57, 89, 108, 113, 126, 137, 140, 143, 170, 179, 198, 199, 202

Whitman, Walt, 107

Wholeness, religion as, 179

Wieman, Henry Nelson, 45, 108–10, 123, 170

Wilder, Thornton, 139

Willkie, Wendell, 120

Witness, Christian, 8, 113, 145–6, 186, 221ff.

Wonder, sense of, 172–5